Zeno Ackermann, Isabel Karremann, Simi Malhotra, and Nishat Zaidi

Terrains of Consciousness

Zeno Ackermann, Isabel Karremann,
Simi Malhotra, and Nishat Zaidi

Terrains of Consciousness

Multilogical Perspectives on Globalization

Würzburg
University Press

The project New Terrains of Consciousness and the publication of this book have been made possible by funds obtained from the Government of India's Ministry of Education through its Scheme for Promotion of Academic and Research Collaboration (SPARC).

Impressum

Julius-Maximilians-Universität Würzburg
Würzburg University Press
Universitätsbibliothek Würzburg
Am Hubland
D-97074 Würzburg
www.wup.uni-wuerzburg.de

©2021 Würzburg University Press
Print on Demand

Coverabbildung: Jantar Mantar, New Delhi (Rama Yantra 2 inside).jpg / AKS.9955.
https://commons.wikimedia.org/wiki/File:Jantar_Mantar,_New_Delhi_(Rama_Yantra_2_inside).jpg , CC BY-SA 4.0 International
Coverdesign: Jule Petzold

ISBN 978-3-95826-168-6 (print)
ISBN 978-3-95826-169-3 (online)
DOI 10.25972/WUP-978-3-95826-169-3
URN urn:nbn:de:bvb:20-opus-243936

Preface

This book grew out of the project "New Terrains of Consciousness: Globalization, Sensory Environments and Local Cultures of Knowledge." Funded by the Government of India's Ministry of Education through its Scheme for Promotion of Academic and Research Collaboration (SPARC) over a two-year time span, our transnational project originally represented a collaboration between the English departments at Jamia Millia Islamia, New Delhi, and the Julius-Maximilians-Universität, Würzburg. Due to the contingencies of academic life and work, however, the project eventually brought together scholars affiliated with three universities in three (quite differently positioned) countries: SIMI MALHOTRA and NISHAT ZAIDI (from JMI), ZENO ACKERMANN (from JMU), as well as – last not least – ISABEL KARREMANN (from UZ, i.e. the University of Zurich).

We would like our readers to receive the conspicuously 'vast' title of our project not as an instance of academic grandiloquence but as expression of our serious wish to work out new perspectives on big issues and urgent problems. Most importantly, the metaphor of *new terrains of consciousness* indicates our conviction that these issues and problems can only be tackled by determinedly exploring multilogical perspectives and by practically forging frameworks for deeply connected transnational collaboration – collaboration, that is, in both research and teaching.

Indeed, our SPARC project has been designed as a scholarly response to globalization – or, more precisely speaking, as a scholarly response to the dramatic economic, political, social, and cultural processes that are usually referred to as 'globalization.' Accordingly, the title of the project invites a twofold reading: on the one hand, the project set out to examine the 'new terrains of consciousness' productively or destructively created by globalization; on the other hand it might not be too bold a claim that the project has been intended as a practice of *worldmaking* in its own right, i.e. as an endeavour of performatively creating 'new terrains of consciousness' from which or on which globalization can be freshly – and critically – assessed.[1]

This approach is decisively informed by the concept of *situated knowledges* – especially by the expectation, most powerfully expressed by Donna Haraway, that a sufficiently grounded awareness of such knowledges would result in a "more

---

[1] See the introduction below for a systematic exploration of the contrastive terminological collocation of 'globalization,' 'worldmaking' and 'worlding.'

adequate, richer, better account of a world, in order to live in it well and in criti-cal, reflexive relation to our own as well as others' practices of domination and the unequal parts of privilege and oppression that make up all positions."[2] Our key programmatic idea has been to strive towards the recognition and appreciation of such situated knowledges by working towards a *phenomenology of globalization*. This means to lay conceptual foundations for systematically studying how globalization transforms locally situated and individually experi-enced socioeconomic terrains, everyday practices, and cultures of knowledge. We have tried to gain an understanding of such terrains, practices, and cultures through phenomenologically accessing them as specific *sensescapes*. Throughout, our approach has been informed by the uncomfortable question of how the 'lib-erating' effects of globalization relate to its limiting, destabilizing and disrupting consequences. In these respects, it is vital to ask how globalization affects the less advantaged or the systematically dispossessed inhabitants of the world and its various societies. The following are the three most salient scholarly propositions laid down in our original funding application:

- to offer *new perspectives on globalization* and to assist in the evolution of a more symmetrical and more productive discourse of globalization;

- to transnationally combine *sensory studies, globalization studies* and *eco-criticism* in order to contribute to the evolution of a *multilogical phe-nomenology of globalization*;

- to compare cultural practices and legacies of *sensory worldmaking* in In-dia and the 'West' – not only asking how the processes, discourses and media of globalization impinge on grounded everyday routines in spe-cific localities but also assessing the processes by which locally specific practices or legacies of worldmaking come to be represented in and pro-jected into the sphere of global negotiation.

The character of the project as a collaboration not only in research but also in *teaching* manifested itself in two intensive courses that Zeno Ackermann and Isabel Karremann conducted for and with Indian graduate and postgraduate students. The first of these seminars or workshops, taught by Zeno Ackermann at Jamia Millia in August 2019, explored the concept of *articulation* – a concept that we take to be central in understanding the transformative interrelationships of languaging, worldmaking and networking in a globalizing world. Under the

---

[2]   Donna Haraway, "Situated Knowledges: The Science Question in Feminism and the Privilege of Partial Perspective," *Feminist Studies* 14.3 (1988): 575-599, here: 579.

title "Rethinking Articulation: Social Phenomena and Vocal Phonomena in Poetry, Pop & Cultural Studies," the course focussed on the dual applicability of its core concept as a seminal device not only in linguistic theory but also in cultural studies and social philosophy. The key idea was to test the potential of the concept to build bridges between cultural studies and linguistics in order to examine the interconnectedness of social *phenomena* with acoustic *phonomena*, and in particular with cultural practices of vocal performance. The governing hypothesis was that in responding to the complex entanglements of 'the local' and 'the global' we urgently need to develop new practices of listening as well as a new scholarly terminology for assessing sound cultures. With over a hundred applications, the course – which met on a nearly daily basis for over two weeks – was attended by forty shortlisted participants from all over India.

The seminar taught by Isabel Karremann in July 2021 followed a similar organizational format. However, due to the exigencies of the COVID-19 crisis – which hit India and its people in a particularly devastating way – it had to be conducted as an online-seminar. Under the title "Inhabiting a Globalized World: Concepts, Theories, Critical Perspectives" the course explored new critical approaches to the problematic of globalization by discussing key texts from the fields of *phenomenology, ecocriticism, queer studies, design theory* and *globalization studies.* Aiming at developing novel understandings of inhabiting and experiencing the world through imaginary as well as material acts of 'worlding,' the seminar asked what happens to situatedness in a globalized world. In particular, the participants were encouraged to dwell on the inclusion of sense perceptions and sensory entanglements into material ecologies of being, so as to arrive at situated ways of knowing and of learning about environments and one's relation to them. The final trajectory of the seminar was concerned with questions of temporality, asking how globalization relates to modernity and how a global perspective challenges and changes our sense of the planet's history and of our place in it. Again, over a hundred applications came in from all around India, and the seminar was finally attended by 34 shortlisted participants.

The most visible manifestation of our SPARC project as an endeavour of transnational research and scholarly multilogue was our exhilaratingly successful *international (online) conference* "Globalization and New Terrains of Consciousness: Phenomenologies of the Global/Local/Glocal," which took place from 8th to 10th February 2021 – and whose densely packed programme (consisting of a total of 16 lectures and 26 presentations) reached an international audience of more than 1,000 participants. The conference was opened by ARJUN APPADURAI (New York University), whose inaugural address on "The Haptic and the Phatic in the Twilight of Globalization" discussed the ever more significant tension between the (paradoxically) growing powers of touch in the era of digitality and the diminishing valence of phatic forms of communication. The valedictory address was delivered by DIPESH CHAKRABARTY (University of Chicago) under the title "The Global and the Planetary: Some Thoughts on Our Times." It explored the diverse meanings of terms such as 'globe' and 'globalization,' suggesting how humankind – in spite of its long-standing habit of positioning itself as the main protagonist of globalization – is seriously out of step with the demands of the planet and making a case for the necessity of multiscalar thinking.

Among the keynote speakers of the conference there were also PEGGY LEVITT (Wellesley College), speaking on "Disrupting the Cultural and Intellectual Inequality Pipeline," and TOM MOYLAN (University of Limerick) speaking on "Becoming Utopian: Exploring the Praxis of Making a Better World." The plenary sessions included key presentations by (among others) JOFF P. N. BRADLEY (Teikyo University, Tokyo), MANOJ NY (Kyung Hee University, Seoul), ANANYA JAHANARA KABIR (King's College London), who teamed up with the author ARI GAUTIER, DAVID SCHALKWYK (Queen Mary University of London), MIRIAM WALLRAVEN (JMU Würzburg), AVISHEK PARUI (IIT Madras), RAHUL K. GAIROLA (Murdoch University, Perth), BRANDON LABELLE (University of Bergen), YASMEEN ARIF (Shiv Nadar University, Delhi), SUMAN GUPTA (Open University), RADHIKA SUBRAMANIAM (Parsons School of Design/The New School, New York), FRANCESCA FERRANDO (NYU) and SHRADDHA A. SINGH (JMI).

Within the confines of the present preface, it is of course impossible to offer a more detailed account of topics covered, approaches suggested, conclusions reached and aporias spotted by such a long list of distinguished speakers – all of whom we remember gratefully. The various methodologies drawn on and connected under the umbrella of the critical reflection on globalization and worldmaking included phenomenology, object theory, literary studies, memory studies, postcolonial studies, the digital humanities, sound studies and sociology – and a particular impression was made by an "open letter," transcribed and read out by RADHIKA SUBRAMANIAM, in which Rattus Norvegicus eloquently confronted humankind with its short-sighted egocentrism and general lack of situated comprehension.

Even this cursory glance at the list of speakers presenting and on the variety of world regions thus represented at the conference testifies to its resonance as a striking manifestation of 'worlding.' We thus feel justified in claiming – with heartfelt thanks to all students, scholars, secretaries and helpers involved – the productive success of our SPARC project on "New Terrains of Consciousness."

Simi Malhotra, with Zeno Ackermann, Isabel Karremann, and Nishat Zaidi

Contents

Introduction: New Terrains of Consciousness in a Globalized World

– Isabel Karremann & Zeno Ackermann

Our SPARC project has followed a twofold agenda: setting out to examine the 'terrains of consciousness' that have been transformed, destroyed or created by globalization, we also have been eager to discover '*new* terrains of consciousness' on which fresh assessments of globalization might be possible. What both endeavours insistently demand is to unsettle the stipulated one-ness or totality of globalization. Indeed, our task has consisted in (and continues to consist in) multilogically opening up globalization, becoming aware of the variety of phenomena, experiences, and perspectives so often speciously subsumed under the term.

In other words, we have taken on the task of re-examining (theoretically as well as concretely) the old dichotomy of 'the global' and 'the local.' As most people would feel, it is unwise to firmly place oneself on either side of the binary by naively buying into progressivist visions of globalization or by stubbornly insisting on the felt primacy of the immediate. Rather, it has become commonplace to follow a dialectical approach – as expressed in the precept 'Think global – act local.' In her book *Hegel, Haiti, and Universal History* (2009), Susan Buck-Morss interestingly twists this idea around: "The contemporary slogan, Think Global – Act Local, requires modification. We need first to ask what it means to Think Global, because we do not yet know how." Significantly, Buck-Morss suggests that in trying to find out "what it means to Think Global" one ought to begin by working through particulars: "We need to find ways through the *local* specificities of our own traditions toward a conceptual orientation that can inform *global* action."[1]

The notion of 'terrains,' which our project and the present book foregrounds as a generative motif for thinking globalization differently, evokes the "local specificities" and "traditions" mentioned by Buck-Morss. By clearly displaying its Latin root 'terra,' the word also thematizes the material aspects of worldly situations: the specific physical, (agri-)cultural, and sensorial conditions in which 'life' and 'reproduction' ground themselves. Moreover, both the Latin word 'terra' and its English companion 'earth' *contain* the tension between extremely large-scale and rigorously small-scale perspectives: spelt with a capital initial,

---

[1] Susan BUCK-MORSS, *Hegel, Haiti, and Universal History* (Pittsburgh: U of Pittsburgh P, 2009) x.

'Earth' refers to the entire globe (even figuring in the globe's cosmic situated-ness); with a small 'e,' however, the word 'earth' draws attention to the unique material 'terroir' that (according to wine lovers) gives a grape its sensual power.

'Terrain' and 'globalization' thus make an interesting pair of concepts. In terms of a determined paradox, discourses of globalization often go along with a tendency to fetishize certain constructions of local terrains. At the same time, it might be posed that local terrains are what globalization is bent to subsume and abolish through processes of mapping, abstracting, and linking. Indeed, the concept of 'terrain' figures situated idiosyncrasies that are heterotopically resistant to globalization as a process of (potentially total) integration. Simultaneously, the ecological crisis brought about or heightened by globalization forces a shift from abstract towards concrete forms of awareness: it demands switching from an economistic to an ecological framework by rethinking the 'globe' as a 'terra.'

In originally designing our research project we became fixated on a term that is thought-provoking as well as precarious: "terrains of consciousness." The term crept in through Lawrence Buell's book *The Future of Environmental Criticism* (2005). Introducing the concept of the 'bioregion,' Buell quotes Peter Berg's and Raymond Dasmann's explanation that it "refers both to *geographical terrain* and a *terrain of consciousness.*"[2] A major part of the attraction of the term 'terrain of consciousness' – or, indeed, 'terrains of consciousness' – is in its validation of locally placed and sensorially embedded practices of creative resistance to ab-straction. We propose that thinking in terms of 'terrains of consciousness' might be a way of re-conceptualizing the conditions of inhabiting a globalized world by emphasizing the concrete material and sensual processes of such inhabitation. Along these lines, we ask about the relationships between the more abstract ge-ographies, power dynamics or ideologies of the global and topographically situ-ated practices or knowledges that are more readily accessible through the senses. Through attending to the senses, and the kinds of knowledge they produce, we hope to begin to re-negotiate the relationships between 'local' and 'global,' 'na-tional' and 'transnational,' 'traditional' and 'modern' sites of agency and identity.

Such an approach is connected to recent developments in globalization stud-ies as they are conducted mainly in the humanities – in philosophy, sociology, social anthropology, historiography, area studies, literary studies and cultural studies. In particular, we have taken up impulses from three major meth-odological shifts in globalization studies. We will begin by revisiting these shifts

---

[2]   Lawrence Buell, "Space, Place, and Imagination from Local to Global," *The Future of Environ-mental Criticism: Environmental Crisis and Literary Imagination* (Malden, MA: Blackwell, 2005) 62-96, here: 83 (emphasis added). Buell quotes Peter Berg and Raymond Dasmann, "Reinhabit-ing California," *Ecologist*, 7 Dec. 1977, 399-401 here: 399-400.

and by conceptualizing them as a progression of methodological turns in globalization studies: a media turn; a phenomenological turn; and an environmental turn.[3]

The media turn

Pondering *The Consequences of Modernity* in 1990, Anthony Giddens identified globalization as one of its key results: "Modernity is inherently globalising."[4] Understanding globalized modernity as "the intensification of worldwide social relations which link distant localities in such a way that local happenings are shaped by events occurring many miles away and vice versa,"[5] he highlighted the importance of social relations and the reflexive interconnection of the local and the global that had hitherto been ignored by theories of globalization. Political theory, which understood globalization in terms of large-scale relations between nation states and analysed its challenges to governance and sovereignty, as well as Immanuel Wallerstein's world-system theory, which focussed on international business corporations and the capitalist world economy, provided separate accounts that in Giddens' view could explore only isolated aspects of globalization. Giddens responded by integrating politics and economics into a model that also acknowledged the importance of culture: a "cultural globalization" that is brought about by "[m]echanised technologies of communication [which] form an essential element of the reflexivity of modernity."[6] He illustrates "the globalising impact of media" by analysing how modern newspapers around 1900 brought knowledge of world-affairs to inhabitants of a local village. While this example might sound quaintly outmoded today, Giddens' general point became highly productive for further analyses of the role of mass media for our everyday experiences of globalization.

Arjun Appadurai's *Modernity at Large* (2003) took up where Giddens had left off. For both, modern technologies of communication and a consequent reordering of time-space lie at the core "of what it feels like to live in the world of modernity" – necessitating a specific "Phenomenology of Modernity"[7] that is, by

---

[3]   The following overview is largely based on the discussions in the SPARC research seminar "Inhabiting a Globalized World," conducted by Isabel Karremann in July 2021 with advanced students from all across India. The author and the project team would like to thank the participants for their highly insightful contributions to an exhilaratingly engaged discussion.

[4]   Anthony GIDDENS, *The Consequences of Modernity* (Cambridge: Polity Press, 1990) 63.

[5]   GIDDENS 64.

[6]   GIDDENS 77.

[7]   GIDDENS 137.

virtue of the inherent links between the two, always also a phenomenology of globalization. Appadurai argues that such a phenomenology needs to be understood through the conjunction of media and migration: reminiscing about his own "early life in Bombay" before moving to the US to study social sciences, Appadurai remembers how he "saw and smelled modernity reading *Life* and American college catalogs."[8] In particular, his book explores the "joint effect" of media and migration "on the work of the imagination as a constitutive feature of modern subjectivity."[9] If "electronic media provide resources for self-imagining as an everyday social project" – think of social media like Twitter, Instagram and YouTube, which had not yet pervaded popular culture at the time Appadurai was writing: his examples are TV programmes and music cassettes – they do not provide a stable, localised identity; on the contrary, with the de-localised structures of the internet and "the rapid flow of mass-mediated images, scripts, and sensations, we have a new order of instability in the production of modern subjectivities."[10] This instability is intensified and becomes a cultural and political challenge where "moving images meet deterritorialized viewers." Because "both viewers and images are in simultaneous circulation" in material and virtual space, they "often meet unpredictably, outside the certainties of home and the cordon sanitaire of local and national media effects."[11]

Appadurai captures the public effects of what seem individual habits of media use in the concept of "the diasporic public sphere." Drawing on Jürgen Habermas' notion of the public sphere as an extra-parliamentary opposition enabled through the mass-mediated circulation of knowledge about political decisions,[12] Appadurai posits that the diasporic public sphere is "a space of contestation in which individuals and groups seek to annex the global into their own practices of the modern."[13] This contestation challenges state-sponsored national identities. Appadurai further appropriates Benedict Anderson's famous definition of the nation as an "imagined community"[14] – another concept closely linked to the historical emergence of the public sphere in the eighteenth century – and stresses the importance of the imagination for the diasporic public sphere as an alternative to that of the nation state. The experience of diaspora, he claims, "bring[s]

---

[8]   Arjun APPADURAI, *Modernity at Large: Cultural Dimensions of Globalization* (Minneapolis: U of Minnesota P, 1996) 1.
[9]   APPADURAI, *Modernity at Large* 3.
[10] APPADURAI, *Modernity at Large* 4.
[11] APPADURAI, *Modernity at Large* 4.
[12] Jürgen HABERMAS, *Strukturwandel der Öffentlichkeit* (1962; Frankfurt: Suhrkamp, 1990) 82-83.
[13] APPADURAI, *Modernity at Large* 4.
[14] Benedict ANDERSON, *Imagined Communities: Reflections on the Origin and Spread of Nationalism* (London: Verso, 1983).

the force of the imagination, as both memory and desire, into the lives of many ordinary people"; and "the images, scripts, models and narratives that come through mass mediation" drive a collective imagination of subjectivities that enable agency and political action even for the dispossessed, the marginalized, the migrants. "There is growing evidence," Appadurai claims, "that the consumption of the mass media throughout the world often provokes resistance, irony, selectivity, and, in general *agency*."[15] Examples from recent history abound. The Arabic Spring in 2011 was significantly carried by the use of social media through which discontent was articulated, solidarity forged, and action coordinated. The Umbrella Movement for democracy in Hong Kong is another example.

Importantly for a phenomenology of globalised modernity, this imagined community of the diasporic public sphere is "a community of sentiment, a group that begins to imagine and feel things together."[16] This sentiment is both localized and globalized, both embodied and generated virtually – it is an effect of a "situated and embodied difference" that is articulated and circulated globally through mass media.[17] However, it does not give rise to yet another totalising vision of a homogenous unity that would override the nation state while following its script. Instead, Appadurai posits a "plurality of imagined worlds" that may, perhaps, afford a "cultural freedom and sustainable justice in the world" which have been promised but not delivered by either "the uniform and general existence of the nation state" or global capitalism.[18]

The phenomenological turn

If globalised modernity understood in terms of media and migration can give rise to 'imagined worlds,' it also necessitates a reimagining of what we mean by 'the world.' In order to avoid the politico-economic language of 'the globe,' new concepts and terms are needed. Jean-Luc Nancy proposes the French notion of *mondialisation*, or 'worlding,' as an alternative to the international lingo of globalization.[19] Globalization discourse, in his account, is driven by the abstract idea of the world as a totality, integrated into a whole by the international networks of politics, commerce and communication technologies. The problem with this

---

[15]   APPADURAI, *Modernity at Large* 7.
[16]   APPADURAI, *Modernity at Large* 8.
[17]   APPADURAI, *Modernity at Large* 13.
[18]   APPADURAI, *Modernity at Large* 5, 23.
[19]   Jean-Luc NANCY, *The Creation of the World or Globalization*, transl. by François Raffoul and David Pettigrew (Albany: SUNY Press, 2007).

is that the world understood in this way appears as an undifferentiated sphere in which everything is available everywhere in the same form – the phenomenon of shopping malls housing the same combination of fashion brand stores in Delhi, London or Buenos Aires – while this semblance of sameness obscures the structures of social inequality and injustice in countries where the goods consumed at such malls are outsourced to the cheapest producer. Such a system leads to a reduction and reification of the world to an agglomeration of commodities and people, following the capitalist logic of proliferation and accumulation.[20] Moreover, the reifying impetus underlying globalization discourse is closely linked to a unifying world view: "It is as if there was an intimate connection between capitalistic development and the capitalization of views or pictures of the world."[21] This capitalist world view also determines a specific viewing-position of the human subject: "A world 'viewed,'" Nancy explains, "is a world dependent on the gaze of a subject of the world. A subject of the world (that is to say as well a subject of history) cannot itself be in the world."[22] Here, then, is the ideological crux of the discourse of globality: it posits the human subject vis-à-vis the world as an object that can be possessed and exploited; and historically, this subject has been located in western culture, reifying the population of non-western countries as part of the object-world appropriated through colonialism.[23]

Mondialisation, by contrast, points to an understanding of the world "as a space of possible meaning for the whole of human relations," for the "interconnection of everyone in the production of humanity" rather than of goods. 'Worlding' or 'world-forming' understood in this sense also implies an acknowledgement of immanence: "it is in 'this' world, or as 'this' world, that what Marx calls the production and/or creation of humanity, is being played out."[24] The production of humanity here means "the production of a humanized world [as] a sphere

---

[20] NANCY's model of capitalist globalization and its 'unworlding' consequences is the "urban network" of megacities, where "city crowds, the hyperbolic accumulation of construction projects (with their concomitant demolition) and of exchanges (of movements, products, and information) spread, and the inequality and apartheid concerning access to the urban milieu […], accumulate proportionally. The result can only be understood in terms of what is called *agglomeration* […]. This network cast upon the planet – and already around it, in the orbital band of satellites along with their debris – deforms the *orbis* as much as the *urbs*. The agglomeration invades and erodes what used to be thought of as globe and which is nothing more now than its double, *glomus*" (33-34).

[21] NANCY 40.

[22] NANCY 40.

[23] See Betty JOSEPH, "Worlding and Unworlding in the Long Eighteenth Century," *Eighteenth-Century Studies* 52.1 (2018): 27-31.

[24] NANCY 36-37.

of freedom" and its enjoyment by all human beings.[25] What sounds traditionally humanistic or impossibly utopian is in fact a plea to redefine just what counts as valuable: not the use-value of goods, but the enjoyment of something that is use-less, that has no reason or end in itself but rather extends beyond, to the world and the meaningful others inhabiting it. Affectivity, participation and interconnection are the modes of inhabiting such a shared world. In Nancy's terms, whereas a world view is a mode of representation, worlding is a mode of experience; *mondialisation* is what includes us but what also always eludes us – an experience of alterity that is captured by the untranslatable French term.[26] In opposition to the commodifying world view of globality, "the decisive feature of the becoming-world of the world [...] is the feature through which the world resolutely and absolutely distances itself from any status as object in order to tend toward being itself the 'subject' of its own 'world-hood'—or 'world-forming.'"[27] This "non-objective status of the world" which humans inhabit as beings-in-the-world is what connects Nancy's phenomenological account with environmentalist and ecocritical visions of the world as the space of co-habitation of companion species.[28]

Drawing on Heidegger rather than Marx, Pheng Chea's study of world literature likewise develops a phenomenological account of the world as what holds all beings together in a way that is prior to and makes possible human activity because it gives us access to other beings. This notion gives rise to the idea of a shared "dwelling"[29] in the world in "non-thematic relations of care" (the non-

---

[25] NANCY 45. Cf. Dipesh CHAKRABARTY, *The Crises of Civilization: Exploring Global and Planetary Histories* (Oxford: Oxford UP, 2016) 174, where – in the context of a critical reassessment of the discourse of freedom – Chakrabarty notes the connection between this Marxist understanding of freedom as "escape [from] the injustice, oppression, inequality, or even uniformity foisted on them by other humans and human-made systems" and the costs its realization meant for the planet: "The mansion of modern freedoms stands on an ever-expanding base of fossil fuel use. Most of our freedoms so far have been energy-intensive."

[26] NANCY 28. Another untranslatable term that tries to capture the incommensurability of the world is Spivak's notion of "planetarity." See esp. Gayatri Chakravorty SPIVAK, "Planetarity," *The Death of a Discipline* (New York: Columbia UP, 2003) 71-102. The planetary is not pitched against the unifying logic of capitalist globalization as a simple contrast or reversal, following the same logic, but as the other to globalization: "the planet is in the species of alterity." Planetarity, moreover, positions human beings differently: not as global agents, but as "planetary subjects" and "planetary creatures." This gesture decentres the human in the sense that the planet's "alterity remains underived from us" (72-73).

[27] NANCY 41.

[28] NANCY 41. Cf. Donna HARAWAY, *When Species Meet* (Minneapolis: U of Minnesota P, 2005) 5-6.

[29] See also Tim INGOLD, "Building, Dwelling, Living," *The Perception of the Environment: Essays on Livelihood, Dwelling and Skill* (New York: Routledge, 2011) 172-188.

thematic corresponding with Nancy's notion of use-lessness).[30] These are relations of looking *after*, not looking *at* the world, and they result in a shared worldmaking rather than a making of things. Hence, the relation between humans and
things changes: no longer mere objects to be possessed or handled, Chea re-
thinks human-object relations (with Heidegger) in terms of "handy things."
Tools, for instance, are not merely objects in the world used for the purpose of
producing a work, but become part of the "work-world" together with the human
wielding it, the materials of the work, as well as the users and consumers of the
finished work.[31] Extending this notion to relations between humans as well as
between humans and non-human beings makes phenomenological worlding relevant as a tool – a handy thing – for criticizing the reifying exploitation of other
people[32] and the natural environment. Importantly, it also deconstructs the very
status of the human subject: if the world is no longer an object, the subject too is
converted into a being among other beings. "The world" understood in Heideg-
gerian terms is "an irreducible openness where we cannot avoid being-with others" in a "mutual dependency that is based on and in turn supports our shared
world."[33] It is peopled by handy things and handy beings that are placed in meaningful relations to each other.

This "placement" in which "each being has a proper place and can be placed
in relation to other beings"[34] is the very opposite of the alienation brought about
through the displacement that Giddens describes as one element in the "frameworks of experience" that constitute his "phenomenology of [globalized] moder-

---

[30] Pheng CHEA, "Worlding: The Phenomenological Concept of Worldliness and the Loss of World
      in Modernity", *What is a World? On Postcolonial Literature as World Literature* (Durham: Duke
      UP, 2016) 95-130, here: 98.

[31] CHEA 99.

[32] See CHEA 120: "Whereas our original being-with people propels us outside ourselves and gives
      rise to authentic community with others, the interpretation of our relations to others as a relation
      of geometrical distance [...] turns them into a passive belonging to an average neutral subject."
      Cf. Sara AHMED, "The Orient and Other Others," *Queer Phenomenology: Orientations, Objects,
      Others* (Durham: Duke UP, 2006) 109-156, who uses Heideggerian phenomenology to revisit
      Said's concept of orientalism and queries how non-white bodies are made to inhabit a 'white'
      world that has resulted from the spatial expansion of the West through colonial imperialism
      which also, of course, underpins capitalist globalization. Her "phenomenology of whiteness"
      (138) demonstrates how spaces – public, institutional, global – become racialized by how they
      are oriented around a normative body-image, and how in turn race is spatialized through the
      allocation of spaces that can be inhabited by some bodies more comfortably than others
      (129-142).

[33] CHEA 105.

[34] CHEA 100.

nity." Yet the processes of globalization do not only pull us from the local environment but are also accompanied by a re-embedding. The experience of globalized modernity, as many critics concur, is marked by often paradoxical juxtapositions of proximity and distance: what is felt to be "comfortable and nearby is actually an expression of distant events and was 'placed into' the local environment rather than forming an organic development within in."[35] Again, the globalized shopping mall provides an example: it constitutes both a space and a set of social practices that are detached from their ties to a local place; it forms an air-conditioned, sanitized bubble in the local environment.

But it is "not just that local places have changed through increased connectivity but also the structures of perception, cognition, and social expectations associated with them," as Ursula Heise observes. Hence, any account of globalized modernity must also have a phenomenological dimension. This is even more true when we think about globalization from an environmentalist perspective, as Heise does: the sense of place must be complemented by "a sense of planet – a sense of how political, economic, technological, social, cultural and ecological networks shape daily routines."[36]

The environmental turn

Such a sense of planet is developed and enacted in Donna Haraway's recent work. She follows a method of storytelling that draws together the threads of multi-species-worlding. A famous example of this critical practice can be found in *When Species Meet* (2005), where Haraway offers a 'thick description' (Geertz) of the multiple threads of personal bonds, human-animal relations, technological devices, genetic encoding, biological environment and sense perceptions that converge in a photograph taken of a moss-covered tree stump that looks like a dog:

> We touch Jim's dog with fingery eyes made possible by a fine digital camera, computers, servers, and e-mail programs through which the high-density jpg was sent to me. Infolded into the metal, plastic, and electronic flesh of the digital apparatus is the primate visual system that Jim and I have inherited, with its vivid color sense and sharp focal power. Our kind of capacity for perception and sensual pleasure ties us to the lives of our primate kin. Touching this heritage, our worldliness must answer to and

---

[35] GIDDENS 140-141.
[36] Ursula HEISE, *Sense of Place and Sense of Planet: The Environmental Imagination of the Global* (Oxford: Oxford UP, 2008) 54-55.

for those other primate beings [...]. Also, the biological colonizing op-
portunism of organisms, from the glowing but invisible viruses and bac-
teria to the crown of ferns on top of this pooch's head, is palpable in the
touch.[37]

The aim of such an analysis is to make visible the interconnectedness of our existence across all scales, from microbiological to planetary. By changing our
thinking about the world, it seeks to effect a different kind of worlding. In *Staying
with the Trouble* (2016), Haraway calls her method "SF," playfully drawing on the
string figures of a game of cat's cradle as well as the modes of "speculative fabu-
lation, science fiction, science fact, speculative feminism, *soin de ficelle*, so far."
These string figures are a rhetorical pattern-weaving as well as a "theoretical
trope, a way to think-with a host of companions in sympoetic threading, felting,
tangling, tracking and sorting." It entails a collective doing and knowing that results in new stories for our time that Haraway calls the *Chthulucene*, after a spider
that dwells in the ground and embodies, for Haraway, the "chthonic powers of
Terra."[38]

This term tellingly diverges from the much-debated term *Anthropocene* that
designates the epoch in which the impact of human beings on the planet has increased to such a degree that humanity has become a geological force.[39] Globalization is an important, indeed a critical chapter in this historical epoch of our
planet, as Dipesh Chakrabarty has pointed out: capitalist globalization and the
industrialisation that went hand in hand with it were – and still are – built on the
exploitation of fossil fuels that by now influences the most basic physical processes of the earth to such a degree that we are facing a climate crisis. And yet,
the discourse of capitalist globalization alone is not able to comprehend what the
climate crisis means, or how we should respond to it: "The problematic of globalization allows us to read climate change only as a crisis of capitalist management. While there is no denying that climate change has profoundly to do with
the history of capital, a critique that is only a critique of capital is not sufficient
for addressing questions of human history [...] once we accept that the crisis of
climate change is here with us and may exist as part of this planet for much longer
than capitalism."[40] While capitalist globalization is clearly the problem, it cannot
offer a solution. Chakrabarty suggests therefore that we integrate it into the perspective of a planetary history. While the main protagonist in global history are

---

[37] HARAWAY, *When Species Meet* 5-6.
[38] HARAWAY, *Staying With the Trouble: Making Kin in the Chthulucene* (Durham: Duke UP, 2016)
      31.
[39] Paul J. CRUTZEN, "Geology of Mankind," *Nature*, 3 January 2002, 23.
[40] CHAKRABARTY, *The Crises of Civilization* 179.

humans, the planetary perspective decentres humans: our life depends on processes that were not made *for* us, but that make us, or make us possible (e.g. the production of an oxygen atmosphere). The planet reduces humans to our creatureliness, our existence as a species – and planetary history tells a story of survival, not of supremacy.[41]

Such an approach harbours at least two problems, however, a political and a phenomenological one. The collective self-recognition as a species may have the potential to forge a unity of action needed to battle the climate crisis; yet this all-inclusive species-thinking also harbours the danger of hiding "the reality of capitalist production and the logic of imperial [...] domination," namely, that it is the West (and in its imitation China, Japan, India, Russia and Brazil) who are mainly to blame for the current crisis.[42] The other problem is that 'species' is an abstract category removed from our everyday experiences as individuals or even collectives such as the nation, or a religious community. The scale on which a species exists, like that of the planetary, is simply too big to be meaningful. "We humans never experience ourselves as a species," Chakrabarty explains: "We can only intellectually comprehend or infer the existence of the human species but never experience it as such. Even if we were to emotionally identify with a word like mankind, we would not know what being a species is [...]. We experience specific effects of the crisis but not the whole phenomenon." While discussions about the climate crisis can produce both "affect and knowledge about collective human pasts and futures," they "work at the limits of historical understanding," which remains organised primarily around the figure of the human subject.[43]

While Chakrabarty pushes for telling history differently, Donna Haraway, Bruno Latour and Ursula LeGuin insist on telling different stories altogether: Gaia stories,[44] Chthulucene stories,[45] carrier-net stories[46] that change the dramaturgy from one of conflict and survival – the human hero triumphing over an inimical environment, a weapon in his hand – to narratives of collecting, assembling, and sharing of what is crucial for multispecies co-existence. "Unlike the dominant dramas of Anthropocene and Capitalocene discourse, human beings

---

[41] Dipesh CHAKRABARTY, "The Global and the Planetary: Some Thoughts on Our Times," keynote lecture delivered at the SPARC conference "New Terrains of Consciousness" in February 2021.

[42] CHAKRABARTY, *The Crises of Civilization* 182-183.

[43] CHAKRABARTY, *The Crises of Civilization* 188.

[44] Bruno LATOUR, *Facing Gaia: Eight Lectures on the New Climatic Regime*, trans. Catherine Porter (Cambridge: Polity, 2017. For a critical appraisal of Latour's Gaia-stories, see HARAWAY, *Staying With the Trouble* 40-43.

[45] HARAWAY, *Staying With the Trouble: Making Kin in the Chthulucene* (2016).

[46] Ursula LEGUIN, "The Carrier Bag Theory of Fiction," *Dancing at the Edge of the World: Thoughts on Words, Women, Places* (New York: Grove, 1989) 165-70.

are not the only important actors in the Chthulucene, with all other beings able simply to react," Haraway explains. "The order is reknitted: human beings are with and of the earth, and the biotic and abiotic powers of this earth are the main story." These new stories do not absolve human beings of responsibility, on the contrary: they endow them with "response-ability."[47] Nor do they offer an escape from history – Haraway urges throughout that we "stay with the trouble" – but engender "historically situated relational worldings." Moreover, the new stories suggested by Haraway and others enable the historical narratives of the Capital-ocene to be "relationally unmade in order to compose in material-semiotic SF patterns and stories something more liveable."[48] The point is not a naïve hope that such stories might change the world. Rather, they may help to change how we experience the world and our place in it. If storytelling is a mode of worlding, then different stories can make a difference.

---

[47] HARAWAY, *Staying With the Trouble* 55, 34.
[48] HARAWAY, *Staying With the Trouble* 50.

1 From Insular Territory to Global Terrains of Consciousness: The Case of *Robinson Crusoe* and *The Farther Adventures*

– Isabel Karremann

This chapter discusses the terrains of consciousness explored in eighteenth-century narratives of colonialism and globalization. Departing from the assumption that such narratives are attempts at understanding the world on a global scale it examines the cognitive as well as emotional geographies these narratives chart.

Daniel Defoe's adventure novel *The Life and Strange Surprizing Adventures of Robinson Crusoe* (1719) is now habitually read as a master-narrative of Western superiority and colonial appropriation, yet its sequel *The Farther Adventures of Robinson Crusoe*, published in the same year, takes a different approach to its protagonist-narrator's encounters with the world.[1] The difference, I maintain, is due to a necessary recalibration of the relationship between consciousness and environment on a global scale. This recalibration is visually indicated by the frontispieces to the different parts of the novel: the first shows the figure of Robinson Crusoe on his island wearing goat-skin coat and breeches, a wide-brimmed hat on his head, two guns over his shoulders and a sword by his side (fig. 1). The island-made clothes, the ship sailing off in the background left, and a fence in the background right indicate a collapsing of time, as events from different moments in the story are brought together in the frame of the engraving.[2] Everything is focussed on Crusoe's island existence and the formative experience he makes there. The visual narrative is expanded by the frontispiece to part three, *Serious*

---

[1] I will be using the following edition: *The Novels of Daniel Defoe*, vols. 1 and 2, ed. by W. R. Owens (London: Pickering & Chatto, 2008). References to this edition will be indicated in brackets in the main text.

[2] Cf. David Blewett, "The Iconic Crusoe," *The Cambridge Companion to 'Robinson Crusoe'*, ed. by John Richetti (Cambridge: Cambridge UP, 2018) 159-190, here 161, who suggests that "the ship in the background is not actually there. Rather, he imagines it, both remembering the ship that brought him to the island and longing for one that will come to take him away."

 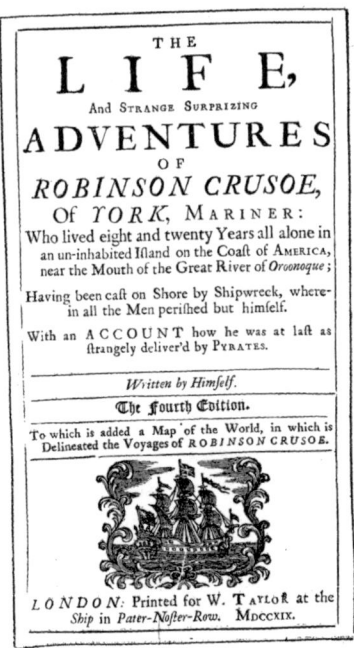

Fig. 1: Frontispiece to *The Life and Strange Surprizing Adventures of Robinson Crusoe* (1719; source: HathiTrust / University of Michigan, https://hdl.handle.net/2027/mdp.39015078548396, Public Domain).

Reflections,[3] which presents a bird's-eye view of the whole island, with several episodes involving Crusoe and the indigenous "savages" as well as the small com-

---

[3]   I am here neglecting the third part, *Serious Reflections* (1720), as it changes from an adventure narrative about encounters with the world to an inner world of moral-didactic commentary, religious meditation and at times polemic opinion on keywords like "Honesty" or "Providence." *Serious Reflections* never achieved the popularity of the first two parts, lacking their action-packed plot of adventure. Nevertheless, the three parts were usually published together until the end of the eighteenth century, with the popularity of *Farther Reflections* continuing into the early twentieth century, after which the readers' view of *Robinson Crusoe* was dominated by the first part only. It is one purpose of the present chapter to demonstrate the importance of reading Parts 1 and 2 together so as to understand the novel's relevance for a literary history of globalization. On the reception history of the three volumes see Melissa FREE, "Un-erasing Crusoe: *Farther Adventures* in the Nineteenth-Century," *Book History* 9 (2006): 89-130.

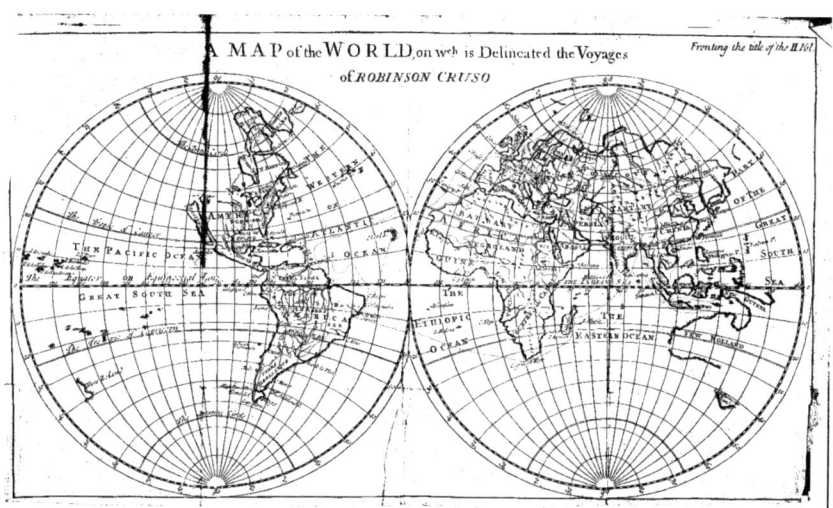

Fig. 2: Frontispiece to *The Farther Adventures of Robinson Crusoe* (1722; source: Internet Archive / Boston Public Library, https://archive.org/details/fartheradventure1722defo/page/n7/).

munity which develops on the island toward the end of the first part and occupies a large section of the narrative in the second part. The second part, *Farther Adventures*, opens up the perspective to the global scale by showing "A Map of the World, on which is Delineated the Voyages of Robinson Crusoe" in a thin dotted line (fig. 2). Such world maps were meant to convey a sense of overview and control, to "overcom[e] the fear of the unknown by slowly integrating the outer regions into the visual schema of the world" as "a single homogenous space" with "familiar territories."[4] Yet the main impression is the vast expanse of the world across which Crusoe makes his haphazard journeys, leaving hardly a trace. Moreover, the logic of periphery and centre is suspended: the map gives no clue as to what would count as "outer regions" and what, conversely, might be the central position at which a spectator is located. For all intents and purposes, such a world map could as well have provided a disconcerting experience of marginalization to a European, let alone a British viewer – and this is precisely the experience that Crusoe, too, makes on his further voyages to the East Indies, to China and back to Europe across the vast steppes and deserts of Tartary and Russia. Crusoe will not respond well to this marginalization, insisting on a self-centred, metaphorically 'insular' perspective throughout. But this is precisely the point the novel is

---

[4]   Cristian JACOB, *The Sovereign Map: Theoretical Approaches in Cartography through History*, trans. Tom Conley (Chicago: Chicago UP, 2006) 273.

making, I would suggest: inhabiting a globalized world demands an adjustment of one's cognitive and emotional responses to this experience.

The visual modification of scale prefigured through the engravings points at the two different modes of inhabiting the world which are figured in the different volumes of the narrative. While on 'his' island, Crusoe experiences and shapes the environment according to his mental preconceptions, fencing off sections of it, cultivating or fortifying them, and turning them into a manorial "estate," "a fortress," a "kingdom" and, explicitly, a "colony." His geomorphing activities are a function of the larger master narrative the novel is generally thought to advocate in order to effectively turn the island into a colonial territory. The second part, by contrast, takes Crusoe – after a return to the island that is quite brief but recounted in detail – on a ten-year voyage of trade through South-East Asia to China and back to Europe. Driven by commercial interest as well as curiosity, Crusoe encounters foreign cultures at first with the culturally relativist, open mind-set of a trader, a tourist, even an anthropologist: not possession of a territory, but knowledge of foreign terrains and the ways of living there inform his experience of the world. As he enters China, however, his frame of consciousness narrows down to that of a British chauvinist and a Christian crusader. His at times almost hysterical fits of xenophobia and religious fundamentalism can be read, as Robert Markley and others have pointed out, as compensations for the experience of Western economic and cultural inferiority, especially when facing China as a leading global power.[5] We can also productively understand them as a response to multifaceted global terrains that utterly defy any cognitive appropriation on Crusoe's part: rather than subsuming them under Western paradigms of thought – individualism, capitalism, colonialism – Crusoe is constantly forced to adapt to the material and sensory conditions of a globalized world. His failure to do so successfully manifests itself in xenophobic invectives and a constant longing to be back on his island territory where he could still experience himself as master.

In reading *Robinson Crusoe* as a novel about imaginative world-making, I propose that we move away from the narrow focus on colonialism that has come to dominate readings of the novel. Such readings tend to be based on the first part only, and in it, on the island episode. If we include the second part, in which Crusoe articulates misgivings about the colonization project, and consider his encounters with the wider world, a different (critical) narrative emerges. Taking the cue from Betty Joseph, we should ask: "How do literary texts […] change their

---

[5]   See Robert MARKLEY, *The Far East and the English Imagination: 1600–1730* (Cambridge: Cambridge UP, 2006); Eun Kyung MIN, *China and the Writing of English Literary Modernity, 1690–1770* (Cambridge: Cambridge UP, 2018).

orientation if they are read as part of a stage within a larger history of globalization?"[6] While the answer will not be a redeeming counter-narrative – instead of embracing a tolerant cosmopolitanism, Crusoe soon develops into a chauvinist Christian fundamentalist – the 'global' perspective "offer[s] a much-needed critique of Eurocentrism, especially for historians of the eighteenth century and the Enlightenment."[7] Roxann Wheeler has noted with regard to the first part that "it is possible to read *Robinson Crusoe* as a vindication of the European, specifically the British, colonial spirit *and* an exploration of its fissures,"[8] a view that has more recently been substantiated by Dennis Todd's revisionary account of colonialism in the novel, stating that "it is often difficult to see how exactly *Robinson Crusoe* offers a straightforward and unalloyed defense of his country's colonial ventures."[9] If we include in our considerations the second part and the global range of imaginative worlding this narrative enacts, then the fissures of Crusoe's insular mind-set become increasingly explicit and are exposed for critique.

1.1 Territory and Terrain

In her article on "Worlding and Unworlding in the Long Eighteenth Century," Betty Joseph adopts Jean-Luc Nancy's terminology of *mondialisation* to describe the processes of worlding through and at the behest of colonialism, which has an effect of 'unworlding' on those who are excluded from this world-picture or show up in it as objects. "When women, non-Europeans, animals, materials, or foreign

---

[6] Betty JOSEPH, "Worlding and Unworlding in the Long Eighteenth Century," *Eighteenth-Century Studies* 52.1 (2018): 27-31, here: 28.

[7] Cf. Ann Marie FALLON, *Global Crusoe: Comparative Literature, Postcolonial Theory and Transnational Aesthetics* (Farnham: Ashgate, 2011) 2, who suggests that modern adaptations of the Crusoe-myth can be read as registering complex experiences of inhabiting a globalized world: "I propose that we see Crusoe today no longer as just a lone, struggling survivor, and individualist as Ian Watt has convincingly argued, but as a cosmopolitan figure of connection to and a representation of our own moment of anxiety around a rapidly globalizing world."

[8] Roxann WHEELER, *The Complexion of Race: Categories of Difference in Eighteenth-Century British Culture* (Philadelphia: U of Pennsylvania P, 2000) 55.

[9] Dennis TODD, "*Robinson Crusoe* and Colonialism," *The Cambridge Companion to* Robinson Crusoe, ed. John RICHETTI (Cambridge: Cambridge UP, 2018) 142-156.

lands show up," she asks, "do they show up in a determined way?"[10] In the first part of *Robinson Crusoe*, there are precious few women, but non-Europeans, animals, and materials do show up as objects to be possessed, sold, and used: the boy Xury, with whom Robinson flees from captivity in Sallee, a city on the Atlantic coast of Morocco, is sold by him as a servant boy (1: 69-73, 81); Crusoe himself orders servants from England and buys slaves to run his Brazil plantation (1: 84). Similarly, the Caribbean island on which he is shipwrecked for twenty-eight years shows up mainly as territory. The *OED* lists as the historically relevant meaning of 'territory' "an extent of the land belonging to or under the jurisdiction of a ruler, state, or group of people" (1b) as well as the figurative use "an area of knowledge; a sphere of thought or action, a province" (3a). The first meaning is evidently in operation when Crusoe sets himself up as the ruler of his island territory by building walls,[11] fencing off ground (1: 142, 165), conducting surveys (1: 129-30), turning his "Habitation" into a "Fortress" by means of a double wall as well as creating "a little kind of Bower [surrounded] with a strong fence," which he calls his "Country House" (1: 136), and – early in Part Two – providing the island community with a legal codex on the basis of which he executes justice. The second meaning of 'territory' is at work throughout and is conveyed by the act of narrative ordering: the island is Crusoe's territory to the extent that he brings his systems of representation to bear on it, apprehending it in terms of European modes of cognition and world-making, such as keeping a calendar (1: 134, 155) as well as a journal (1: 109-134), making lists of his provisions and possessions that follow the accumulative logic of trade, and employing a Christian rhetoric of divine providence that retrospectively imposes meaning and order on his precarious, bewildering existence. Together, these have been identified as the cognitive disposition of bourgeois, capitalist subjectivity at the heart of the colonial enterprise.[12]

---

[10]   JOSEPH, "Worlding and Unworlding" 29. Jean-Luc NANCY, *The Creation of the World, or Globalization*, trans. François Raffoul and David Pettigrew (New York: SUNY, 2007), seems to employ the terms 'globalisation' and '*mondialisation*' (or world-forming) synonymously; as his translators point out, however, "they reveal two quite distinct, if not opposite, meanings" (1): globalisation points to "the uniformity produced by a global economical and technological logic […] leading toward the opposite of an inhabitable world, to 'the un-world,'" while *mondialisation* refers to "the possibility of an authentic world-forming" (ibid.) that is creative rather than destructive. I will follow Joseph's synonymous usage because it allows me to distinguish between colonialism and globalisation as two different narratives of imaginative world-making in which the latter is much closer to Nancy's meaning of *mondialisation*.

[11]   On Crusoe's obsession with building walls, see MIN 58-59.

[12]   Robert MARKLEY, "'I have now done with my island, and all manner of discourse about it': Crusoe's *Farther Adventures* and the Unwritten History of the Novel," *A Companion to the Eight-*

For the purpose of turning the island into his territory, Crusoe employs a rhetoric of sovereignty whose power and legitimacy is directly bound to the possession of land:

> I descended a little on the Side of that delicious Vale, surveying it with a secret Kind of Pleasure, (tho' mixt with my other afflicting Thoughts) to think that this was all my own, that I was King and Lord of all this Country indefeasibly, and had a Right of Possession; and if I could convey it, I might have it in Inheritance, as completely as any Lord of a Manor in *England*. (1: 131)

Here, the activity of surveying is identified as an act of taking-in-possession.[13] Defoe has his protagonist speak the language of political philosophy and law: his "Right of Possession" as sovereign is "indefeasible," that is, without risk of forfeiture, inalienably his. When he likens himself to "the Lord of a Manor in *England*," he projects a foreign territorializing concept onto the local island-terrain: in England, the owner of a landed estate had special rights of lordship over tenants and held court (1: 304, note 312). By using this term, in conjunction with the idea of inheritance, Crusoe also prospectively fills his world (albeit imaginatively) with people who by definition appear as his subjects and heirs. He thereby carries out an act of worlding in terms of territory, (re)making the world in the image of England.[14]

Crusoe will go on to people his island with ersatz-subjects – a dog, cats, and a parrot – whose presence bolsters his sense of territorial sovereignty: "It would have made a Stoick smile to have seen, me and my little Family sit down to Dinner; there was my Majesty the Prince and Lord of the whole Island; I had the Lives of all my Subjects at my absolute Command. I could hang, draw, give Liberty, and take it away, and no Rebels among my Subjects" (1: 166). His domesticated animal-subjects function as props for Crusoe's self-image as "Prince and Lord" with absolute power over all that live in his territory.[15] The household, in

---

eenth-Century English Novel, ed. Paula R. BACKSCHEIDER and Catherine INGRASSIA (Oxford: Blackwell, 2008) 25-47.

[13]   This has long been recognized as a technology of imperial expansion. See esp. Mary Louise PRATT, *Imperial Eyes: Travel Writing and Transculturation* (London: Routledge, 1992).

[14]   Such rhetoric is supplemented by activities like fencing off parts of the island or building a wall around his habitation, thereby creating "a perfect Enclosure." This mimics a particularly English way of inscribing ownership on land through acts of enclosure, which was perpetuated in the American colonies (see MIN 62).

[15]   See R. John WILLIAMS, "Naked Creatures: *Robinson Crusoe*, The Beast, and The Sovereign," *Comparative Critical Studies* 2.3 (2005): 337-48; Philipp ARMSTRONG, *What Animals Mean in the Fiction of Modernity* (New York: Routledge, 2008), see esp. 5-48; and Alex MACINTOSH, "Cru-

the political philosophy of the time an established analogy for the state, thus becomes the pattern through which "the whole Island" is worlded. This household will later include Man Friday.

The reassuring presence of submissive subjects is set off by the absence of other, less tractable human beings. Crusoe's taking possession of the island as his territory is premised on the assumption that it is a "solitary desart" and therefore available for appropriation. This premise featured in early modern natural law as *terra nullius*, no man's land, and was an enabling fiction of the discourse of colonialism. *Terra nullius* does not so much mean that a country is indeed uninhabited; it rather distinguishes between settled, cultivated land as possession and land that is merely used by indigenous people.[16] The second case constitutes a terrain, as it were, that is available for territorial appropriation by colonial settlers. Hence Crusoe's panic at discovering a naked footprint on the beach which threatens his very premise of property right. As Wolfram Schmidgen explains, in contemporary legal discourse "even a very partial contact of feet with soil could suffice to indicate 'intent to possess,' and it is this possibility that Crusoe's extravagant response registers."[17] Another category of human co-presence that is successfully discounted in Part One but will become a disturbing reality in Part Two is the presence of others laying claim to a territory. "I was Lord of the whole Manor; or if I pleas'd I might call my self King, or Emperor over the whole Country which I had Possession of," Crusoe declares before he makes the telling addition: "There were no Rivals. I had no Competitor, none to dispute Sovereignty or Command with me" (1: 152). The idea of having rivals points to political conflict and civil war resulting from competing claims to sovereignty and command. The passage further includes mercantile competition in this idea when Crusoe goes on to illustrate his absolute power in terms of exploiting the land for profit in global trade: "I might have rais'd Ship Loadings of Corn, […] I had Timber enough to have built a Fleet of Ships […] I had Grapes enough to have made Wine, or to have cur'd into Raisins, to have loaded that Fleet" (ibid.).

In hindsight, this will have been Crusoe's happiest moment: inhabiting a territory without competitors who challenge his sovereignty. As the novel continues and moves into the second part, this premise is revealed as an enabling fantasy that increasingly collides with the resistant agency of other humans: savages who fight back, settlers who disregard Crusoe's decrees, competitors outdoing him in

---

soe's Abattoir: Cannibalism and Animal Slaughter in *Robinson Crusoe*," *Critical Quarterly* 53.2 (2011): 24-43.

[16] See Wolfram SCHMIDGEN, *Eighteenth-Century Fiction and the Law of Property* (Cambridge: Cambridge UP, 2002) 33.

[17] SCHMIDGEN 40-41.

trade, foreign civilizations that remain unavailable for appropriation and exploitation. In particular after he has left his island for good in the middle of *The Farther Adventures*, Crusoe's accustomed modes of apprehending the world undergo a significant change. No longer a fixed territory, the world becomes a 'terrain,' a "tract of country considered with regard to its natural features, configuration, etc." (OED 2a). Unable to possess the global terrain (often because it is the territory of others), Crusoe can at best apprehend it in terms of "its military use esp. as affecting its tactical advantages, fitness for manœuvring, etc." (ibid.), for which the frequent, hostile encounters with native people give ample opportunity. In that global terrain, non-Europeans show up not as objects but as subjects – as agents with their own agendas, knowledge, and tactics. Crusoe must adapt his cognitive and emotional responses to foreign cultures accordingly. Driven by commercial interest as well as curiosity, he encounters them at first with the culturally relativist, open mind-set of a trader, a tourist, sometimes an explorer: not possession of a territory, but knowledge of a foreign terrain and the ways of being there inform his experience of the world.

In fact, the territorializing impetus was already challenged by uncomfortable moments on the island. At these moments Crusoe is confronted with the surroundings as a terrain that determines his consciousness, rather than the other way round. Consider the following scene which strikes a contrapuntal note in his territorializing fantasies:

> [A]s I walk'd about [...] the Anguish of my Soul at my Condition, would break out upon me on a sudden, and my very Heart would die within me, to think of the Woods, the Mountains, the Desarts I was in; and how I was a Prisoner lock'd up with the Eternal Bars and Bolts of the Ocean, in an uninhabited Wilderness, without Redemption: In the midst of the greatest Composure of my Mind, this would break out upon me like a Storm, and make me wring my Hands [...]. (1: 140)

No longer something to be appropriated through enclosure, now the combined terrain of landscape and seascape – hyperbolically pluralized as woods, mountains, and deserts – encloses Crusoe as a prisoner. The reassuring idea of *terra nullius* gives way to "an uninhabited Wilderness" to which he is helplessly exposed. This scene is followed by religious reflections on divine providence, from which Crusoe draws the mental strength to transform terrain into territory again: "But now I began to exercise my self with new Thoughts", and "From this Moment I began to conclude in my Mind" (I: 141). Rather than stubbornly holding on to preconceived notions, such moments signal a shift in Robinson's consciousness induced by his experience of the island terrain. As Dennis Todd points out, "Crusoe repeatedly has to abandon attitudes and assumptions he brought with him and see the world anew: the rhythm of the seasons, the flux of the currents, the relative value of money and things of use, the importance of human bonds, and most of his religious views. [...] The New World is, after all, a new world, and Defoe's point is that to survive in it, Crusoe will have to look at it more closely and with new eyes."[18] This consciousness-shaping capacity of the terrain will become the dominant note of the latter half of *Farther Adventures*.

The resistance of material objects is another dimension through which the tension between terrain and territorializing impetus shows up. For instance, a crucial part of Crusoe's occupation of the island is his attempt at building a canoe from a whole tree. In this *periagua*, he wants to circumnavigate the island, thereby extending his scope of surveying. Yet the first attempt fails because he chooses too big a tree, and the canoe is too heavy to be moved to the water: "It lay about one hundred Yards from the Water, and not more: But the first inconvenience was, it was up Hill towards the Creek; well, to take away this Discouragement, I resolv'd to dig into the Surface of the Earth, and so make a Declivity" (1: 151). Misreading the terrain as he has misjudged the object's properties, however, these geomorphing activities likewise are to no avail. Only a reduction of his ambitions to a smaller canoe and a submission to the given terrain allow Crusoe to follow through on his plan (1: 157-9). The cannibals are, of course, the supremely resistant human 'objects.' Their arrival on the island shakes Crusoe's sense of possession profoundly and at least momentarily turns the territory into a terrain: their presence and agency force him to inhabit 'his' world differently. And the landscape of the terrain is in league with the savages who visit it: Crusoe indulges in triumphant fantasies of violent destruction, yet his cognitive response changes toward a more moderate, tolerant view due to the physical exertion of having to climb a steep hill each day for several months to keep lookout for the savages.[19]

These instances show how the terrain shapes Crusoe's consciousness as much as he cognitively and materially shapes it into a territory. To read *The Life and Strange Surprising Adventures* as a straightforward tale about colonization, therefore, does not do justice to the anxieties that this dialectic of territory and terrain engenders. The tension becomes even more prominent in *Farther Adventures* when Crusoe, after a three-week stay on his island during which he reconciles conflicts among the settler colony he left behind, determines to give up entirely

---

[18] TODD 143.

[19] See Nicholas SEAGER, "Crusoe's Crusade: Defoe, Genocide, and Imperialism," *Études Anglaises* 72.2 (2019): 196-212, here: 203. Cf. TODD 146, who likewise argues that Crusoe has to "rethink cannibalism," mainly because Defoe and his contemporaries had to: treating indigenous people as brute savages had led to a deterioration of "Anglo-Indian relations in the colonies," to the extent that "the British empire in the Americas was in danger."

on the project of territorial colonization: "I have now done with my Island, and all manner of Discourse about it" (2: 125), he writes. This is followed by a brief but detailed sketch of an alternative narrative of the proper colonizing process that retrospectively (if not entirely convincingly) frames the story told in Part One as something different altogether. Crusoe lists specific colonizing practices and their legal conditions: "Had I taken a small Vessel from *England*, and went directly to the Island; had I loaded her […] with all the Necessaries for the Plantation […], took a Patent from the Government here, to have secur'd my Property, in Subjection only to that of *England*; had I carry'd over Cannon and Ammunition, Servants and People, to plant, and taking Possession of the Place, fortify'd and strengthen'd it in the Name of *England*" – yet none of this has actually taken place: "But I never so much as pretended to plant in the Name of any Government or Nation; or to acknowledge any Prince, or to call my People Subjects to any one Nation more than another; nay, I never so much as gave the Place a Name; but left it as I found it belonging to no Body" (2: 125-6).

Crusoe imaginatively restores here the colonial territory to the state of terrain, *terra nullius*. Markley reads this as a final "self-conscious *rejection*" of the "colonialist parable,"[20] recognizing that *Farther Adventures* is not an unsuccessful sequel along the same lines as the first, but offers instead a different narrative of global modernity characterized by commercial relations and intercultural entanglements. That narrative both "depicts and seeks to counter" a globalized world for which Defoe's protagonist, however, turns out to be poorly equipped: Crusoe's "limited set of imaginative and intellectual tools to deal with cultural difference"[21] mean that he is constantly thrust into a terrain he finds threatening and foreign and to which he responds with a "compensatory Eurocentrism."[22] In the same measure, the narrative of *Farther Adventures* also distances itself increasingly from its narrator, as John Richetti has recently pointed out: Crusoe's extreme chauvinism is implicitly bracketed as prejudice, due to its sheer arbitrariness and hyperbole.[23]

But again we need to be cautious and to differentiate carefully. For between his colonial mind-set and his Eurocentric chauvinism – both of which are expressions of an ideology of insularity – Crusoe does exhibit moments of enlightened reflection in the face of cultural alterity. Early on in his global travels, he approaches the world with curiosity, respect, and a willingness to submit himself to

---

[20]   MARKLEY, *The Far East* 26.
[21]   MIN 53.
[22]   Betty JOSEPH, "Capitalism and Its Others: Intersecting and Competing Forms in Eighteenth-Century Fiction," *Studies in Eighteenth-Century Culture* 45 (2016): 157-173, here: 160.
[23]   John RICHETTI, "Eurocentric Crusoe: *The Farther Adventures of Robinson Crusoe*," *Études Anglaises* 72.2 (2019): 213-224, here: 222.

the rules of foreign territories. Richetti argues that "Crusoe's moral enlightenment and thoughtful reservations about cross-cultural imperial violence" can be
understood as direct responses to the experience of being in a foreign terrain:
they are "unintended side effects of his compelling desires to have new experiences and to see new places, locales where Europeans were often enough not welcome."[24] This becomes evident in an episode set on Madagascar, where Crusoe
and the ship's crew enter into small-scale trading relations with the natives before
one of them presumes to rape a girl and the ensuing violence escalates into a
massacre. Crusoe condemns the massacre, in which a whole town is destroyed,
as "altogether barbarous" and "beyond what was human" (1: 135). His moral cen-
sure is the reason why he has to leave board eventually. This episode will remain
relevant throughout the *Farther Adventures*, as we will see later, although its
meaning for Crusoe will change profoundly. It thereby also functions as a touch-
stone for the character development of the narrator.[25] What is important for our
purpose now is that Crusoe's respect for the native population is conveyed
through his acceptance of local practices of managing social relations through
marking space as mutually respected (rather than unilaterally imposed and
dominated) territory. Defoe apparently drew on existing travel accounts from
Africa for this passage,[26] and it conveys a sense of anthropological authenticity
that makes it well worth quoting at length:

> We were obliged to stay here some Time after we had furnish'd ourselves
> with Provisions; and I, that was always too curious, to look into every
> Nook of the World where ever I came, was for going on Shore as often as
> I could; it was on the East Side of the Island that we went on Shore, one
> Evening, and the People, who by the Way are very numerous, came
> thronging about us, and stood gazing at us at a Distance; but as we had
> traded freely with them, and had been kindly used, we thought ourselves
> in no Danger; but when we saw the People, we cut three Boughs out of a
> Tree, and stuck them up at a Distance from us, which it seems, is a Mark
> in the Country, not only of Truce and Friendship, but when it is accepted,
> the other Side set up three Poles or Boughs, which is a Signal, that they
> accept the Truce too; but then, this is a known Condition of the Truce,
> that you are not to pass beyond their three Poles, and all the Space be-
> tween your Poles and theirs, is allow'd like a Market, for free Converse,
> Traffic and Commerce: When you go there, you must not carry your
> Weapons with you[.] (2: 128)

---

[24] RICHETTI 215.
[25] See RICHETTI, passim.
[26] See *The Novels of Daniel Defoe*, note 198 on 2: 232.

The neutral space between the two sets of poles becomes a market place in which people of different tribes, nations and ethnicities can meet in "free Converse." Trade is what connects people and ensures peace, because it offers an alternative to armed conflict, a view that the liberal Defoe held with conviction. Unfortunately, the neutrality of the market place is not respected as one English sailor abducts a native woman from this protected space, and is tortured and killed in punishment. While Crusoe stresses the sailor's unlawful and immoral actions, his companions' thirst for revenge has them – much against Crusoe's advice and admonitions – burn down the town and kill its inhabitants. Moral enlightenment proves powerless to prevent the deterioration of peaceful commercial relations into armed conflict and bloodshed fuelled by chauvinism.

Crusoe's refusal to condone this massacre results in his being set ashore in Bengal, with "all [his] necessary Things" and "a sufficient Sum of Money" (2: 143), further away from England than he had been on his Caribbean island. Crusoe first takes his bearings in this foreign terrain by calculating the relative distances of possible routes home. But instead of returning to England he joins an international community of expatriates and, encouraged by an English merchant, decides "to go [on] a trading Voyage to *China*" that will take several years and make him incredibly rich. This is a protracted episode enjoyable for the protagonist as well as his readers, who are presented with "a great variety [of] strange and surprising things" as Crusoe easily slips into the life of a global trader – even though he keeps insisting that he is not motivated by "getting more Money": he is "rich enough" (2: 145). Instead of trying to possess the world, or parts of it, Crusoe travels across its terrains in pursuit of profitable deals and adventure. Markley identifies these episodes as a "vision of infinitely profitable trade to the Far East and the South Seas."[27] *Farther Adventures* appeared at the height of the 'South Sea'-craze that held English investors in its grip. The South Sea Company sold shares to private people and businessmen that rendered fantastic profits until the bubble burst in the late summer of 1720 and plunged many of them into ruin. Defoe's sequel, written as the South Sea Bubble was about to burst, would have provided a warning to those who looked for it: for while Crusoe is made rich through the Asia trade, his narrative signals clearly that the most profitable trade, that with China, was mere wish-fulfilment.

---

[27]   MARKLEY, *The Far East* 28.

1.2 Perfect Insularity: China as Utopia of Self-Sufficiency

Crusoe dismisses China as a source of economic profit for Europeans, concluding that China is "not [...] worth naming, or worth my while writing of, or any
that shall come after me to read" (2: 173). His utter contempt for all things Chinese stands in striking contradiction, however, to the wide-spread contemporary
admiration for China. Inspired by early travel reports of Jesuit missionaries, a
myth of China as an ancient civilization, whose untold riches and sophisticated
culture were protected against hostile incursions by an impenetrable Great Wall,
dominated the European view in the seventeenth and early eighteenth centuries.

Crusoe's oddly negative response can be understood as the result of a complicated relation of economic rivalry in which European countries, and England
in particular, stood at a serious disadvantage vis-à-vis a self-sufficient Chinese
empire that exported exotic luxury goods for a high prize while remaining largely
uninterested in European produce. In *New Voyage Around the World* (1725), for
instance, Defoe articulated his criticism of the export deficit characteristic of the
Asia trade along with a mortifying sense of inferiority: "[W]e carry nothing or
very little but money [to the Orient], the innumerable nations of the Indies,
China, &c., despising our manufactures and filling us with their own."[28] As Min
explains, the economic rivalry was complemented by a cultural contest over technological progress and modernity, an imbalanced fight largely conducted again
on the European side. For Defoe in particular, it seems, "the definition of European modernity was challenged by the reputation of the Chinese" as an ancient
civilization which had "invented much of mankind's basic technology." China
stood "for an alternative modernity that put[] to shame the European modernity
'we admire ourselves so much for'" and thus posed an "obstacle to European self-
love."[29]

In order to make a bid for the superiority of European modernity, Defoe had
to come to terms with the myth of China. He did so by what is recognized as the
key cognitive and representational structure of European modernity: realism,
and the novel as its most popular form. Crusoe explicitly states after observing
an ingenious piece of Chinese workmanship – a house built of porcelain, that
mysterious substance the secret of which was inaccessible to Europeans – that his
aim is to debunk suchlike myths through his realistic eye-witness account: "As
this is one of the singularities to *China*, so they may be allow'd to excel in it," he
grudgingly concedes, "but I am very sure they excel in their Accounts of it; for

---

[28] Daniel DEFOE, *A New Voyage Round the World by a Course Never Sailed Before*, ed. George A.
      AITKIN (London: Dent, 1902) 155.
[29] MIN 50.

they told me such incredible Things of their Performance in *Crockery Ware*, for such it is, that I care not to relate, as knowing it could not be true" (2: 181). The representational structure of myth ("they excel in their Accounts of it") is replaced by the representational structure of realism, indicated by the truth-claim Crusoe is able to make as an eye-witness as well as by insisting to reduce the refined product of a complicated alchemical procedure to its crude materiality of earthen-ware ("for such it is").[30] At a macro-textual level, Defoe's novel of realism "attempt[s] to write China into a new kind of narrative that he helped invent."[31] *Farther Adventures*, in other words, writes China out of myth and into history. Crusoe's strategy is to expose Chinese degeneration, pomposity and ignorance, and to cut it down to size by comparing Chinese culture unfavourably with England or other European countries, whose superiority is belligerently asserted. His initially positive, brief description of the city of Nanquin, for instance, is immediately followed by a lengthy comparison with European cities in which he makes somewhat improbable claims about their superiority:

> [W]hen I compare the miserable People of these Countries with ours, their Fabricks, their Manner of Living, their Government, their Religion, their Wealth, and their Glory as some call it, I must confess, I do not so much as think it is worth naming [...] what are their Buildings to the Pallaces and Royal Buildings of *Europe*? What their Trade, to the universal Commerce of *England*, *Holland*, *France* and *Spain*? What are their Cities to ours, for Wealth, Strength, Gaiety of Apparel, rich Furniture, and an infinite Variety? What are their Ports, supplied with a few Jonks and Barks, to our Navigation, our Merchant Fleets, and our large and powerful Navys? Our City of *London* has more Trade than all their mighty Empire: One *English*, or *Dutch*, or *French* Man of War, of 80 Guns, would fight and destroy all the shipping of *China*. (2: 173)

If his readers at home are impressed by the fabled Chinese wealth, trade, military strength, and power of government – which Crusoe cannot dismiss altogether – this is because previous reports have overstated them in their surprise to find "a barbarous Nation of Pagans, little better than Savages" to possess them at all: "otherwise it is in itself nothing at all" (ibid.). Again the aim is to cut Chinese civilization down to size and to elevate European culture by comparison.

---

[30] On the significance of the porcelain house as one of the "symbolic architectures" through which Crusoe negotiates his relationship to the Other, see Scott NOWKA, "Building the Wall: Crusoe and the Other," *Digital Defoe* 2.1 (2010): 41-57. Nowka highlights the undeniable admiration the China house elicits from Crusoe, and sees the protagonist's response "as characteristic of his reaction to China as a whole: he sees why others are impressed at a distance, yet he eagerly looks into details to dismiss the achievement" (50).

[31] MIN 52.

The effect is ambivalent, however, because even in this new narrative China remains central to "definitions of English modernity [...] in terms of unprecedented maritime expansion, commercial opportunity, and racial and cultural conflict." If Defoe's novel is, as Min remarks, a "response to the 'integration of global space' produced by the early modern forms of global exchange," then the problem is that England, and Crusoe as its representative, does not emerge as the unchallenged hero of the narrative of globalization offered in *Farther Adventures*. Instead, China newly "become[s] a modern economic, political, and cultural problematic" that Crusoe (and, by implication, England) is poorly equipped to solve.[32] In Markley's reading, Chinese independence functions as both a model for and a threat to European mercantile ambitions: "The promise that the Far East holds, and the myth it embodies for Europeans, then, is that it can sustain an unending, and infinitely profitable trade. The reality that Defoe must deal with is that the Chinese cannot be transformed into the subjects or dupes of European imperialism."[33] Unable to factually match Chinese military and mercantile power, Crusoe resorts to rhetorically and imaginatively belittling it. By the same token, his boastful claims of English superiority are, Markley argues convincingly, compensation fantasies to come to terms with the historical reality of the overwhelming Chinese competition in the global trade. While Part One offered a reassuring image of the Englishman's economic self-sufficiency and cultural superiority on his island that functioned as "a colonialist parable," this self-image is threatened in part in Part Two by the realisation of global interdependencies and mercantile rivalries: *Farther Adventures* "depicts and seeks to counter nightmare visions of an embattled English identity in a hostile world."[34]

Against this historical background, *Farther Adventures* can be read as an attempt at negotiating the appropriate measure of British involvement in global trade relationships. The old ideal of splendid isolation,[35] indulged in the island episodes of Part One, increasingly has to give way to a recognition of the modern entanglement into global networks of commerce and consumption. However, insularity as an ideal does not entirely disappear in Part Two. It is invoked – enviously – in the myth of China as island, and Crusoe's dismissal of that myth can be understood as a compulsory repetition of, or perhaps a revenge for Britain's loss of a protective insularity. Moreover, in a complex act of compensatory back-projection, it is imaginatively reasserted as a cognitive and symbolic structure

---

[32] MIN 53.
[33] MARKLEY, *The Far East* 29.
[34] MARKLEY, *The Far East* 26.
[35] Already in Shakespeare's time this trope was available as a nostalgic ideal, most notably in John of Gaunt's "scepter'd isle" speech in *Richard II*, 2.1.

that simultaneously mimics China's most admired feature and proclaims Englishness. As Min remarks perceptively, "Crusoe is haunted by an ideal of a perfectly fortified independent self that hyperbolically mimics the political fantasy of China's Great Wall" which turns China into "a naturally protected, self-sufficient and self-enclosed island."[36] Crusoe's encounter with Chinese culture is filtered through an attitude that is best described as ideological insularity. His responses to the – in his view – vast terrains of China (which would appear as territory in a Chinese perspective, of course) are figured in terms of enclosed spaces that he unconsciously identifies as islands. Yet, such island-imagery says less about the Chinese territory than about Crusoe's uneasy cognitive and emotional responses to the experience of being exposed to the terrain of the global.

Already when he arrives in China, Crusoe perceives this environment in terms of guns, fortresses and walls, the very tools of self-sufficiency and self-enclosure that had structured his island existence.[37] All his comparisons between China and Europe, for instance, quickly narrow down to the question of military prowess (2: 173-4). The insistence on this aspect is ambivalent, however: it might be read as a chauvinistic boasting of European superiority, yet given the fact that technologies like black powder had been invented in China itself, Crusoe's claims begin to sound somewhat overstated, pointing to an anxiety this fantasy of European might compensates for. When it comes to China's most impressive achievement of military defence, the Great Wall, Crusoe's dismissal of this famous fortification becomes revealingly ridiculous. Moreover, given the fact that building walls had been Crusoe's key technology of turning terrain into territory, and that the Great Wall effectively turned China into an island-territory sealed off from the rest of the world, we begin to realise that Crusoe's contempt is more significant than can be explained by mere chauvinism or even compensation.

1.3 Europe in a Globalized World: Crusoe's Ideological Insularity

I think what the narrative does in such moments is to signal the profound similarity of interests, tactics and technologies of nations entangled in a global modernity. Such a similarity runs counter to ideologies of superiority, of course; hence Crusoe's vehement objection to it. What also emerges in those moments, moreover, is that the narrative increasingly distances itself from the protagonist.

---

[36] MIN 54.
[37] MIN 58.

As several critics of the *Farther Adventures* have noted, its Crusoe is not the hero readers encountered, admired, and possibly identified with in *Robinson Crusoe*. His "wildly extravagant remarks" and "almost comical and over-elaborated chauvinism," Richetti points out, undercut the objective description and more or less levelled judgment that are the hallmarks of the narrative mode of realism.[38] Driven by his "defining compulsions,"[39] Crusoe becomes an unreliable narrator to the extent it raises the question of whether "author and character [have] fully parted ways."[40] I would like to conclude with two conspicuous moments from the last pages of *Farther Adventures* that illustrate the global similarities that are uncomfortably felt but remain unacknowledged by Crusoe, and the ironic distance that the narrative builds toward its protagonist, to the point that we are offered a new model of inhabiting a globalized world embodied by a Russian Prince.

The first moment comes as Crusoe travels west with a trading caravan, crossing the vast deserts and steppes of Central Asia on the way back to Europe. As they reach the dominions ruled by the Czar of Muscovy, they come across a village that worships a wooden idol. Crusoe, who had constantly and vociferously condemned the paganism of non-Christian heathens on his travels, now devotes considerable attention to describing this "Idol made of Wood, frightful as the Devil":

> [I]t had a head certainly not so much as resembling any Creature that the World ever saw; Ears as big as Goats Horns, and as high; Eyes as big as a Crown-Piece, a Nose like a crooked Ram's Horn, and a Mouth extended four Corner'd like that of a Lion, with horrible Teeth, hooked like a Parrot's under Bill; it was dressed up in the filthiest manner that you could suppose; its upper Garment was of Sheep-Skins, with the Wool outward, a great Tartar Bonnet on the Head, with two Horn growing through it. (2: 192)

The description is followed by an account of the rites of worship conducted on that idol. The "Stupidity and brutish Worship" of the villages incenses Crusoe so that he attacks the idol with his sword; unable to do more in the face of the villager's resistance, he resolves to return at night and destroy it completely.

Interestingly, Robinson's account of this scene evokes memories of his Caribbean island. The circle of worshippers around the idol is explicitly described as an island: "A little way off from *the Island*, and at the Door of that Tent or Hut, made all of Sheep-Skins and Cow-Skins, dry'd, stood three Butchers, I thought

---

[38]   RICHETTI 219.
[39]   RICHETTI 214.
[40]   SEAGER 197.

they were thus" (2: 192, my emphasis). The epithet "Butchers" had been repeatedly used to describe the violent actions of the three English deserters on the island (2: 33ff.; interestingly, they are also prospectively likened to "a Hoord of *Tartars*", 2: 36), who now seem to enter into Crusoe's description of the three priests standing by for the sacrifice. What is more, the figure of the idol itself – standing at the centre of the 'island' of villagers, commanding their adoration – can be recognized as a grotesque version of Crusoe himself: not only does his description of it incorporate all the animals he encountered on his travels (the lion shot on the coast of Africa) or lived with on the island. The figure of the idol, clad in clothes and a large hat of goat-skin, moreover, looks a lot like Crusoe in his island dress: he too had worn "a great high shapeless Cap, made of Goat's Skin" as well as "a short Jacket of Goat-Skin, the Skirts coming down to about the middle of my Thighs: and a Pair of open-knee'd Breeches of the same, the Breeches were made of the Skin of an old He-goat, whose Hair hung down such a Length on either Side" (1: 167). The "old He-Goat" is present in the "Ram's Horn" sported by the idol as well as the skins worn "with the Wool outward." Carrying a basket on his back, "on my Shoulder my Gun, and over my Head a great clumsy ugly Goat-Skin Umbrella," Robinson is turned into "a most barbarous Shape" that appears "monstrous" and "frightful" (1: 168), much like the idol.

The comparison is lost on Crusoe, however, who regards the idol as utterly alien. Yet, instead of merely vilifying it as a token of barbarous heathenism, as he usually does, this time Robinson steps into action. Gathering around him a small group of European merchants from the caravan, he persuades them to join his "Project" to destroy the "Idol Monster" (2: 193). The "Design" for the raid on the village is provided by the massacre on Madagascar: "Well, *says I*, I'll tell you a Story; so I related the Story of our Men at Madagascar, and how they burnt and sack'd the Village there, and kill'd Man, Woman and Child, for their murdering of one of our Men, just as it is related before; and when I had done, I added, that I thought we ought to do so to this Village" (2: 194). This is a shocking moment indeed, designed to distance the reader from Crusoe as he performs a complete turn-around: where before he had condemned the massacre as "an exemplar of European atrocity,"[41] now he recommends it as the right course of action, fired by a religious "Zeal" (2: 194) that seems every bit as abominable as the heathens' worship. The effect is to make the readers, who are not taken in by this faux-moralizing righteousness, take a step back and realize just how thin the veneer of civilization is, and that it therefore does not provide a stable criterion by which to define a global hierarchy. Quite the contrary, it brings the Christian European civilization on a par with Asian civilizations, as Crusoe himself admits: "I thought

---

[41] SEAGER 206.

long before this, that as we came nearer to Europe we should find the country better peopled, and the People more civiliz'd, but I found myself mistaken in both" (2: 202). While this is only a half-hearted admission, followed by condemning numerous "Nations" of what today would be Eastern Europe as "entirely Pagan" and therefore "barbarous," it does qualify the stark contrasts by which Crusoe had before conceived of the world and considerably narrows down the territory of the – in his view – "more civiliz'd" Christian Europe. Mapping the globe according to relative states of "Ignorance and Paganism" (ibid.) as Crusoe does here, has thus the unintended side-effect of revealing the "embattled, precarious state of Christianity" in a global context.[42]

The second moment is again marked by a cross-mapping of the Caribbean island onto Eastern civilizations, and this time the effect is to expose Crusoe's ideological insularity explicitly as inferior. Already well advanced on his way west, Crusoe is forced to hibernate in the Siberian capital Tobolski. He now evokes the island episode in an effort to describe the conditions of living in Tobolski: "I was now in a quite different climate from my belov'd Island, where I never felt Cold […]. Now I made me three good Vests, with large Robes or Gowns over them to hang down to the Feet, and button close at the Wrists, and all these lin'd with Fur to make me sufficiently warm" (2: 204). In Tobolski he meets a Russian prince who has been exiled from Muscovy for political reasons. Crusoe introduces himself, in attempt to be witty, with a "Riddle[] in Government" that mainly displays his boastfulness: alluding to but not revealing his territory to be a small island, he claims to be "a greater and more powerful Prince than ever the Czar of Muscovy was" because he "had the absolute Disposal of the Lives and Fortunes of all my Subjects," "all the Lands in my Kingdom were my own […] and that never Tyrant, *for such I acknowledged myself to be*, was ever so universally belov'd, and yet so horribly fear'd, by his Subjects" (2: 205). The Prince – formerly a powerful potentate himself – is charmed with the following story of Crusoe's island-life, yet for quite different reasons than Crusoe advances: not the trappings of power, but peace of mind and resignation appeal to him. His eloquent elaboration on the pleasures of retirement and his dismissal of the "fancy'd Felicity" of power and its "dark Side" (2: 206) becomes a subtle yet pointed critique of Crusoe's world-view when he describes his own exile in analogy as being shipwrecked: "[W]e live perfectly retir'd, as suited to a State of Banishment; we have something rescue'd from the Shipwreck of our Fortunes, which keeps us from the meer Necessity of hunting for our Food" (2: 207). He is as shipwrecked as Robinson was on his island in a city which the surrounding countryside effec-

---

[42] SEAGER 197.

tively turns into a prison (2: 209). Likening his prison to an island offers a counter-narrative to that of absolute mastery over the island-territory and evokes instead, for the mindful reader, Crusoe's own experience of being subjected to a frightening, overpowering terrain.[43]

The narrative thus subtly punctures Crusoe's boastful claims by recalling what his account has conveniently left out. Moreover, because the Prince's state of imprisonment is no reason for despair but a "blessed Confinement" (2: 210), he becomes a counter-figure to Crusoe. He is presented as a truly enlightened person who has achieved a degree of autonomy from his environment through accepting it. By contrast, Crusoe constantly struggles against his environment, seeking to shape, form and master it. Seeking to re-establish his master-narrative, Crusoe offers to the Prince to liberate him from this prison, then urges him to accept the offer by saying "That he ought to look upon this as a Door open'd by Heaven for his Deliverance, and a Summons by Providence, who has the Care and Disposition of all Events, to do himself good, and to render himself useful in the World" (2: 210). This is the discourse of providence and of being useful in the world which has long been recognized as the hallmark of the Puritan middle-class bourgeois mind-set that *Robinson Crusoe* had advocated. In *Farther Adventures*, this ideology is exposed as arrogant and sinful: "Here I am free from the Temptation of returning to my former miserable Greatness," the Prince replies with some indignation to Crusoe's repeated offer, "there I am not sure but all the Seeds of Pride, Ambition, Avarice and Luxury, which I know remain in Nature, may [...] again overwhelm me, and then the happy Prisoner, who you see now Master of his Soul's Liberty, shall be the miserable Slave of his own Senses, in the Full of all personal Liberty" (2: 210).

Crusoe's much-prized personal liberty – which for him translates into the right to capitalist self-fulfilment in the possession, or at least exploitation of the inhabited world to his own advantage – is revealed as a form of slavery to worldly interests. Importantly, this is not a rejection of the world and of human nature for an ascetic ideal: "I am but Flesh," the Prince says, "a Man, a meer Man, have Passions and Affections as likely to possess and overthrow me as any Man" (ibid.). True liberty consists in an acceptance of human nature that projects a global levelling of differences – we are all merely human. This is a kind of enlightened universalism that is not the handmaid of imperial colonialism, as is often claimed, but a critique of it. At this point, the Prince is offered to all readers as a superior, positive model for inhabiting the world. Crusoe himself stands "surpriz'd" and "quite dumb" (ibid.). He overcomes his admiration quickly, though, setting out for England which he reaches at last, at the age of 72, richer

---

[43] "The Island was certainly a Prison to me, and in the worst Sense of the Word" (1: 128).

than ever before and at least now having "learn'd sufficiently to know the Value of Retirement" (2: 217).

1.4 How to Inhabit a Globalized World

Taken together, this chapter has shown two modes of worlding at work in *Robinson Crusoe* and *Farther Adventures*. The first explores how consciousness shapes the world into a territory and enables a fantasy of self-sufficient mastery, the other how consciousness is shaped by a material, resistant terrain and introduces an idea of adaptation and cohabitation. Crusoe experiences the latter mainly as a nightmare of dependency, exposure, and vulnerability to which he responds with further, compensatory fantasies of cultural superiority. These fantasies are connected with frequent and increasingly nostalgic recollections of his island: insularity as a concept shapes Crusoe's responses to the global terrain. His narrative is determined by this 'insularity' in both senses of the word, as he perceives everything in terms of island-ness and exhibits what we may call an ideology of insularity. Yet such an insular mind-set is marked negatively by the narrative: to insist on treating the entire world as a territory to be mastered and possessed is ridiculed as megalomania. Thus, the second part of Defoe's novel offers a counter-narrative to that of the first: to be part of a globalized world necessitates a different frame of consciousness than to colonize it. Crusoe's failure to see this foreshadows the eventual demise of imperialism and suggests ex negativo the cognitive and emotional dispositions necessary for successful participation in a global world. The historically prescient warning that the *Farther Adventures* spell out is that while colonialism is premised on the ability to control a territory, the global terrain cannot be controlled but only experienced and shared.

2 Phenomenalizing the Global: Women's Movements in India, 1813–2020

– Simi Malhotra

There is indeed a noumenon of the 'global': certain ideas and practices which arose in the global North or West and which have since been presumed as axiomatic and imposed or adopted across the global South and East – first in the course of European colonization and thereafter by the different means of neo-colonialism. The abstract notion of 'gender equity' may be one of these noumenal global axioms. However, if one moves beyond official social reforms for women that the colonial administration and later the postcolonial state introduced (almost always at the hands of male social reformers) and if one looks at actual women's movements in India in the last two hundred years, a very different picture – a richly and diversely phenomenalized, locally experientialized and corpo-realized one – of the global quest for women's rights emerges.

This chapter studies some specific women-led movements in India from 1813 to 2020. It wishes to show how these movements – while they definitely did log on to the processes of a global worldmaking inspired by the vision of a more gender-equitable planet and while they often were articulated in the more global feedback loops of the media – were in fact resolutely grounded in peculiarly local everyday routines and very localized legacies of worldmaking. More importantly, since being a 'woman' is fundamentally a corporeal experience, many of these movements can be seen to foreground the body of the woman as the site of oppression and struggle, making sensory perception and affective engagement the tools to deal with the same. These movements thus can be seen to constitute a multilogical phenomenology of globalization, where the noumenal idea of 'women's rights' is articulated, but phenomenally, through localized and experientialized issues and strategies.

This phenomenological question also leads us to the issue of hermeneutics. For some time now, we have been governed by a postcolonial hermeneutics, which makes us think of social and cultural processes in India primarily through a postcolonial critical lens. However, there is a need to rethink this predominant signifier under which everything Indian has to be thought. We have to make it possible to read social and cultural movements through a dialogue between modes of indigenous sociocultural musings and the predominantly colonially defined hermeneutic practice that we have curricularly imbibed under the rubric of the postcolonial.

In the context of how the global impetus of Feminism gets phenomenalized through specific women-led movements in India we thus need to first understand what the features of a postcolonial hermeneutics of feminism are. The first is the most obvious feature, which is that our reading formation about women's issues or feminism is primarily induced through our colonial contacts, primarily accessed through our colonial discursive legacy, and even our postcolonial renegotiation of the same relies primarily on Northern and Western sources of global Feminism. A colonially/globally received, and therefore mostly North/West-induced, notion of what women's issues are and what the lines of resistance could be informs this postcolonial feminist hermeneutics. This automatically leads to local feminisms being elided under a global Feminism generated from the North/West.[1]

The second feature is that even when one tries to move away from Northern and Western reading formations in order to look at women's issues and movements in India more locally, one views the same as essentially tied to the colonial period and, more often than not, centred around reforms initiated during the colonial period – for instance the abolition of the practice of sati or the introduction of widow remarriage. This is not to say that these reforms have not benefited Indian women, especially considering the many misogynist practices that were followed traditionally in India. However, such a postcolonial feminist hermeneutics ends up partly ameliorating colonialism and partly attributing reforms initiated for women's emancipation to enlightened native men – spearheaded by male social reformers and oriented at abolishing misogynistic traditional practices – with either colonial administrators or indigenous male reformers seen as championing women's rights, rather than the women themselves.

Third, even when we move away from social reforms induced by the colonial administration or enlightened native men and do talk of the participation of actual women in movements, a postcolonial hermeneutics mostly restricts the same to women who were part of the anticolonial struggle, the history of Indian women's participation in movements being seen as a part of the narrative of the nationalist movement alone. So, we often still end up privileging only those women who were connected to the nationalist project of the freedom movement, to the prospect of nation building, etc. This nationalist co-optation is also evident in the iconography of the Nation as a woman – as Mother India or Bharat Mata.

To understand how the noumenal and global issue of women's rights gets phenomenalized in local women's movements in India, one has to problematize

---

[1]   For perspectives on specific forms of 'feminism' and 'women's studies' in India, see: Maitrayee CHAUDHURI, ed., *Feminism in India* (New Delhi: Kali for Women / Women Unlimited, 2004); Mary E. JOHN, ed., *Women's Studies in India: A Reader* (New Delhi: Penguin Books India, 2008).

these three features of postcolonial feminist hermeneutics. The first problem – i.e. the problem that our reading formation into Feminism primarily comprises sources that have been made available colonially – can be easily addressed if we no longer restrict our theoretical knowledge of the field to Northern and Western sources alone but also incorporate other theorizations and practices, including those from Indian contexts. As to the second issue – that women's emancipation has been tied to reforms during colonial times initiated by either colonial administrators or enlightened Indian men – there is a need to move beyond this to look at women's movements during the colonial period which were led by women. This also entails uncoupling women's movements from the grand colonially-induced nationwide reform agenda against traditional misogynistic practices alone and engaging with local grassroots women's movements in colonial times. Finally, to address the third issue – that women get subsumed within the rubric of nationalism – there is a need to go beyond the narrative of the Nation and look at how many post-independence women's movements offer critiques of existing models of Nationalism. This would also contest the axiomatic presumption that the establishment of the postcolonial Indian state would have necessarily delivered freedom unto all sections of its population, including women.

In order to look at the phenomenalization of the global through women's movements in India and in order to transcend the easily available model of a postcolonial feminist hermeneutics, this chapter will present ten specimens of women-led movements that have happened in India from 1813 to 2020, arranging them chronologically. As one would notice, the first three of these movements occurred during colonial times, while the remaining happened after independence. Irrespective of whether they took place during the colonial or the postcolonial era, however, the resistance offered by women through these movements will be seen as refusing the homogenizing tendencies of the Nation. Instead, in the face of a national project which tries to subsume women and make them complicit with the State's and the dominant Civil Society's policies of exclusion, exploitation, moral policing, and demonization of the female body, these women's movements will be seen to have forged localized, experientialized, corporealized, and phenomenalized trajectories of resistance.

Specimen 1: The Channar Revolt (1813–1859)

The Channar Revolt, also referred to as *Channar Lahala* (Channar is a surname of Ezhavas and a term that refers to Nadars too) or the *Maru Marakkal Samaram* (literally 'struggle for the right to cover breasts') was a movement led by the Nadar and Ezhava women in the Kingdom of Travancore (today's southern Kerala and south-western Tamil Nadu) fighting for the right to be able to cover their breasts, against the humiliating rule that they (and women of some other 'lower' castes) had to compulsorily stay topless. The movement was also aimed at fighting against the even more discriminatory rule that these women could cover their breasts only if they paid a 'breast tax', or *mulakkaram*, whose amount was determined according to the size of their breasts, beginning right from their attaining puberty, and measured physically through periodic visits by male government officials.

Initially, some Nadar women embraced Christianity, under the presumption that stepping out of the Hindu caste system they would be able to cover their breasts. Indeed, in 1813 Colonel John Munro, the British *dewan* at the Travancore court, issued an order granting permission to Christian Nadar women to cover their breasts if they so wished. However, the order was withdrawn under pressure from the *pindakars*, members of the King of Travancore's council, and while converted Nadar women were allowed to wear *kuppayam*, a type of blouse worn by other Muslims and Christians of the kingdom, they were forbidden to cover themselves with the traditional long cloth, the 'Nair cloth' as it was called, which the upper-caste Hindu women would wear. The non-converted women, in any case, could not cover their breasts or were subjected to the breast tax. This led to a sustained rebellion, mostly by Nadar and Ezhava women, who fought the system often violently, as in the legendary case of Nangeli, a woman who chopped off her breasts in protest when approached by a breast tax collector and bled to death, who is the subject of many popular cultural texts. In 1859, partly in response to the Channar Revolt, and partly under pressure from Charles Trevelyan, the then British Governor of the neighbouring Madras Presidency, the king of Travancore partially allowed all women in his kingdom to cover their breasts, if they so wished, though the breast tax continued in some form till as late as 1924, when it was finally fully abolished. However, till as late as 1952 one has instances of *maru marakkal* movements being fought.[2]

---

[2] On the Channar Revolt, see esp.: Keerthana SANTHOSH, "Dress as a Tool of Empowerment: The Channar Revolt," *Our Heritage* 22.1 (2020): 532-536; Venkat PULAPAKA, "The History of Breast Tax and the Revolt of Lower Caste Women in 19th Century Travancore," *STSTW Media*, 17 May 2019, web; "The Woman Who Cut off Her Breasts to Protest a Tax," BBC News, 28 July 2016, web; Robert L. HARDGRAVE JR., "The Breast-Cloth Controversy: Caste Consciousness and Social Change in Southern Travancore," *The Indian Economic & Social History Review* 5.2 (1968): 171-187.

Specimen 2: Initiating Dalit and Muslim Women into Formal Education (1847; 1909)

This specimen concerns the efforts of Savitribai Phule, Fatima Sheikh, and Rokeya Sakhawat Hossain to initiate Dalit and Muslim women into formal education from the mid-nineteenth to the early-twentieth century. While I have deliberately chosen to leave out the more obvious educational reforms instigated among upper-caste Hindu women by Christian missionaries and male reformers, I do wish to mention these women-led attempts to educate Dalit and Muslim women.

Savitribai Phule (1831–1897), born in the socially downtrodden Mali community, was illiterate at the time of her marriage to the major anti-caste activist Jyotirao Phule, but got educated after that and undertook two teachers' training programmes – at an institution in Ahmednagar run by the American Missionary Cynthia Farrar, and at the Normal School run by Ms. Mitchell in Pune – to become formally qualified as a teacher. Initially she started teaching girls, particularly from the backward castes and communities, at home along with her accomplice Sagunabai, starting the first such 'school' at Maharwada in Pune on 1 May 1847, but on 1 January 1848, she formally founded at Bhide Wada, also in Pune, the first institutionalised girls' school initiated by an Indian woman.[3] By 1852, Savitribai and her husband had opened as many as eighteen schools for girls, thus

---

[3]   On female education in Bengal, see Firoj High SARWAR, "Christian Missionaries and Female Education in Bengal during East India Company's Rule: A Discourse between Christianised Colonial Domination versus Women Emancipation," *IOSR Journal of Humanities and Social Science* 4.1 (2012): 37-47. This shows that the school Savitribai Phule set up in 1848 was by no means the first girls' school for non-Europeans in colonial India, the claimant for which could be a 1760 girls' school set up in Calcutta by one Mrs. Hedges. Indeed, by the 1810s, at least a dozen girls' schools had already been set up in Bengal alone. The foundation of the Female Juvenile Society of Calcutta in 1819, the Ladies Society for Native Female Education in Calcutta in 1824, and many similar organizations pushed up the number of schools for native Indian girls in Bengal to several hundred by the 1840s. This was not peculiar to Bengal alone, and one can see similar enterprises in all the three Presidencies under EIC rule, like Cynthia Farrar's school itself, set up in 1829. But one could argue that these were all results of European Christian missionary activities. Attempts at setting up girls' schools by Indians themselves would have to wait till 1847-48, when Peary Charan Sarkar started the Kalikrishna Girls' High School in Barasat, a northern suburb of Calcutta, in 1847, the Parsi community started a school for girls in Bombay in 1847, and the Students' Literary and Scientific Society, founded by some native alumni of the Elphinstone Institution, started the SL&SS Girls' High School in Bombay in 1848. However, these were all enterprises by Indian men, and not by women themselves. Savitribai Phule's girls' school set up in Pune in 1848 is thus indeed the first girls' school in India set up by an Indian woman.

revolutionising the field of education for girls, particularly from the backward communities. Her monumental contribution to education was recognised when the University of Pune was renamed Savitribai Phule Pune University in 2015.

As orthodox upper-caste Hindus could not tolerate these enterprises by the lower caste Phules, and that too for girls' education, they persecuted them in all possible ways. In 1849, the Phules were forced to leave Jyotirao's parental home and move in with a Muslim friend, Usman Sheikh. This started an even more spectacular collaboration between Savitribai and Usman Sheikh's sister, Fatima Sheikh (biographical data uncertain), who had also undergone a teacher's training course, and the duo together opened another school in 1849. In 1855, by the time when the Phules had set up several girls' schools, Fatima Sheikh was given the charge of independently running one of them. This monumental collaboration between a Dalit and a Muslim woman to set up the first girls' schools in India founded by Indian women themselves for the education of girls from the minority and backward communities was no less than a revolution, and it is hardly surprising that the 2019–2020 anti-CAA protests at Shaheen Bagh, Delhi (which I discuss in specimen 10 below), would see the opening of an open access library – the Fatima Sheikh & Savitribai Phule Library – in their memory.[4]

Rokeya Sakhawat Hossain (1880–1932), also known as Begum Rokeya (at times spelt as Roquiah), was a major early-twentieth-century Bengali author, who also wrote in English, apart from being an educator and a political activist. Her fictional works in Bengali and English and her non-fictional essays which express her feminist ideas are well-known and I do not discuss them here. Instead, I want to bring to focus how – much like Savitribai Phule and Fatima Sheikh, though more than half a century after them – Begum Rokeya established the first school for Muslim girls started by a Bengali woman, when, on 1 October 1909, she founded the Sakahawat Memorial Girls' High School in memory of her recently deceased husband at Bhagalpur (in today's Bihar), which was moved to Calcutta on 16 March 1911. A pioneer of Muslim women's education and emancipation in Bengal, in 1916, she founded the Anjuman-e-Khawateen-e-Islam (Muslim Women's Association), and devoted her entire life to the cause. Begum Rokeya is well-revered in both West Bengal and Bangladesh, particularly in the latter

---

[4]   On Savitribai Phule and Fatima Sheikh, see: Dilip MANDAL, "Why Indian history has forgotten Fatima Sheikh but remembers Savitribai Phule," *The Print*, 9 January 2019, web; Velivada Team, "Life Sketch of Savitribai Phule – Timeline," *Velivada: Educate, Agitate, Organize*, 2017, web; Leah VERGHESE et.al. (script) and Sumon CHITRAKAR (illustrations), *Savitribai: Journey of a Trailblazer* (graphic novel; Bangalore: Azim Premji University, 2014).

where her birthday, 9 December, is celebrated as Begum Rokeya Day, and the University of Rangpur has been renamed Begum Rokeya University in 2009.[5]

Specimen 3: The Nupi Lan Movement (1904; 1939)

In the Nupi Lan (literally 'women's war') Movement in Manipur women organized themselves and rose in direct war against the local king, the north-Indian traders, and the British administrators, who, in complicity with each other, were forcefully relocating Manipuri males for lumbering labour (first Nupi Lan, 1904) and who were contributing to an agrarian crisis (second Nupi Lan, 1939).

The Kingdom of Manipur, which was a British Protectorate from 1824, became a Princely State of British India in 1891. Within just thirteen years of this annexation, in 1904, John Maxwell, the British Political Agent at Manipur, re-introduced the *lalup* system, which was otherwise abolished in the rest of British India from 1892 on. *Lalup* was a system of forced labour which required men between 17 and 60 years of age to work without payment for ten days in every forty days of work. The first Nupi Lan was fought by Manipuri women against the British order to send Manipuri men on *lalup* to the Kabaw Valley in today's Myanmar to get timber to re-build a Police Agent's bungalow destroyed in a fire. More than 5,000 women participated in the first Nupi Lan, and this week-long agitation, though eventually suppressed by the British, was successful insofar as it led to the withdrawal of the *lalup* system. The first Nupi Lan was thus a successful all-women's movement against exploitation by the British colonizers.

The second Nupi Lan was launched by Manipuri women against the 1930s economic and administrative policies of the Maharaja of Manipur, Sir Chura-chandra Singh, which promoted indiscriminate export of rice from Manipur to colonial garrisons outside Manipur by Marwari traders in collusion with the British government, leading to an artificial famine-like situation in Manipur. The acute scarcity of rice and sharp rise of prices of other food grains affected the women of Manipur the most, since they did not only run the households, but were the primary buyers and sellers in the predominantly matriarchal Manipuri agrarian economy. Thousands of women started organising demonstrations, including at the State Durbar Office, demanding an immediate cessation of the export of rice. The State authorities deployed heavy force against the unarmed women protesters. Many women were seriously injured and a few lost their lives,

---

[5]   On Rokeya Sakhawat Hossain, see: Mohammad A. QUAYUM and Md. Mahmudul HASAN, eds., *A Feminist Foremother: Critical Essays on Rokeya Sakhawat Hossain* (Hyderabad: Orient Black-Swan, 2017).

and though the second Nupi Lan was withdrawn after some months due to the outbreak of World War II in the region, the valiant women were victorious insofar as they could secure a ban on exporting rice from Manipur, except to two cantonments of the Assam Rifles.

Some of the prominent leaders of the agitation were Aribam Chaobiton Devi, Tombimacha Devi, Mongjam Leima Devi, Tongbram Sabi Devi and Ibemhal Devi. The second Nupi Lan also produced leaders such as Hijam Irabot, who went on to found the Communist Party in Manipur. The leftist women's organisation Manipur Mahila Sanmelani was also a product of this agitation. The two Nupi Lan movements together not only constitute important milestones in the history of women's movements in India, but they led to many long-term ecological, economic, political, and administrative reforms that have come to constitute the very fabric of Manipur and have also provided inspiration for future women's movements in Manipur, as will be discussed later in connection to my fifth specimen.[6]

Specimen 4: The Chipko Movement (1973–1974)

In the Chipko (literally 'hug and stick [to a tree]') Movement, which took place from 1973 to 1974 in today's Uttarakhand, women organized themselves into brigades and started hugging and sticking to trees in huge numbers to stop government-aided corporate agencies from large-scale timber logging and thus from causing irreversible damage to the fragile Himalayan ecology.

The Chipko Movement exposed vested interests in the government-corporate nexus. Its primary achievement, however, was in making women of the local marginalised hill communities become the true agents of ecological awareness and activism as well as of social change. Though the names of a couple of more recognised male social activists like Chandi Prasad Bhatt and Sunderlal Bahuguna are often associated with the movement, the Chipko Movement was primarily led by rural women activists like Gaura Devi, Suraksha Devi, Sudesha Devi, Bachni Devi, Virushka Devi and others. These women were the agitators on ground. They spread the movement all around the area and brought success

---

[6] On the first and second Nupi Lan, see: Rakhee BHATTACHARYA, "Identity Consolidation of Meitei Women: Reflections on Women's War," *Nationhood and Identity Movements in Asia: Colonial and Post-Colonial Times*, ed. Swarupa GUPTA (New Delhi: Manohar, 2012); Malem NINGTHOUJA, "Nupi Lan: Women's War in Manipur," *Reflections* 1.2 (2007): 27; N. Joykumar SINGH, *Colonialism to Democracy: A History of Manipur, 1819–1972* (Guwahati & Delhi: Spectrum Publications, 2002); Sanamani YAMBEM, "Nupi Lan: Manipur Women's Agitation, 1939," *Economic and Political Weekly*, 21 February 1976: 325-331.

to the movement by ensuring the reversal of many of the deforestation contracts. The women also played an instrumental role in the afforestation work that followed the success of the movement.

While sporadic demonstrations against the logging policies of the government were already held in the Gopeshwar area of Uttarakhand in October 1971, things came to a pass in late 1972 when the Forest Department turned down the request of the Dasholi Gram Swarajya Mandal (DGSM was set up by Chandi Prasad Bhatt in Gopeshwar in 1964 as a rural self-sufficiency organisation) for ten ash trees to make agricultural tools, and instead awarded a contract for felling 300 trees to a sporting goods manufacturer from Allahabad. When the contractors and lumberjacks of this company came to the area to cut down the trees, hundreds of villagers, mostly women, took recourse to hugging the trees on 24 April 1973 to protect them, and the contract was finally cancelled and DGSM's request was acceded.

However the ordeal was far from over, as the same sporting goods manufacturer was instead awarded trees in the Phata forest around 80 kilometres from Gopeshwar, and in January 1974 the government announced an auction of an even greater number of 2,500 trees near the Reni village close by. On 25 March 1974, when lumberjacks arrived to start logging operations in the Reni area, Gaura Devi, the head of the Mahila Mangal Dal (Women's Welfare Force) at Reni village led a team of 27 women who braved all threats and kept hugging the trees throughout the night. They were joined by more people the next morning, which caused the contractors and lumbermen to withdraw. Similarly, from 20 June 1974, women of Phata and the neighbouring Tarsali village started guarding trees in their area, a vigil which continued till December 1974, when the lumberjacks at Phata also withdrew.

The success of the three original Chipko Movements – at Gopeshwar (April 1973), Reni (March 1974) and Phata (June–Dec. 1974) – encouraged people from many areas in the Uttarakhand Himalayas to adopt the same strategy of tree-hugging to fight against ecological and economic exploitation. Till 1979, over 150 villages got involved with the Chipko Movement, resulting in 12 major protests in the Uttarakhand region. The wildfire of Chipko gained its greatest success when in 1980, the government totally banned the felling of trees in the Himalayan regions for fifteen years. From 1981 to 1983, Sunderlal Bahuguna, a leading male Chipko activist and one of the most prominent environmentalist leaders of the region, undertook an almost 5,000 kilometre-long Trans-Himalayan March, from Kashmir to Nagaland, on foot, to spread the message of the Chipko Movement and the ecological strategies learnt from it to other areas of the Himalayas beyond Uttarakhand.

The Chipko Movement won the Right Livelihood Award in 1987, and though it is ironic that its male leaders got more recognition – Chandi Prasad Bhatt was awarded the Ramon Magsaysay Award in 1982, and Sunderlal Bahuguna was awarded the second highest civilian award in India, Padma Vibhushan, in 2009 – the movement continues to be a great inspiration to environmentalist and women's movements all over the world. Indeed, the strategies of the Chipko Movement were replicated in several parts of the globe by ecofeminist activists.[7]

Specimen 5: Meira Paibi Movement (1977 till date)

In the Meira Paibi (literally 'women torchbearers') Movement, which started in 1977 in Manipur and is still ongoing, women with flaming torches have come out to the streets to protest against human rights violations and atrocities against women by organs of the Indian State, particularly through the draconian Armed Forces Special Powers Act (AFSPA).

Women's movements in Manipur have a long history, and the genealogy of Meira Paibi can be traced back not only to Nupi Lan, as has already been discussed earlier, but also to the more immediate 1970s Nisha Bandi (literally 'stop addiction') Movement, where women would take to the streets on night-long marches with *podons*, or lanterns, in their hands, often burning down liquor shops, leading finally to an official prohibition of alcohol in the state. When in 1977, women's vigils in Kakching replaced the lanterns with flaming torches, or by some accounts, when in the early morning of 29 December 1980, close to a hundred women marched with torches to the Langthabal Army Base Camp near Manipur University to free a youth, Lorembam Ibomcha, who was arrested on false charges of planting a bomb, they started getting called 'Meira Paibi.'

While Meira Paibi as a movement, and torch-carrying as the preferred mode of protest by women spread all over Manipur, it was not only the lantern that was replaced with a torch, but the agenda of the agitating women was also broadened to include protests against drug abuse, crimes against women, and specifically the AFSPA, which allowed the security forces unrestricted power, leading to numerous cases of human rights violation. The Meira Paibi movements not only

[7]   On the Chipko Movement, see: Ramachandra GUHA, "Chipko: Social History of an 'Environmental' Movement," *The Unquiet Woods: Ecological Change and Peasant Resistance in the Himalaya* (Delhi: Oxford UP, 1991) 152-184; Vandana SHIVA, "Women in the Forest," *Staying Alive: Women, Ecology and Development* (New Delhi: Zed Books, 1989) 55-95; Thomas WEBER, *Hugging the Trees: The Story of the Chipko Movement* (New Delhi: Viking Penguin, 1988); Anupam MISHRA and Satyendra TRIPATHI, *The Chipko Movement* (New Delhi: People's Action / Gandhi Peace Foundation, 1978).

held mass rallies and demonstrations, and organised strikes and road closures, but they also often stopped army vehicles and marched to army camps to rescue the apprehended youth, as in Lorembam's case already mentioned above. The sustained nature and effective forcefulness of the Meira Paibi movements all over the state have also earned them the sobriquet of the 'third Nupi Lan'.

The iconic protest on 15 July 2004, where twelve elderly Manipuri women, calling themselves 'Mothers of Manipur' or *Ima*, stepped out in front of the Kangla Fort in Imphal in the nude, carrying a banner that read "Indian Army Rape Us" to protest against the rape and murder of Thangjam Manorama by the Indian Army, is seen as an extension of the Meira Paibi movement, though the protesters did not carry flaming torches. Women's protests in Manipur against atrocities committed by the Indian security forces and gross human rights violations in the state continue till this day, and they can all be considered a legacy of Meira Paibi. It is in recognition of this that in 2013 *The Times of India* awarded the "TOI Social Impact Awards: Lifetime Contribution" to Meira Paibi and its five *Ima* leaders: Thokchom Ramani (who led both the 29 December 1980 and the 15 July 2004 protests), Ak Janaki Leima, L Memchoubi Devi, Y Leirik Leima, and Purnimashi Leima.[8]

Specimen 6: The Krantikari Adivasi Mahila Sangathan (1986 till date)

The Krantikari Adivasi Mahila Sangathan (literally 'Revolutionary Tribal Women's Organization') is a currently banned women's organization in the tribal-dominated and mostly Maoist-controlled Bastar-Dandakaranya region of today's Chhattisgarh. It supports and organizes resistance both against the atrocities of the State Police, aimed at dispossessing the communities of their traditional habitats, and against the ingrained patriarchal practices of their own male tribal companions.

In 1986, the Maoists, who de facto control that part of India, set up the Adivasi Mahila Sanghathana to organize women and address their issues, and it later

---

[8]   On the Meira Paibi, see: Minu BASNET, "Disrobed and Dissenting Bodies of the Meira Paibi: Postcolonial Counterpublic Activism," *Communication and the Public* 4.3 (2019): 239-252; Sunil OINAM, "TOI Social Impact Awards: Lifetime Contribution – Meira Paibi," *Times of India*, 10 January 2013; Binalakshmi NEPRAM, "A Narrative on the Origin of the Meira Paibis," webcast lecture, 9 January 2005, *Now the World Knows*, web; Ksh. Bimola DEVI, "Women in Social Movements in Manipur," *Social Movements in North-East India*, ed. M.N. KARNA (New Delhi: Indus, 1998) 75-81.

evolved into the Krantikari Adivasi Mahila Sangathan (KAMS), with the word *krantikari* or 'revolutionary' added to its name. The KAMS reportedly has around 90,000 to 100,000 registered members and is probably the biggest women's movement in India. The KAMS, while active in organizing movements, along with other banned Maoist outfits, against state excesses meted out to the tribal population in the region, also campaigns against the misogynistic practices of the tribal men themselves, like forced marriage and abduction, traditional prejudices against menstruating women, polygamy, sexual assault, domestic violence, etc. It also operates against the exploitation of natural resources of the forested and mineral-rich it is active in.

For instance, in Dandakaranya, tribal women were not allowed to sow seeds in the fields, and the KAMS, with help from the Maoist insurgents fought against this practice and, at least in theory, reversed it. Apart from fighting against state atrocities and traditional patriarchal practices, the KAMS has also been successful in agitating against rampant mining in the region by Posco and Vedanta. In the overall Bastar area of their operation, the women cadre of the KAMS have fought against the atrocities committed not only by the police, but also by Salwa Judum (literally 'peace march' or 'purification hunt'), a now banned, allegedly state-sponsored, vigilante, anti-Maoist militia.

It should be noted that women comprise 60-70% of the total Maoist cadre, are deployed in sensitive combat roles, and are at the receiving end of the gravest atrocities at the hands of the security forces, and yet there is hardly any female presence in the top leadership of the Maoist organization. The KAMS, while being a wing of the Maoists, fights for women's rights on both these fronts – against harassment in the hands of both the state and the militia.[9]

Specimen 7: Pink Chaddi Campaign (2009)

In 2009, the Pink Chaddi (literally 'pink underwear') Campaign was led by a 'Consortium of Pub-Going, Loose and Forward Women' against an attack on women in a pub in Mangalore in Karnataka by the Hindu fundamentalist organization Sri Ram Sena (SRS) and their threat to marry off any young couple seen together on Valentine's Day, whereby, through a nationwide successful cam-

---

[9]   On KAMS and other movements operational in Bastar, see: Nandini SUNDAR, *The Burning Forest: India's War in Bastar* (Delhi: Juggernaut, 2016); Arundhati ROY, *Broken Republic* (New Delhi: Penguin, 2013) and *Walking with the Comrades* (New Delhi: Penguin, 2011); Rahul PANDUIT, *Hello Bastar: The Untold Story of India's Maoist Movement* (Chennai: Westland/Tranquebar Press, 2011).

paign, women from all over India sent thousands of pink panties to the Sri Ram Sena's office in protest.

It all started on 24 January 2009, when a mob of around forty SRS activists barged into a pub (Amnesia – The Lounge) at Hotel Woodside in Mangalore and assaulted several women for being in the pub, since they believed that women's going to pubs was against 'Indian culture.' More women were assaulted on 6 February 2009 on similar grounds by members of this moral-policing Hindu fundamentalist outfit. In continuation of their pogrom against women in the name of defending 'Indian culture,' Pramod Muthalik, the leader of the SRS, announced that on 14 February, i.e. Valentine's Day, activists of his organization would target couples found together in public and would forcefully get them married . The Pink Chaddi Campaign was launched against this threat of vigilantism, and the media attention it received led to Muthalik and 140 members of his organization being taken into preventive custody on the eve of Valentine's Day, averting any major untoward event.

Initiated by Nisha Susan, a journalist working with the *Tehelka* magazine, a group called 'Consortium of Pub-going, Loose and Forward Women' was formed, which invited everyone, through Facebook and its blog, to courier pink panties to the SRS office by Valentine's Day, as a mark of protest. The choice of pink underwear was poignant, with its obvious connection to the assertion of female sexuality, but the choice of the word *chaddi* instead of 'underwear' or 'panty' was even more significant as this Hindi colloquial word for 'underwear' is also a slang to refer to Hindu fundamentalists, because of the shorts that members of the parent organization of the Hindu Right in the country – the RSS – wear.

The movement gained a major fillip when it was joined in by Jasmeen Patheja of Blank Noise fame.[10] Irreverent, ironic, and yet assertive, the movement spread like wildfire through massive media traction, and not only were thousands of pink panties sent to the SRS office, the campaign also raised nationwide and even global consciousness about women's right to freedom of movement and lifestyle. As Nisha Susan writes, "[w]ithin a day of starting the campaign we had 500 odd members. In a week we hit 40,000. From Puerto Rico to Singapore, from Chennai to Ahmedabad, from Guwahati to Amritsar, people wrote to us, how do I send

---

[10] Cf. the website *Blank Noise*. Jasmeen Patheja founded the women's organization 'Blank Noise' in 2003. It organized several 'Take Back the Night' marches all over the country from 2006 onwards, on similar lines as the 'Reclaim the Night' movement that started in Leeds in 1977 to assert women's rights to move around freely in public areas at night, without fear of sexual assault and social disapproval. Though significant as a women's collective in India, I do not discuss Blank Noise separately in this chapter, as its organization of actual women's movements has been sporadic.

my chaddis? [...] Elderly men and women, schoolchildren, middle-aged house-wives, gravelly-voiced big men from Bihar who did not quite want to say the word chaddi aloud called us."[11]

More than a decade after it happened, the Pink Chaddi Campaign remains a landmark event in women's movements in India, which not only showed the Indian woman's readiness to assert her body in public discourse but also the power of social media in forging feminist solidarities cutting across religion, region, and even gender. It also set off several similar campaigns, beginning with the 'Pub Bharo Andolan' ('fill the pubs movement') initiated by Renuka Choudhary, the then Minister of State for Women and Child Development of India herself on Valentine's Day 2009, the 'Take Back the Night, Take Back Our Streets' campaign in March 2009 and leading to several other campaigns by women for freedom of movement, access to public spaces, and the right of asserting their sexuality, over the next decade, which will be discussed in relation to specimen 9 below.[12]

Specimen 8: The Anti Female Genital Mutilation Campaign (c. 2010 till date)

The Anti Female Genital Mutilation Campaign (c. 2010 till date) led by Masooma Ranalvi, Aarefa Johari, and others, works to end the practice of Female Genital Mutilation (FGM) or *khatna* (literally circumcision, in this case, clitorectomy) of young girls amongst the Dawoodi Bohra sect of Shia Muslims, predominantly from western India. In this movement mothers have started pledging not to allow their daughters to be subjected to this practice.

Though there is some debate as to the extent of female genital cutting in the Dawoodi Bohra practice of *khatna, khafd, or khafz* – whether only the clitoral hood is lightly nicked, thus amounting to circumcision akin to that done to males, or whether it is usually a full clitorectomy, aimed at curbing female sexual pleasure, and thus amounting to FGM – there is no doubt that a major campaign has arisen from within women of the community itself against this practice.

---

[11] Nisha SUSAN, "Valentine's Warriors: The Pink Chaddi Campaign – Why It Began and How," *Tehelka Magazine* 6.8, 28 Feb. 2009.

[12] On the Pink Chaddi Campaign, see: Sonakshi SRIVASTAVA, "The Pink Chaddi Campaign: Women's Fight for Right to Public Spaces," *Feminism in India: Intersectional Feminism – Desi Style!*, 20 June 2019, web; Rita BANERJI, "The Pink Panties Campaign: The Indian Women's Sexual Revolution," *Intersections: Gender and Sexuality in Asia and the Pacific* 23, January 2010, web; Consortium of Pub-Going, Loose and Forward Women, "The Pink Chaddi Campaign," blog, 8 Feb.–11 Apr. 2009, web.

While organized campaigns are recorded to have begun at least from November 2011, when Tasneem, a Dawoodi Bohra woman, started an online petition on *change.org*, now the campaign is led primarily by two women's groups 'We Speak Out' and 'Sahiyo' – founded by Masooma Ranalvi and Aarefa Johari, respectively.

Masooma Ranalvi, herself a survivor of FGM, could muster the courage to speak out about her horrific childhood memories of the same only at around fifty years of age, when in October 2015, she wrote a blog describing her own experience of *khatna* at the age of seven. As many women who underwent the same experience shared their responses to the blog, Ranalvi initially created a WhatsApp group, which soon took the form of an organization called 'Speak Out On FGM,' which has also collaborated with the Lawyers Collective Women's Rights Initiative (LCWRI) to seek legal recourse to ending FGM in India. In 2016, Ranalvi founded another organization called We Speak Out, aimed at ending FGM in India through mass sensitization. Apart from encouraging women to break their silence over FGM, We Speak Out has also organized campaigns like #NotMyDaughter, where parents would take the pledge of not subjecting their daughters to *khafz*, #MenAgainstFGM, aimed at sensitizing males of the community against the practice, and several other campaigns like #KhafzNoMore, #EndFGMinIndia, etc.

In 2015, Aarefa Johari, another Dawoodi Bohra woman and a survivor of FGM, co-founded Sahiyo (literally 'female friends', a Gujarati equivalent of *saheliyan*), along with Mariya Taher, Priya Goswami, Insia Dariwala and Shaheeda Tavawalla-Kirtane, which also is engaged in activities to end FGM in India through public awareness campaigns, through dialogue within the community, and through petitions. In February 2016, the two groups, Sahiyo and We Speak Out, came together to launch a joint campaign called 'Each One Reach One,' which encourages members of the community to break the silence around the practice and speak out against it, with an aim towards building sensitization towards ending FGM in India. Apart from addressing the ills of the practice to the community and encouraging community members to themselves end it, the two organizations have also taken the matter to higher bodies – as in their December 2016 petition to the United Nations Human Rights Council and their May 2017 Public Interest Litigation, which is currently pending before the Supreme Court of India – with the aim to formally ban FGM in India. [13]

---

[13] On anti-FGM movements in India, see: *Sahiyo – United against Female Genital Cutting*, web; *We Speak Out*, web; Debangana CHATTERJEE, "Masooma Ranalvi – Fighting the Odds of Female Genital Cutting in India" (excerpts from interview with Masooma RANALVI, 22 August 2018), *Be! Life Beyond Numbers*, 28 April 2020, web; LCWRI (Lawyers Collective Women's Rights Initiative) and Speak Out On FGM, *Female Genital Mutilation: Guide to Eliminating the FGM Practice in India*, *Lawyer's Collective*, 21 May 2017, web.

Specimen 9: Recent Urban or Campus-Based Movements (2011 till date)

This section focuses on the numerous, primarily urban and young-women-driven, often campus-based, movements like the Besharmi Morcha (literally 'the shameless brigade') SlutWalks (2011–2013), the Red Alert / Pads Against Sexism Campaign (2014–2015), the Pinjra Tod (literally 'break the cage') Movement (2015 till date), etc., where women's collectives fight against sexual harassment, curbs on female mobility or the demonization of the female body and sexuality, etc.

It has been reported earlier in specimen 7 of this chapter how Blank Noise and its 'Take Back the Night' marches, the Pink Chaddi Campaign, and its immediate spinoffs like Pub Bharo Andolan, etc. had already set up a milieu of a certain kind of urban women's protest movements in India. It is, however, from 2011 onwards that one sees a fruition of these in a sustained series of similar women's movements.

Inspired by the first SlutWalk in Toronto, Canada, held on 3 Aril 2011 – in protest against comments by the police that women get raped and assaulted when they dress like 'sluts' – an initiative where women stepped out to the streets wearing what they pleased, and which spread like wildfire all over the world in the months that followed – in India the first SlutWalk was held in Bhopal on 16 July 2011, which was called the Besharmi Morcha, or 'the march of the shameless', and in which only about 50 people participated. However, when on 31 July 2011, Besharmi Morcha took place in Delhi, and on 21 August 2011, in Lucknow, hundreds of women participated. Though the 4 December 2011 Bangalore Besharmi Morcha had to be cancelled due to threats of reactive violence, Kolkata had two SlutWalks in consecutive years, on 24 May 2012 and on 7 June 2013. Though not officially connected with the Besharmi Morcha, one can also note how the Delhi-based Citizens' Collective against Sexual Assault organised a 'Take Back the Night' sort of a march on New Year's Eve, 31 December 2012, to project how women also had the right to be out on the streets at night by themselves, dressed as they please, and participate equally in public revelry and merry-making.[14]

Discrimination faced by menstruating women and the general situation of sexual harassment and discrimination saw the innovative use of sanitary napkins as a medium of protest all over the country from December 2014 through 2015. It all started when, upon a used sanitary napkin being found in the toilet of Asma Rubber Private Limited in Kochi, the management of the company strip-

---

[14]   On the Besharmi Morcha, see: Rita BANERJI, "SlutWalk to Femicide: Making the Connection," *The WIP* (Women's International Perspective), 2 September 2011, web; "Besharmi Morcha, 'Shameless Protest,'" *Remember Our Sisters Everywhere*, 24 July 2011, web.

searched forty female employees on 10 December 2014, and in protest, the already successful 'Kiss of Love'[15] campaign hosted another Facebook campaign called 'Red Alert: You've Got a Napkin!', urging women from all over the country to mail sanitary napkins to the manager of the rubber company, in the fashion of the Pink Chaddi Campaign. The Red Alert campaign, apart from addressing this immediate issue, also led to the use of sanitary napkins as a means of women's protests against sexual violence and discrimination. Inspired also by the #PadsAgainstSexism campaign by Elonë Kastrati – a young German woman of Albanian descent, who wrote messages against sexual violence on sanitary pads and put them up in public spaces in Karlsruhe, Germany, on International Women's Day, 8 March 2015 – a group of four women students of the university Jamia Millia Islamia in Delhi – Mejaaz, Mohit, Sameera and Kaainat – stuck sanitary pads with messages against sexual harassment all over the Jamia campus, starting on 12 March 2015. Though they were show-cased by the university administration, the movement reached other universities of the country like Jadavpur University in Kolkata, where the Sanitary Pad Movement took off in continuation of its own Hok Kolorob[16] (literally, 'let there be noise') movement against sexual harassment on campus, which had just concluded in January 2015.[17]

---

[15] See "Kiss of Love," Facebook page. The page was launched when, following a Malayalam news channel Jai Hind TV's October 2014 telecast of footage of a young couple kissing and hugging in the parking lot of Downtown Cafe in Kozhikode, Kerala, vigilantes of the Hindu right-wing Bharatiya Janata Yuva Morcha, vandalized the cafe. Kiss of Love organized massive protests against such moral policing, by gathering young people to kiss in public, beginning in Kochi, Kerala on 2 November 2014, and spreading all over the country through similar protests soon. However, I do not discuss the Kiss of Love protests here, since they involved protesters from all genders against moral policing and was not strictly a women's movement, to which I have restricted this chapter. However, I do discuss how this same group launched the 'Red Alert' campaign, involving sanitary napkins, which was indeed a women's movement.

[16] See Devjyot GHOSHAL, "A brief history of #HokKolorob, the hashtag that shook Kolkata," *Quartz India*, 9 October 2014, web; Sajni MUKHERJEE, "The movement that shook Kolkata," *India Today*, 27 February 2015, web. The Hok Kolorob Movement was a major students' uprising at Jadavpur University, Kolkata from September 2014 to January 2015, held against the sexual assault on 28 August 2014 of a female student on campus, and the inaction of the university authorities regarding the same. While the protest started on a small scale on 3 September 2014, the police brutality on the assembled protesters on 17 September 2014 led to the protests becoming massive and garnering national and international support across campuses, which continued for several months, till the resignation of the Vice Chancellor of the University on 12 January 2015. Though organized against the sexual assault of a female student, I do not discuss Hok Kolorob here: it was not really a women's movement, as its leadership and participants were from all genders.

[17] For details on women's movements involving sanitary pads, see: Emma ANDERSON, "German teen launches global feminist trend," *The Local* (German Edition), 20 March 2015, web; Aarefa JOHARI, "'Red Alert: You've Got a Napkin' campaign – Kerala activists fight menstrual taboos #Vaw," *Kractivism: Bridge the Gap Bring the Change*, 1 January 2015, web; Kainat SARFARAZ, "In

Probably the most remarkable movement in this regard has been the Pinjra Tod or 'Break the Cage' – a collective of female students from different colleges and universities of Delhi, with significant influence across campuses in other parts of the country too – which has been challenging anti-women policies on campuses from 2015. Pinjra Tod's primary work has been aimed against discriminatory curfew hours imposed on women in hostels, imposition of dress codes and moral policing of female students, and sexual harassment in educational campuses, but with time they have broadened their political spectrum. When in August 2015, the Delhi Commission for Women (DCW) issued a notice to Jamia Millia Islamia about its discriminatory rule that female students could not stay out of their hostels after 8 pm, the Pinjra Tod collective was formed to draw the DCW's attention to the fact that this kind of curfew was not peculiar to Jamia alone, but practised in most other hostels in Delhi, and to urge female students to break such cages. Some of the earliest activities of Pinjra Tod were graffiti on walls of university campuses of birds escaping from cages in September 2015, a protest march in the North Campus of the University of Delhi on 8 October 2015, a petition to DCW on 10 October 2015, a protest at the Ministry of Human Resource Development (the Education Ministry) on 24 October 2015, a multi-city demonstration, simultaneously undertaken in Allahabad, Kolkata, Pune, Bangalore, Delhi, Darjeeling, Chandigarh, and Patiala, called 'Bus Teri Meri, Chal Saheli' (literally, 'the buses are yours and mine, let's go female comrades') on 16 December 2015, aimed at girls taking late night public transport all by themselves, etc. Pinjra Tod's fervent activism bore immediate fruit, as on 2 May 2016, the University Grants Commission (the parent body that regulates universities in India) issued a directive concerning "Prevention, Prohibition, and Redressal of Sexual Harassment of Women Employees and Students in Higher Educational Institutions," and on 7 May 2016, DCW issued notices to 23 universities and seven colleges regarding their discriminatory hostel curfew timings for men and women. However, the initial positive response from government agencies notwithstanding, the stridently feminist collective soon started having frequent run-ins with the students' organization of the right-wing ruling party as well as the government. While it would be impossible to exhaustively list all such instances over the last five years, the most memorable one surely is the 23 May 2020 arrest by the Delhi Police of two founding members of Pinjra Tod, Natasha Narwal and Devangana Kalita – both research scholars of JNU – under the draconian Unlawful Activities Prevention Act (UAPA), for allegedly and baselessly being 'masterminds' of the February 2020 Delhi riots that followed the anti-CAA

Jamia – How #PadsAgainstSexism Turned Into People Against Sanitary Pads," *Youth Ki Awaz*, 26 March 2015, web.

agitation, which will be discussed in greater detail as the next and final specimen of this chapter. Natasha and Devangana were held in custody at Tihar Jail, a maximum security prison in Delhi, for more than a year unlawfully without any proper charges or trial, till the courts released them on bail on 17 June 2021, with scathing comments against the government's attempts to muffle dissent. This episode shows the sheer power that movements like Pinjra Tod, a small-scale organization of young female students demanding non-discrimination on campuses, actually have. Thus, while the women's movements described in this section are often charged as being frivolous, elitist, and restrictive in their class and caste positions and urban campus locations, how the state perceives them as threats bears out the proof of the efficacy of these movements.[18]

Specimen 10: The Dadis of Shaheen Bagh (2019–2020)

The Dadis (literally 'grannies') of Shaheen Bagh (2019–2020) are not necessarily restricted to grandmothers alone but metonymically represent the women who led the movement against the discriminatory Citizenship Amendment Act (CAA) that seeks to discriminate against Muslims in terms of granting them citizenship of India.

When, on 11 December 2019, the Indian Parliament passed the Citizenship (Amendment) Act 2019, whereby for the first time a religious criterion was introduced for granting citizenship of India, with certain communities being named and Muslims being excluded from the list, protests broke out all over the country against this blatant violation of the secular fabric on India. When, on 15 December 2019, the police acted particularly brutally against protesters on Jamia Millia Islamia campus in Delhi, residents of the neighbouring Shaheen Bagh area, primarily Muslim women residents, took to the streets to protest against not only the discriminatory CAA but also the police assault. From 15 December 2019 till 24 March 2020, when the lockdown due to the COVID-19 pandemic caused them to disperse, women protesters – ranging from infants to grandmothers – sat round the clock, blocking a major road that ran through the area. The protest

---

[18] For details on Pinjra Tod, see: Madan B. LOKUR, "Five Questions on the Shameful Proceedings against Natasha Narwal, Devangana Kalita, Asif Iqbal," *The Wire*, 22 June 2021, web; Anagha TAMBE, "(Hyper)Visible 'Women'/Invisible (Dalit) Women: Challenging the Elusive Sexism in Indian Universities," *Strategies for Resisting Sexism in the Academy: Higher Education, Gender and Intersectionality*, ed. Gail CRIMMINS (Cham, Switzerland: Palgrave Macmillan, 2019) 129-152; Nikita AZAD, "Pinjra Tod: Stop Caging Women behind College Hostel Bars," *Feminism in India: Intersectional Feminism – Desi Style!*, 30 September 2015, web.

inspired women all across India and several similar round-the-clock sit-in protests against the CAA were replicated all over the country, till the pandemic-induced new restrictions led to their premature cessation.

At the helm of the Shaheen Bagh protests were elderly women, three of whom – the octogenarian Bilkis Bano, and her friends Asma Khatoon (90) and Sarwari (75) – gained particular prominence, earning them, and their innumerable comrades, the moniker 'Dadis of Shaheen Bagh.' Bilkis Bano – Bilkis Dadi or Grandma Bilkis – who did not miss a single day of the three-month-long protest held in the open under tents in the bitter Delhi winter, and who led from the front, taking part in open-mic sessions and addressing the people at the protest, emerged as the face of the movement, and was recognized internationally. On 23 September 2020, she was included in *Time* magazine's list of the 100 most influential people in 2020; in November 2020, BBC named her in the list of 100 inspiring and influential women from around the world for 2020; and the 2021 edition of *The Muslim 500: The World's 500 Most Influential Muslims 2021* named her 'Woman of the Year'.

Personal accolades and honours aside, what Grandma Bilkis and the Dadis of Shaheen Bagh really came to represent was that women – including elderly women from poor and lower middle-class Muslim families who would have spent their entire lives tending to their households alone – did not need men to lead them, but could forge and fight a movement themselves, when the situation so demanded. That the fight was, and would continue to be, against something as serious as attempts to rewrite the very contours of the secular fabric of India, becomes further poignant as their alternate female public sphere emerges as a bulwark against the toxic masculinity of the xenophobic hatefulness of fundamentalists.[19]

****

Apart from the theoretical points raised at the beginning of this chapter concerning the phenomenology and hermeneutics of women's movements in India, there are several other points to be noted from the above sections. First, not all these movements may qualify as 'women's movements' from a noumenal global perspective of the same, because some of them do not address what are exclusively

---

[19]   For details, see: Rana AYYUB, "Bilkis. The Hundred Most Influential People of 2020," *Time*, 22 September 2020, web; "BBC 100 Women 2020: Who is on the list this year?" *BBC News*, 23 November 2020, web; Zehra NAQVI, "The Nanis and Dadis of Shaheen Bagh … not just Dadis," *The Indian Express*, 3 February 2020, web; S. Abdallah SCHLEIFER, ed., *The Muslim 500: The World's 500 Most Influential Muslims 2021* (Amman: Royal Islamic Strategic Studies Centre, 2020), web.

women's issues (like ecology in specimens 3 and 4, or citizenship in specimen 10), but they are 'women's movements' indeed, because they were led by women, involving the actual corporeal, experiential engagement of the phenomenal woman into practice. Similarly, even for those movements discussed above, which are kind of tied with the usual global feminist agendas of educational reforms or negotiating the woman's role vis-à-vis the state and civil society (like specimens 2, 5, or 6), the focus here has been on women-led movements, once again foregrounding actual phenomenal practices by women.

Second, one must note that many of these movements are extremely context-specific (like the covering of breasts in specimen 1, or FGM in specimen 8) and the issues as well as the strategies for struggle cannot be grasped without a localized and phenomenalized understanding of the same, which may be impossible to fathom out of context.

Third, many of these movements directly concern the female body (specimens 1, 5, 7, 8, for instance – involving covering of breasts, nude protests, pink underwear, and genital mutilation, respectively), thus specifically foregrounding the acutely corporeal. Even the two movements which voice environmental and agrarian concerns (specimens 3, 4) are also where women's bodies had to be directly thrown into a sensorium of the corporeal and implicating it in ecofeminist terrains of consciousness, issues of great pertinence in theorizing a 'phenomenology of globalization.'

Fourth, some of these movements are of exclusively urban occurrence (specimens 7 and 10, but particularly those in specimen 9, which are mostly urban-youth and campus-based movements), thus possibly bringing to the fore how such a phenomenal worldmaking is negotiated in the megacity space, another issue that this book wants to bring to focus. And finally, some of these movements (particularly specimens 9 and 10) have given rise to a rich and popular body of slogans and songs with lasting 'acoustemological reverberations', which also can be thought of as one of the registers of phenomenalizing the global, that this book as a whole wants to present.

These movements in India over the last 200 years – led by women in local contexts, implicating their bodily experiences into specific ecological or urban milieus, with lasting reverberations – thus indeed mark a phenomenalizing of the global idiom of women's struggles for equity.

3 Phenomenologies of Urban Space and Urban Existence: The Literature of Delhi, 1940–2017

– Zeno Ackermann & Nishat Zaidi

The present chapter discusses textual representations of India's capital produced between the 1940s and the second decade of the third millennium. If, in the first chapter of this book, Isabel Karremann has analysed *Robinson Crusoe* as an early projection of the economically driven transformation of the world, we will now take the discussion of the interplay between globalization and literature from origins to recent manifestations. We will do so by considering various attempts of imaginatively mastering the seemingly uncontrollable dynamic of urbanity in the context of rapid 'globalization' – and, specifically, in the context of rapid 'globalization' playing out within a (still) 'developing country.'

The two chapters in this section will look at texts ranging from Ahmed Ali's *Twilight in Delhi* (1940) to Arundhati Roy's *The Ministry of Utmost Happiness* (2017). Experimental and non-fictional texts such as the seminal Sarai Reader *Cities of Everyday Life* (2002) or Rana Dasgupta's incisive literary reportage *Capital: A Portrait of Twenty-First-Century Delhi* (2014) will also be taken on board. We are interested in how writings on and of Delhi have traced and accompanied the movement from the colonial city to the postcolonial metropolis and from there to the globalized megacity. The main focus of the analysis, however, is on the ways in which literary and quasi-literary texts have registered political, spatial and social changes sensorially: as transformations in or as disruptions of 'structures of feeling.' How do the texts selected for discussion fathom the big city as a sensorially and affectively charged terrain, or as a vast assemblage of such terrains? How do socioeconomic structures – especially the socioeconomic structures created by transnational cultural exchange and global capitalism – come to be spatially and experientially concrete in terms of sensescapes? How are social differences felt sensorially, how are they implemented through sensorial regimes? And how might such differences be (imaginatively) transgressed by interventions in rhetorics or by practices of sensorially interacting with the world?

The approach sketched by these questions is based in an extensive scholarly debate on the city and the senses – a field of research that has received new impetus through recent systematizations of sensory studies,[1] and in particular of

---

[1]   The following titles can be singled out as markers of the current discourse of urban sensory studies: Alexander COWAN and Jill STEWARD, eds., *The City and the Senses: Urban Culture Since 1500*

sound studies.[2] Richard Sennett's *Flesh and Stone: The Body and the City in Western Civilization* (1994) represents an important earlier milestone in this discussion. The book argues that "urban spaces take form largely from the ways people
experience their own bodies."[3] It is particularly interested in how modern media
and urban planning have colluded with hegemonic strategies of control in creating a "sensate apathy"[4] that makes people indifferent to difference. Sennett's ideas
continue to play a significant role in the debate on "cities and citizenship,"[5] which
hinges on the assumption that such an indifference to difference is both a boon
and a curse – that it enables urban 'tolerance' and cosmopolitan openness at the
same time that it makes glaring inequality liveable.

These questions are particularly acute in relation to the major cities (or so-
called 'megacities') in countries such as India, where severe underdevelopment
and extreme poverty exist side by side with vibrant technological innovation and
exalted forms of globalized capitalism.[6] Drawing these problematics into the domain of sensory studies is not meant to deflect from societal problems or admin-

---

(Aldershot: Ashgate, 2007); Mădălina DIACONU, Eva HEUBERGER, Ruth MATEUS-BERR and Lukas Marcel VOSICKY, eds., *Senses and the City: An Interdisciplinary Approach to Urban
Sensescapes* (Wien: LIT, 2011); Kelvin E. Y. LOW and Devorah KALEKIN-FISHMAN, eds., *Senses in
Cities: Experiences of Urban Settings* (London: Routledge, 2017). Note also Kimberly DEFAZIO's
study *The City of the Senses: Urban Culture and Urban Space* (Basingstoke: Palgrave, 2011),
which vocally criticizes extant approaches in order to tie the sensitivity to sensory experience to
a materialist approach, emphasizing the importance of paying attention to the ways in which the
urban experience is based in global structures of production and exploitation.

2   As examples of the interaction between urban studies and sound studies or musicology, see: R.
Murray SCHAFER, *The Vancouver Soundscape* (Burnaby: World Soundscape Project / Simon Fra-
ser University, 1973); Michael BULL, *Sound Moves: iPod Culture and Urban Experience* (London:
Routledge, 2007); Brandon LABELLE, *Acoustic Territories: Sound Culture and Everyday Life* (New
York: Continuum, 2010); Karin BIJSTERVELD, ed., *Soundscapes of the Urban Past: Staged Sound
as Mediated Cultural Heritage* (Bielefeld: transcript, 2013); Ricciarda BELGIOJOSO, *Constructing
Urban Space with Sounds and Music* (Farnham: Ashgate, 2014); Matthew GANDY and B. J. NIL-
SEN, eds. *The Acoustic City* (Berlin: Jovis, 2014); Brett LASHUA, Stephen WAGG, Karl SPRACK-
LEN and M. Selim YAVUZ, eds., *Sounds and the City*, 2 vols. (Houndmills: Palgrave Macmillan,
2014-2019); Lorraine PLOURDE, *Tokyo Listening: Sound and Sense in a Contemporary City* (Middletown: Wesleyan UP, 2019).

3   Richard SENNETT, *Flesh and Stone: The Body and the City in Western Civilization* (New York:
Norton, 1994) 370.

4   Sennett, *Flesh and Stone* 323.

5   See esp. James HOLSTON and Arjun APPADURAI, "Cities and Citizenship," *Public Culture* 8
(1996): 187-204. Cf. HOLSTON and APPADURAI, eds., *Cities and Citizenship* (Durham, NC: Duke
UP, 1999).

6   See for example: Amita BAVISKAR, "Between Violence and Desire: Space, Power, and Identity in
the Making of Metropolitan Delhi" (2003), rpt. in *International Social Science Journal* 68 (2018):
199-208; Gautam BHAN, "The Impoverishment of Poverty: Reflections on Urban Citizenship and

istrated inequalities that may be more directly apparent from hard socioeconomic data. Rather, the approach of discussing social experience and social structure
in terms of sensorial placings and affective responses is meant to provide access
to 'Other' terrains of consciousness – i.e. to everyday strategies of existing (or
resisting) and thus to sociocultural subjectivities that need to be recognized as
'equal' and 'equally relevant.' Tripta Chandola's dissertation *Listening in to Others: In between Noise and Silence* (2010) may be among the most plausible examples of such an agenda: coupling social anthropology with sound studies, Chandola not only offers insightful close-readings of urban life in a Delhi slum cluster,
but also draws critical attention to a "politics of sensorial ordering" that predominantly operates in the service of the "bourgeois cultural imagination," producing
"a sanitised experience of the city" by "situat[ing] the 'other' sonically."[7]

In contrast to Chandola, we access the topic of socio-sensorial experience and
ordering from the point of view of literary studies – more precisely speaking:
from the point of view of a culturally sensitive mode of literary studies. Doing so,
we are paying homage to the belief that literary texts provide a partially privileged
access to 'terrains of consciousness' – that they facilitate deep insights into 'life-
worlds,' not only in the sense of culturally and materially determined ensembles
of everyday practices but also in the sense of horizons of awareness and possibility. Moreover, by approaching urban life and experience through the lens of literary or quasi-literary textualizations we are drawing on the well-established notion of "the city as text."[8] Respective approaches have argued that the "imagined
city" is as important as – and in fact can be shown to be instrumental in producing – the practically inhabited city. As Alev Çınar and Thomas Bender put it in
the introduction to their edited volume *Urban Imaginaries: Locating the Modern
City* (2007), it is "the collective imagination" that "conjures up a city," so that we

---

Inequality in Contemporary Delhi," *Environment and Urbanization* 26.2 (2014): 547-560; Karen
COELHO, Lalitha KAMATH and M. VIJAYBASKAR, eds., *Participolis: Consent and Contention in
Neoliberal Urban India* (New Delhi: Routledge, 2013).

[7]   Tripta CHANDOLA, *Listening in to Others: In between Noise and Silence*, PhD thesis, Queensland
University of Technology, 2010, web, quotations: 4-5; 17-18. Chandola conducted her research
mainly in a South Delhi cluster of settlements consisting of Lapatagunj, Gandhipuri and Pura-
nihaweli 'camps.' By reference to an adjacent lower-middle-class settlement, the cluster is com-
monly known as the 'Karimnagar slums' (cf. 21-22; 98-101).

[8]   The *locus classicus* of such approaches is James DONALD, "Metropolis: The City as Text," *Social
and Cultural Forms of Modernity*, ed. Robert BOCOCK and Kenneth THOMPSON (Cambridge:
Polity Press / Open University, 1992) 417-461, see esp. 422-424 ("'The City' as Imagined Environment").

"need to look for the city" in literary texts and other "media of the collective imagination."[9]

Throughout the following chapters on writing Delhi, the notion of 'articulation' will serve as a conceptual tool and terminological link. As used in various disciplines from anatomy to musicology and from dentistry to sociology and linguistics, the term basically refers to processes of matching, combining and structuring. The purchase of 'articulation' as a concept in social and cultural analysis is in gesturing towards the ambivalence and complexity of such processes: every articulation can simultaneously be understood as a joining and as a disjoining; the combinations established are both relatively stable and relatively flexible; moreover, social systems and positionalities are constituted through chains and networks of articulations, so that it becomes impossible to establish unidirectional hierarchies of cause and effect. Finally, the concept of articulation is particularly generative because it holds a central position in linguistics as well as in cultural studies or social philosophy: on the one hand, students of society and culture deploy the concept for engineering solutions to the problem of mediation; on the other hand, 'articulation' addresses the (still 'mysterious') interplay between the phonetic work of the tongue and the semantic work of the mind – and thus between environment, body and consciousness.[10]

Our readings of texts on Delhi will substantiate the proposition that cities can be viewed – and have explicitly or implicitly been viewed in various kinds of writing, both scholarly and non-scholarly – as sites, systems, or machines of articulation. Within the domain of the city, the complex processes of social, ideological and linguistic articulation and disarticulation – of linking or separating spheres of life and production, of joining or disjoining agents, of making or unmaking

---

[9]   Alev ÇINAR and Thomas BENDER, "Introduction: The City – Experience, Imagination, and Place," *Urban Imaginaries: Locating the Modern City*, ed. BENDER and ÇINAR (Minneapolis: U of Minnesota P, 2007) xi-xxvi; quotations: xiv-xv. See also Anthony D. KING, "Re-Presenting World Cities: Cultural Theory/Social Practice," *World Cities in a World-System*, ed. Paul Leslie KNOX and Peter J. TAYLOR (Cambridge: Cambridge UP, 1995) 215-231, who claimed already in the 1990s that a "current concern with representation" had "opened up the opportunity for otherwise marginalized voices, alternative representations, to be heard from below" (216).

[10]   Probably, the respective entry in the *Oxford English Dictionary* provides the best starting point for examining the concept of articulation and for gauging the provocative interrelations between the term's various usages in different disciplinary and historical contexts. Helpful digests of 'articulation theory' in social and cultural scholarship are offered by Jennifer Daryl SLACK, "The Theory and Method of Articulation in Cultural Studies," *Stuart Hall: Critical Dialogues in Cultural Studies*, ed. David MORLEY and Kuan-Hsing CHEN (London: Routledge, 1996), 113-129, and Petra SABISCH, "Outline of the Notion of Articulation," *Choreographing Relations: Practical Philosophy and Contemporary Choreography* (München: epodium, 2011) 106-115.

subjectivities through various interrelated economic projects, cultural and communicative practices or ideological endeavours – not only come to be spatially concrete but also are felt with particular acuteness. It is these processes that create and dissociate specific terrains of consciousness or structures of feeling. How, then, have writings on and of Delhi grasped the sensorial aspects of the economically, politically and culturally grounded dis/articulation of the urban population? How, and with what implications, have they portrayed the sensorial aspects of the ruptures created by colonial administrations, by the projects of postcolonial nationhood, and by the post-postcolonial experiment of economic liberation?

3.1 Writing Older Delhis: Traditional Structures of Feeling and (Post-)Colonial Ruptures
– Nishat Zaidi

> His world had fallen to pieces all around him, smothered by indifference and death.
>
> > – Ahmed Ali, *Twilight in Delhi* (1940)[11]
>
> In Delhi, death and drink make life worth living.
>
> > – Khushwant Singh, *Delhi: A Novel* (1990)[12]
>
> Can you rinse away this city that lasts / like blood on the bitten tongue?
>
> > – Agha Shahid Ali, "Chandni Chowk, Delhi"[13]

Most writings on Delhi can be located between the axes of celebration and mourning, pulsating energy and profound exhaustion, surfeit of sensuous excess and inertia. Is this anomaly, this Dionysian pull, common to all cities of the world or it is unique to cities of the Global South? Is the ubiquitous morbid imagery an imaginary construct or it is anchored to substantive referents? Are moments of the city's emergence into the global economy also moments of *emergencies*, forcing people to make adjustments between the inner rhythms of their life and the redrawn external environment? Cities are sites of complex geographies "where

---

[11]   Ahmed Ali, *Twilight in Delhi* (1940; New Delhi: Rupa, 2007) 275.
[12]   Khushwant Singh, *Delhi: A Novel* (New Delhi: Penguin Books India, 1990) 12.
[13]   Agha Shahid Ali, "Chandni Chowk, Delhi," *The Veiled Suite: The Collected Poems* (New York: Norton, 2010) 51.

'far away events' mix with proximate fears," posits Arjun Appadurai.[14] Scholars of urban studies have theorised the city in varied ways.[15] In his iconic essay "The Metropolis and Mental Life," Georg Simmel attributed the metropolitan type of individuality to "the intensification of emotional life due to the swift and continuous shift of external and internal stimuli."[16] Referring to the new precision demanded by the calculating nature of modern life and its money economy, Simmel further posits that "[p]unctuality, calculability, and exactness, which are required by the complications and extensiveness of metropolitan life, are not only most intimately connected with its capitalistic and intellectualistic character but also colour the content of life and are conducive to the exclusion of those irrational, instinctive, sovereign human traits and impulses, which originally seek to determine the form of life from within instead of receiving it from the outside in a general, schematically precise form."[17]

This chapter engages with writings on Delhi, specifically with the way these writings are marked by an acute consciousness of the phenomenological experience of the place, the way the organisation of spaces determines – and is determined by – emotive and sensory responses, and the way in which individuals relate to the place sensorially and in which the cityscape in turn acts upon and shapes human sensibilities. Using Simmel as a central theoretical linchpin, the chapter focuses on the sensory environments constructed in the selected literary and performative texts to tease out from them the tensions between "the attempt of the individual to maintain the independence and individuality of his existence" and an overwhelming magnitude of "social forces, of historical heritage, of external culture, and of the technique of life,"[18] which pose a perennial threat to human autonomy.

It is intriguing why most discussions about Delhi, like most discussions about any other city from the Global South, are marked by the preponderance of the

---

[14]   Arjun APPADURAI, Fear of Small Numbers: An Essay on the Geography of Anger (Durham: Duke UP, 2006) 100.

[15]   See esp. Georg SIMMEL, "The Metropolis and Mental Life," On Individuality and Social Forms, ed. Donald N. LEVINE (Chicago: U of Chicago P, 1903); Richard SENNETT, Flesh and Stone: The Body and the City in Western Civilization (New York: W. W. Norton, 1996); Edward W. SOJA, Postmetropolis: Critical Studies of Cities and Region (Oxford: Blackwell, 2000); and David HARVEY, Spaces of Global Capitalism: A Theory of Uneven Geographical Development (London: Verso, 2006).

[16]   SIMMEL 325.

[17]   SIMMEL 329.

[18]   SIMMEL 325.

organisational logic of nation and nationalism[19] – a logic that blinds one to all other issues. Even though the city is not strictly a new, modern, colonial or post-colonial phenomenon in India, and even though urban existence has always been a part of Indian cultural life,[20] the inherent anti-urban bias of Indian scholarship has resulted in a gap between the lived and the academic significance of cities.[21] Without getting into the trap of nationalist rhetoric, this chapter focuses on urban imaginaries and their exposition of the ruptures of feelings caused by the disjuncture between Delhi's emergence as a global city, on the one hand, and its characteristic rampant underdevelopment ("poverty, environmental toxicity, disease"[22]), on the other. In focusing on sustained diurnal practices, the chapter does not undermine the importance of erupting crises. Within the larger context of the money economy encapsulated in the idea of the metropolis, this chapter examines the terrains of consciousness mapped in creative and performative engagements with Delhi – engagements that trace the city's transition from its pre-modern and colonial phases to the more recent phase of globalization. In their multimodal articulations of the city with its divided, hyphenated existence between the old and the new, these writings capture the various levels of ruptures between the past and the present, the traditional and the modern, the local and the global – all entangled in a complex web of subjectivities, wherein these binaries encroach upon each other. The chapter focuses on the textual and performative reconfigurations of the sensorium of Old Delhi in order to gain a sense of the city's past history and colonial ruptures as well as of the acute realisation of an irreparable loss experienced by its people and indexed by "the realms of hearing, smell and taste," the "haptic architecture of the muscle and the skin."[23]

---

[19] Cf. Partha CHATTERJEE, *The Politics of the Governed: Reflections on Popular Politics in Most of the World* (New York: Columbia UP, 2004), and Sunil KHILNANI, *The Idea of India* (Delhi: Penguin, 2003).

[20] See Vinay LAL, *The Oxford Anthology of the Modern Indian City*, vols. 1 and 2 (New Delhi: Oxford UP, 2013), esp. xvi-xvii.

[21] Cf. Gyan PRAKASH, "The Urban Turn," *Cities of Everyday Life*, ed. Sarai: The New Media Initiative (New Delhi: Sarai, 2002) 2-7; Janaki NAIR, *The Promise of the Metropolis* (New Delhi: Oxford UP, 2005); Madhurima CHAKRABORTY, "Introduction: Whose City?" *Postcolonial Urban Outcasts: City Margins in South Asian Literature*, eds. Madhurima CHAKRABORTY and Umme AL-WAZEDI (New York: Routledge, 2017) 1-18.

[22] Ananya ROY, "Postcolonial Urbanism: Speed, Hysteria, Mass Dreams," *Worlding Cities: Asian Experiments and the Art of Being Global*, ed. Ananya ROY and Aihwa ONG (Hoboken: Wiley-Blackwell, 2011) 279-306, here: 224.

[23] Juhani PALLASMAA, *The Eye of the Skin: Architecture and the Senses* (Sussex: John Wiley & Sons, 2005) 48.

The inhabitants of Delhi negotiate the many historical layers in their daily traversing of the city.[24] The contestation and alliance between the physical fixedness of people in places and their emotional and ethical response to sensory stimuli forms the focus of this chapter. The cityscape of Delhi has been configured and reconfigured in the writings of various settlers, refugees, travellers, and dwellers.[25] Recognising these and many more similar traditions, the chapter will move beyond the ocular to a whole gamut of 'sensorial' phenomena that are present in Delhi's everyday life in the history of the multiple cities embedded in it. By foregrounding sensory modalities, the chapter also reflects on how the politics of the sensorium is played out, embedding contemporary patterns of violence within stories of the past, present and future. By unpacking sonic, olfactory and other sensorial vectors, the chapter attempts to study how articulations of the sensorium allow us to trace the marginalisation of individuals, communities and cultures in a city that lodges distinctive conditions of contemporary life.

Old Delhi today stands at the cusp of the old and the new – between the Islamicate architecture reminiscent of the glorious Mughal past, on the one hand, and activities surrounding it and varying in volume and density according to the time of day and year, on the other. Founded by the Mughal Emperor Shahjahan as Shahjahanabad in 1639, the city of Delhi has been a witness to many transformations, the greatest ones being the transition from the pre-modern to the modern or from the pre-colonial to the colonial – a transition that not only metamorphosed the physical and material structure of the city and its demography but also redefined the very grammar and lexicon of city life, the ordering of everyday activities. In the process, while a new city came up under the sign of colonial power as a symbol of modernity and mobility with its wide roads, rationally organised houses, the old city by contrast became a site of chaos, disorder, noise and stagnation. In the independent India, decimated by the ravages of the Partition and a huge influx of refugees, New Delhi became the seat of power of the newly formed sovereign nation while the Old City (i.e. the walled city of Shahjahanabad with its identification with the Muslim/Islamicate past) further slid back in time. In spite of stagnation, congestion, pollution, dirt, garbage, itinerant vendors, beggars, crime, contagious diseases, noise, squalor and chaos, the Old City

[24]   Cf. Sidharth DEB, *The Beautiful and the Damned: Life in New India* (New Delhi: Penguin, 2010) 220.
[25]   Cf. Saif MAHMOOD, *Beloved Delhi: A Mughal City and Her Greatest Poets* (New Delhi: Speaking Tiger, 2018); Bushra Alvi RAZZAK, ed., *Dilliwali: Celebrating the Women of Delhi through Poetry* (New Delhi: Authorspress, 2018); Semeen ALI, ed., *Dilli: An Anthology of Women Poets of Delhi* (Prayagraj/Allahabad: Cyberwit, 2014); Khushwant SINGH, ed., *City Improbable: Writings on Delhi* (New Delhi: Penguin, 2004); and Tafazzul Husain KAUKAB, *Fughan-i-Dilhi* ["The Lament for Delhi"] (Dehli: Chashma—i-Faiz, 1863).

remains the nerve centre supporting the thriving economy. The medieval architecture of the Old City stands in sharp contrast to its densely populated markets and a flurry of economic activity. Embedded in such overt disjunctures and ruptures are many layers of interactions, interdependencies and negotiations.

3.1.1 City Sensoriums as Metaphors of Memory: The Synaesthetic Mapping of the Changing City in *Twilight in Delhi* (1940)

This section examines Ahmed Ali's *Twilight in Delhi* (1940) to explore how embodied practices of singing, dancing and listening generate emotional responses, how cultural productions like the poetry of Mirza Ghalib and Mir Taqi Mir become markers of the past glory and emotional outgrowth of creative and intellectual pursuits. I will further study the emotional imaginaries of the banal that lay embedded in the Old City lost in inertia and stasis.

Twilight in Delhi is a requiem to Delhi and reconstructs the city through its sounds, through vivid visual depictions and through tactility, which together evoke poignant and melancholic emotions. The writer sets the mood right in the opening paragraph of the novel, which personifies the city as it deploys a synaesthetic mode to underline feelings of melancholy, nostalgia and anxiety. The picture of a night-muffled city, sleeping by-lanes, oppressive heat, half-naked, tired sleeping men, the smell of the flowers getting smothered by the heat, sniffing dogs, slinking cats and stinking gutters draw the reader into the sensorial experience of the city. In the midst of all these olfactory, visual and tactile sensations, the author announces:

> But the city of Delhi, built hundreds of years ago, fought for, died for, coveted and desired, built, destroyed and rebuilt, for five and six and seven times, mourned and sung, raped and conquered, yet whole and alive, lies indifferent in the arms of sleep. It was the city of kings and monarchs, of poets and story tellers, courtiers and nobles. But no kings live there today, and the poets are feeling the lack of patronage; and the old inhabitants, though still alive, have lost their pride and grandeur under a foreign yoke. Yet the city stands still intact, as do many more forts and tombs and monuments, remnants and reminders of old Delhis, holding on to life with a tenacity and purpose which is beyond comprehension and belief.[26]

---

[26]   Ahmed ALI 4.

The threat of the foreign yoke is further amplified in a detailed description of the network of alleys leading to a narrow alleyway and in the design of the house where Mir Nihal resides, rhythms of Mir Nihal's daily life, his passion for breeding pigeons, which are under continuous threat from snakes and cats, pitted against his young son Asghar's "aping of the Farangis."[27] With his red Turkish cap, the collar of his English shirt peeping out of the open upper button of his *sherwani*, his "dirty English boots"[28] and his passion for the dancing girls reflected through the jasmine garland wrapped around his wrist, Asghar stands at the cusp of history.

In his scrutiny of Raymond Williams's notion of "structures of feeling"[29] and its potential use in Affect Studies, Ben Highmore argues that "[t]he joining together of a socially phenomenological interest in the world of things, accompanied by an attention to historically specific moods and atmospheres, is [...] a way of mobilising the critical potential of 'structures of feelings' [sic] towards important mundane cultural phenomena."[30] Ali's novel maps 'structures of feeling' through an extended description of ubiquitous forms of material culture such as clothing, housing, interpersonal interactions, food, and other material practices of daily living. Feelings, in this manner, are not dissociated from the social realm, lifestyle is not removed from historicity.

Set in the period between 1911 and 1919, the novel revolves around Mir Nihal's family, and his social circle. A feeling of gloom, loss and decay haunts all the characters, often spurred by insignificant events like a sound in the distance or a turn in the weather. Like many other narratives of Delhi, the novel weaves Urdu and Persian verses from Ghalib, Meer and Hafiz, and songs to add to the poignancy of feelings. An array of sounds, ranging from wandering *qawwals* singing in the distance, or cries of a child somewhere outside, or mundane sounds like "the peculiar noise of silver-leaf makers beating silver and gold,"[31] the chattering of sparrows, the "heart-rending voice"[32] of a blind beggar and the mournful and haunting sound of the *azaan* constitute the sonic world of the characters – a world that provokes mournful, morbid emotions. The intensity of inevitable loss is further accentuated when, in contrast to these sounds, the novel presents the lively and colourful scenes of Asghar's wedding or the joyous celebrations of

---

[27]   Ahmed ALI 13.
[28]   Ahmed ALI 13.
[29]   The phrase 'structures of feeling' was first used by WILLIAMS in 1954 in his book (with the documentary filmmaker Michael ORROM) *Preface to Film*.
[30]   Ben HIGHMORE, "Formations of Feelings, Constellations of Things," *Cultural Studies Review* 22.1 (2016): 144-167, here: 145.
[31]   Ahmed ALI 19.
[32]   Ahmed ALI 132.

Eid, or the olfactory and the gustatory sensations induced by the smell of "ghee, fat, oil and burning meat" filling the air as the kebab vendors grill kebabs.[33] The helplessness and spiritual paralysis induced by the colonial rule is conveyed through a continuous juxtaposition of actors and actants. Pining for Bilqeece, the daughter of a "low-born" Muslim, Asghar muses about the difference between loving and being loved: "To be loved is sweet, he thought, whereas to love is full of sorrow and grief and pain."[34] Asghar's mother, Begam Nihal, reiterates this dichotomy when she tells her philandering husband: "I know only how to burn. I don't know how to light the fire."[35] Bilqeece, Mushtari Bai, Begam Nihal, Mir Nihal, Asghar, all feel passive at different levels, reflecting the larger inertia felt by the residents of feudal Delhi under colonial rule. In the Introduction, Ahmed Ali says: "[M]y purpose in writing the novel was to depict a phase of our national life and the decay of a whole culture, a particular mode of thought and living, values now dead and gone before our eyes."[36]

Delhi's decline, lamented already at the beginning of the novel, is complete when the city begins to prepare for the Coronation Durbar.[37] The attendant changes include the removal of the deep gutters, the demolition of the city walls, "the disfiguring of the Chandni Chowk,"[38] the demolition of Old Delhi's central causeway and the cutting down of peepul trees. All these disturb city dwellers, who express their resentment by cursing the city: "To hell with you Delhi."[39] The narrative articulates Mir Nihal's fears thus: "The old culture, which had been pre-served within the walls of the ancient town, was in danger of annihilation. Her language, on which Delhi had prided itself, would become adulterated and im-pure [...]. She would become the city of the dead."[40] Mir Nihal's contempt for the English echoes the views of an author who scathingly speaks of "Bentinck's Westernisation and Macaulay's painting our faces brown with a pigmentless brush of anglicization."[41] In the later chapters of the novel, the narrator acknowl-edges: "The glory had gone, and only dreariness remained. The richness of life had been looted and despoiled by the foreigners, and vulgarity and cheapness had

---

[33] Ahmed ALI 106.
[34] Ahmed ALI 24.
[35] Ahmed ALI 45.
[36] Ahmed ALI xxi.
[37] The capital of British India was transferred from Calcutta to Delhi in 1911, after which King George V held his Coronation Durbar in the new capital.
[38] Ahmed ALI 196.
[39] Ahmed ALI 196.
[40] Ahmed ALI 197.
[41] Ahmed ALI xiii.

taken its place."[42] The chapters recurrently end with the words "And life went on," which foreground a worldview that treats loss and longing as normative. The "engulfing sense of futility" is rendered visible through the grand monuments like Jama Masjid or the Grand Mosque and the Chandni Chowk standing in contrast to the narrow lanes surrounding them, the hum-drum of the life in the zenana which Ali describes as "water in the pool," the sounds of music and dance in the red-light area of Chaori Bazaar,[43] the star-studded sky, the beggars and vendors thronging the streets, the tram cars indicating incursions of modernity under the colonial rule.

The influenza epidemic of 1918, which afflicted Delhi immediately after the ravages of the First World War, intensified a sense of disillusionment with the British Empire. The coppery sky, the sand blowing with the hot wind that howls due to the demolition of city walls, quiet dogs and moaning cats invoke sensations of fear and impending death. Towards the end of the novel, Mir Nihal lies paralysed in bed, his wife has lost her eyesight and is condemned to the seclusion of the zenana, some die premature deaths, while others are left to mourn the dead. Rendering historicity to sensory experiences and to the feelings they induce, the novel records: "The sky was overcast with dust and sand. The kites circled and cried; there was dreariness in the atmosphere."[44]

3.1.2 "Stranded in the Backwaters of Time": The Disjunct Sights and Sounds of Post-Partition Old Delhi in Anita Desai's *In Custody* (1984)

In the walled city of Shahjahanabad or present-day Old Delhi, poverty and squalor lived in close proximity with royal opulence. Royal arcades and boulevards were surrounded by clumsy, narrow by-lanes. The colonial town planners of New Delhi visualised the cityscape differently when, in 1911, they began constructing it to the south of what is now known as Old Delhi. The new city was designed by Edwin Lutyens to reflect the idea of the garden city developed by the English architect Ebenezer Howard. The older incarnation of Delhi, however, did not disappear. It survived in a splendid fort, in the Jama Masjid and in many

---

[42] Ahmed ALI 240.
[43] Ahmed ALI 73: "From all around came the sounds of song, whining of sarangis, muffled drums and the tinkling of bells, as the dancing girls entertained their customers. The music made Asghar feel more sad, for it reminded him of his love."
[44] Ahmed ALI 69.

other mosques and temples, in some broken walls and in the names of specific *kuchas* and *mohullas*. It also survived as a culture and a way of life.

If Ali's *Twilight in Delhi* captures the sense of loss suffered by the city's residents at the beginning of colonial rule in the old Indo-Persian tradition of Shahr-e Ashob,[45] Anita Desai's *In Custody* returns to the much beloved city and culture of Mir Nihal within a pronounced modernist framework – a framework in which the city is no longer an object of love and longing. It is rather presented as a distinct site of decay, stagnation and disjuncture, invoking emotions of disdain and odium.[46] The claustrophobic chaos of Old Delhi is seen in Desai's novel as having a debilitating effect on the much-revered Urdu culture of the past, underlining its slide from sublime to vulgar. In post-Partition India, where Muslims constitute a minority, the grandeur of the late Mughal culture, with its celebration of great Urdu poets and poetry, music recitals, and dancing courtesans presented in Ali's novel in all their lyrical charm have degenerated into vulgar excess within the noisy overcrowded slums of Old Delhi in Desai's novel. In place of Mir Taqi Mir (1722–1810), Ibrahim Zauq (1788–1854), or Dagh Dehlavi (1831–1905), who are so reverentially recalled in *Twilight in Delhi*, the "glorious past of Urdu" is now hinged on the figure of the poet Nur Shahjahanabadi, his nom de plume or *takhallus* tying him to the city of Shahjahanabad, a seat of Urdu literary tradition. Embedded in the figure of the poet Nur is the entire glory of the Muslim past of Hindustan, whose grand architecture and literature have now been reduced to cheap sentimental songs sung by the low-class singers of the Bombay cinema.

In Custody is the second novel by Anita Desai that delves into the ruptures between the Muslim past and the Post-Partition present through the spatial juxtaposition of Old and New Delhi. Desai delineated the subject first, in her novel

---

[45]   According to the Urdu scholar Shamsur Rehman FARUQI, the first proper Shahr-e Ashob was written by Mir Jafar Zatalli. Prominent Urdu poets such as Mir Taqi Mir and Sauda wrote a number of poems deploring the diminishment of the Mughals' cultural influence as well as their political hold over Delhi. The noted Urdu poet and critic Altaf Husain Hali (1837–1914) lamented the decline of the Mughal culture of Delhi in "Marsiya-e-Marhum-e Dehli" (Elegy on a Deceased Delhi). For more on Shahr-e Ashob, see Choudhary M. NAIM, *Readings in Urdu: Prose and Poetry* (Honolulu: East-West Center Press, 1965); Pasha Mohamad KHAN, *The Lament for Delhi* (1863).

[46]   In a letter to be found in Daud RAHBAR, ed., *Urdu Letters of Ghalib* (New York: State University of New York, 1987) 133, Ghalib (1797–1869) expressed his sorrow as follows: "Nowadays, the people of Dihli are either Hindus or common workers or men in Khaki or Panjabis or Goras. Which of these do you intend as the speakers of praiseworthy language?" In another letter, Ghalib refers to the changing demography of the city: "This is not the Dihli in which I have lived for the last fifty-one years! Dihli is now a military base. The only Muslims left in the city are either common labourers or else menial servants employed by government officials." (27)

Clear Light of Day (1980), through the three families Ali, Das and Misra, who have been neighbours in Old Delhi "since so long as they could remember."[47] In this novel Bim articulates Desai's perceptions about the Janus-faced city of Delhi when she says: "Old Delhi does not change. It only decays. My students tell me it is a great cemetery, every house a tomb. Nothing but sleeping graves. Now New Delhi, they say is different. That is where things happen."[48]

The novel moves beyond the Manichean pitting of the sepulchral view of Old Delhi against the trendy and modern New Delhi to zoom in on the cesspool that Old Delhi and its rich literary heritage have now become. Young Deven Sharma teaches Hindi in a school in the village of Mirpore. Deven's claim that Urdu is his true vocation and that he teaches Hindi only to gain a livelihood underlines Hindi's participation and Urdu's non-participation in the money economy of post-Partition India. Fed up with the hum-drum of the daily and the mundane, such as the demands of his students, school administrators, his wife and child, Deven dreams of doing something meaningful. When he meets Murad, a brash and crooked journal editor and an old classmate who invites Deven to befriend and interview the great Urdu poet Nur, Deven's subterranean desires are rekindled. Trapped between the opposite poles of nostalgia and ambition, Murad and Deven become victims of their own selves.

Deven's dream of the high ideal of beauty associated with Urdu, as opposed to the vulgar materiality attached to Hindi, receives a violent blow for the first time when he has to navigate through the narrow lanes of Chandni Chowk to meet his icon, the great Urdu poet Nur. The spatial details of Chandni Chowk, with its "shady looking" and "evil smelling" shops, gutters, and narrow alleyways repel Deven:

> If it had not been for the colour and the noise, Chandni Chowk might have been a bazaar encountered in a nightmare; it was so like a maze from which he could find no exit, in which he wandered between the peeling, stained walls of office buildings, the overflowing counters of shops and stalls, wondering if the urchin sent to lead him through it was not actually a malevolent imp leading him to his irrevocable disappearance in the reeking heart of the bazaar. The heat and the crowds pressed down from above and all sides, solid and suffocating as sleep.[49]

---

[47]   Anita DESAI, *Clear Light of Day* (New Delhi: Penguin, 1980) 136.
[48]   DESAI, *Clear Light of Day* 5.
[49]   DESAI, *In Custody* (1984; London: Vintage, 1999) 40.

Deven finds it difficult to reconcile this "pullulating honeycomb of commerce"[50] with the grandeur and beauty of Nur's poetry. The material world of sights, sounds, speech and actions of the Chandni Chowk bazaar encroach on the artistic self of Nur, reducing the poet and his spatial location (Chandni Chowk) to a sight of hopeless degeneration. In Desai's imaginative cartography of the city, Nur and Chandni Chowk become extensions of each other. Relics of a pre-modern past, they both are hopelessly out of tune with the modern present. Nur is appalled at the idea of recording poetry: "Record – like in the cinema? For songs? I am not one of those singing poets, you know, some performer at weddings and festivals."[51] Deven, Nur and Murad, all three fail to reconcile the sordid reality of Urdu's present with its glorious past. Nur echoes Bim's frustration when he says:

> How can there be Urdu poetry when there is no Urdu language left? It is dead, finished. The defeat of the Moghuls by the British threw a noose over its head, and the defeat of the British by the Hindi-wallahs tightened it. So now you see its corpse lying here, waiting to be buried.[52]

The opening scene of the novel foregrounds these tensions through the affective agency of food. When Murad meets Deven in his college, he demands alcohol with food, but Deven takes him to a vegetarian canteen that serves buttermilk, radishes, potatoes and paratha, which Murad terms "food for cows and pigs."[53] Over this pure vegetarian meal, Murad, the aggressive representative of the Urdu-speaking Muslim community, co-opts Deven, a self-proclaimed lover of Urdu, to "keep alive the glorious traditions of Urdu literature." Murad vehemently asks: "If we do not do it, at whatever cost, how will it survive in this era of – that vegetarian monster, Hindi?"[54] Through the narrative strategy of collating the first-person inclusive pronoun "we" with a euphonic attitude towards Urdu, the author enunciates the reader's identification. The tensions between old and new, Urdu and Hindi, Muslim and Hindu are further augmented when the austere meal offered by Deven is contrasted with the meal served by his colleague Siddiqui, where in place of the vegetarian buttermilk and radishes there is rum, kebabs and *pilao*. These contrasts of food are politically charged. They imply Hindu-Muslim contradictions and historical discords between the two communities. As the narrative puts it: "After pressing a glass of rum into Deven's hand, [Siddiqui] gave orders to the servant boy and sent him out to the bazaar for kebabs and *pilao*. They sat there on the terrace, like a pair of nawabs stranded in the

---

[50]   DESAI, *In Custody* 41.
[51]   DESAI, *In Custody* 143.
[52]   DESAI, *In Custody* 43.
[53]   DESAI, *In Custody* 14.
[54]   DESAI, *In Custody* 14.

backwaters of time, thought Deven."[55] Patterns of feelings and tastes reflect processes of worlding. Food stuff and modes of consumption are a function of social class, religious affiliation and local traditions. In this sense, the post-Partition minoritization of Muslims is attributed to their decadent anti-modern lifestyle in the novel. The sight and smell associated with food attains political overtones when both Nur and his wife Imtiaz Begum equate Deven with a carnivore and a jackal, as Deven tries to prod Nur to record his poems. Imtiaz Begum tells Deven:

> I know your kind – jackals from the universities […] trained to feed upon our carcasses. Now you have grown impatient, you can't even wait till we die – you come to tear at our living flesh.[56]

Nur echoes his wife when he admonishes Deven:

> Do you think a poet can be ground between stones, and bled, in order to produce poetry— *for you*? You think you can switch on that mincing machine, and I will instantly produce for you a length of raw, red minced meat that you can carry off to your professors to eat?[57]

By conflating the body with poetry and admirers like Deven with flesh-eating carnivores, Desai articulates a deep sense of insecurity that afflicts Urduwalllahs/Muslims in contemporary India. Their self-proclaimed custodians appear to them as nothing more than carrion-eaters bent on consuming everything that gives meaning to their lives.

The novel abounds in sensory detail to undergird the erosion of the old in the face of changes wrought by modernity, its attendant technology and money economy. The billboard advertisements for refrigerators and cars, reflecting the aspirational realm of Deven's middle-class wife contrast with the barren terrains of Mirpore; spatial details of Old Delhi are deployed to situate the poet within a degenerate present. The recurrent references to the body and bodily fluids linked to ingestion are used to reinforce the contrast with modern notions of health and hygiene. The rhetorical reconstructions of pigeon excreta on the surface of a Mirpore mosque,[58] the description of a lane "that was lined with nothing but gutters and seems to serve as a latrine for the entire neighbourhood,"[59] Chotu's discharge

---

[55] DESAI, *In Custody* 49. As we learn on the same page, Deven "was aware that it was entirely the wrong sort of food for his delicate digestive system and that he would regret it all within a few hours."
[56] DESAI, *In Custody* 126.
[57] DESAI, *In Custody* 170.
[58] DESAI, *In Custody* 20.
[59] DESAI, *In Custody* 32.

of nasal mucus, Nur's vomit,[60] and Deven's diarrhoea contribute to the construction of a grotesque realism that aims at invoking emotive responses from the readers, prompting their active participation. Furthermore, references to smeared train windows, flies hovering over sweets in the food lanes of Chandni Chowk, the mud- and dung-filled houses, the dead dog being eaten by crows, carcasses littering the landscape or the dead fly in Deven's tea,[61] are aimed at foregrounding the cesspool of the Islamic past, Urdu literary culture and Muslims in contemporary India. Deven's shock and "horror at the teashop owner's filthiness,"[62] his refusal to drink the cold drink "at a stall where poison green and red sherbets in bottles topped with lemon and carrot juice in damp oozing earthen jars were in great demand,"[63] his horrified recoil when a shopkeeper offers him a betel leaves with "his fingers"[64] reaches a peak when the feast offered by Nur is brought up by the waiters "in filthy pyjamas, tattered vest, and waiters' napkins."[65] All these identify Muslim culture with "rot, poison and filth."[66]

In representing the complex sensory environment of Old Delhi, which frequently acts as an assault on the senses of visitors and residents, Desai deploys a healthy dose of irony. Rich in subtexts implied by ethos and telos, Desai's novel captures the psychological, emotional and mental responses to sensory experiences based on the author's own perception of disjunctures between the medieval Islamic past and colonial as well as postcolonial modernity.[67] When Deven attempts to preserve the dying world of Urdu poetry by deploying the modern technology of recording, he discovers to his dismay that owing to his assistant Chiku's mishandling of tapes, all that is left after three weeks of recordings is merely one tape of "a bizarre pastiche."[68] The failure of technology to preserve the past articulates Desai's utter despair of the revival of Urdu heritage. In foregrounding poetry as performance, especially through Imtiaz Begum's soulful

---

[60] DESAI, *In Custody* 57: "It isn't ulcers that has made you vomit on my floor, it is drink," says the outraged wife of Nur.

[61] DESAI, *In Custody* 16-23.

[62] DESAI, *In Custody* 23.

[63] DESAI, *In Custody* 40.

[64] DESAI, *In Custody* 113.

[65] DESAI, *In Custody* 48.

[66] Marta DVORAK. *The Faces of Carnival in Anita Desai's 'In Custody'* (Paris: Presses Universitaires de France, 2008) 65-66.

[67] Cf. DESAI, qtd. in YAQIN: "It was very much the voice of North India. But although there is such a reverence for Urdu poetry, the fact that most Muslims left India to go to Pakistan meant that most schools and universities of Urdu were closed. So that it's a language I don't think is going to survive in India. There are many Muslims and they do write in Urdu; but it has a kind of very artificial existence."

[68] DESAI, *In Custody* 98.

renditions, Desai also points towards the degeneration that has beset the Urdu literary sphere as it sinks from elite to mass/popular cultural spheres. Deven's refusal to accept this slide gestures towards his failure in acknowledging the inevitability of change.

Hoping to gain entry into Delhi's literary circles and publish his own Urdu poetry, Deven finds himself trapped in the poet's squalid world: "All he knew was that he who had set out to hunt Nur down was being hunted down himself, the prey."[69] In spite of the unreasonable demands raised by Nur, who no longer writes verses but lives extravagantly, Deven feels bound to the poet. In contrast to the only Urdu teacher at his college, who sells his family property to a real-estate developer, and the other Muslim speakers of Urdu who seek jobs in other countries, Deven has become the custodian of what is left of the Islamicate/Urdu culture in India, reflecting Desai's only hope for the Urdu literary culture and for Old Delhi.

3.1.3 Anxieties of a Postcolonial City:
Khushwant Singh's *Delhi: A Novel* (1990)

Any narrative on Delhi's modernity has to contend with multiple versions of this palimpsestic city. Khushwant Singh's *Delhi: A Novel* deals with a dynamic relationship between spatiality and social processes, foregrounding the ways in which language, architecture, and other cultural practices of older Delhis have endured the impact of changes set in motion by the colonial and the postcolonial worldview. As we have observed in the previous sections, located on two sides of the temporal divide marked by the Partition of India, Ahmed Ali and Anita Desai share an ambivalent relationship with the socio-cultural and historical environment of Old Delhi. If Ali's novel mourns the loss of its pre-colonial grandeur, Desai's works bring out its irredeemable decay in the postcolonial India. They both, however, position Old Delhi as the irreconcilable 'other' of New Delhi and rely on the "scenography or ruptures"[70] in their textual reconstructions of the life in Old Delhi. Singh's novel marks a shift from these modernist engagements to

---

[69] DESAI, *In Custody* 156.
[70] The term used by Charles BONN has been cited by in Arnold in the context of Mauritian writings. See Markus ARNOLD, "Between Post-Colonial and Postcolonial: A Reading Proposal through and for the Contemporary Novel Production of Mauritius (and Beyond)," *Pensée, Pratiques et Poétiques Postcoloniales Contemporaines: Monde Atlantique et Océan Indien*, ed. Rodolphe SOLBIAC (Paris: L'Harmattan, 2018).

postmodern scenographies where identities are more fluid, processual and capable of accommodating differences.

Delhi: A Novel tells the story of the multi-layered city of Delhi, where the past intervenes in the present, and where present perceptions conjure to life a forgotten past not recorded in the dominant historiography. The spatial narrative of the much used, abused and misused city is indexed on the character of a pockmarked eunuch, Bhagmati, who despite overt ugliness attracts the Sikh protagonist with her hidden charms. The novel is a non-linear, polyphonic narrative deploying teleological shifts, indeterminacy, slippages and Rabelaisian bawdy humour to interrogate history and textuality. The materiality of Bhagmati's appearance with her dark complexion, pockmarked face, uneven and yellowed teeth (caused by the long years of chewing tobacco and smoking *bidis*), loud clothes, bawdy speech and manners, matches the protagonist's first response to the disorderly city with little civic amenities and the uncivil habits of its citizens:

> To the stranger Delhi may appear like a gangrenous accretion of noisy bazaars, mean-looking hovels growing round a few tumble-down forts and mosques along a dead river. If he ventures into its narrow, winding lanes, the stench of raw sewage may bring vomit to his throat. The citizens of Delhi do little to endear themselves to anyone. They spit phlegm and bloody *betel*-juice everywhere; they urinate and defecate whenever and wherever the urge overtakes them; they are loud-mouthed, express familiarity with incestuous abuse and scratch their privates while they talk.[71]

But the protagonist is no 'stranger,' and hence is not repelled by odious sights, sounds, smells and habits. According to the protagonist, Bhagmati, the *hijda*, and Delhi, have two things in common: "[T]hey are a lot of fun. And they are sterile."[72] The novel sets out to map the story of Delhi by tracing the disorderly contours of the city, in conjunction with the pockmarked body of the *hijda*. In this anthropomorphising of the city by linking it to the body of Bhagmati,[73] the novel exposes disjunctures and dissonances between what Sennett has termed the "cité" ("a kind of consciousness") and the "ville" ("the built environment"). Drawing upon this distinction, which points towards duality of object and experience, Sennett argues that the way people want to live is often not in harmony with how cities are built, resulting in contradictions and jagged edges.[74] Singh's narrative of Delhi brings out these jagged edges, these contradictions, asymmetries, and

---

[71] SINGH, *Delhi: A Novel* 1.
[72] SINGH, *Delhi: A Novel* 30.
[73] Halina MARLEWICZ, "Heterotopian City: Khushwant Singh and His *Delhi: A Novel*," *Politeja* 40 (2016): 159-176, here: 170.
[74] Richard SENNETT, *Building and Dwelling: Ethics for the City* (New York: Allen Lane, 2018).

glaring inequalities – but not in terms of negative rejection, as the narrator warns in the beginning of the novel: "Delhi and Bhagmati have a lot in common. Having been long misused by rough people, they have learnt to conceal their seductive charm, under a mask of repulsive ugliness. It is only to their true lovers, among whom I count myself, that they reveal their true selves."[75] Love for the city, therefore, is a precondition for appreciating its charms.

The protagonist of the novel is an educated Sikh – a globe-trotter who lives in a modern apartment in Delhi, is friends with journalists, diplomats, politicians and others in the upper echelons of power, and regularly visits the upmarket, elite spaces of modern Delhi like the India International Centre, the diplomatic quarters, the coffee houses, and Connaught Place. He also visits the various monuments of Delhi, and with each monument he visits, a first person narrative of the past is conjured to capture the quotidian life of ordinary individuals of the period when the monument was built. This ruptures the dominant historiography, which only focuses on the lives of rulers and elites. Even though the architectural monuments of the past may appear out of tune with the present ethos surrounding them, closer scrutiny makes it clear that many forms of violence in the present are anchored in the past and that shadows of the past loom large over the present, modifying the textures of its daily life.

The topography of Delhi is presented in the novel through its affective and embodied practices revealed by many real and imagined personas covering 600 years of its past, such as Musaddi Lal (a Hindu clerk under the Muslim rule); Tamerlene (a tyrant much despised in the pages of dominant historiography); an untouchable Sikh; the Mughal emperor Aurangzeb; the Persian king Nader Shah; Meer Taqi Meer (an Agra-born Urdu poet who enjoyed great prestige and power in Delhi's elite literary circles); Bahadur Shah Zafar (an outcaste of history); Alice Aldwell, the half-caste wife of an English civil servant; 'the builder'; and Ram Lakha, a refugee from Pakistan presenting their first person narratives of the place. As we move from one speaking voice to the other, we discover the shifting foci of urban development. These narrators reveal ways in which their lives have been altered by their experiences of the city or how events in their lives have altered cityscapes of Delhi. In this spatio-temporal fictional vision of the city, contours of cartography become alive in interaction with accounts of bodily experiences of the people inhabiting those spaces, much in line with Sennett's perception of cities as made of flesh and stone.[76] Halina Marlewicz sums this up as follows: "Yet Khushwant Singh's novel not only exemplifies how, in each narrative, the autobiographical 'I' constitutes the net of geographical interferences but also

---

[75]   SINGH, *Delhi: A Novel* 1.
[76]   Cf. SENNETT, *Flesh and Stone*.

how it becomes a meaningful constituent of the history of the place."[77] In interspersing all these chapters with chapters on the protagonist's liaison with his mistress Bhagmati, the fictional narrative punctures the linear telos of history to project a hybrid perspective and the simultaneous presence of multiple truths. In an almost Proustian sweep, through a vast assemblage of characters and their perception of various streets, alleys, muhallas, palaces, chowks, bazaars and hospices, Singh's novel produces a collective place consciousness of Delhi.

Henri Lefebvre argued: "What is an ideology without a space to which it refers, a space which it describes, whose vocabulary and links it makes use of, and whose code it embodies?"[78] Singh's novel explores this embodied code by observing the life animating the aggregation of structures of dead stones. Its epigraph is a couplet by Ghalib: "I asked my soul: What is Delhi? / She replied: The world is the body and Delhi its life." This is meant to articulate Singh's perception of the city as the fountainhead of life in the world. In a fascinating intersection of the synchronic and diachronic, the horizontal expanse of the city and its chronological sweep, Singh underlines the inseparability of the city's spatial contours and their temporal axes. The past continues to impinge on the present, just as the present is shaped by events of the past. Collision between past and present is apparent to the narrator as soon as, after a sojourn aboard, he steps out of the airport and drives back to his apartment:

> More roads and roundabouts have had their names changed. The Windsors, Yorks, Cannings and Hardings have been replaced by the Tilaks, Patels, Azads and Nehrus. There are red flags outside a petrol station with three men chanting 'Death to petrolstationwalla.' [...] On the lawns of Connaught Circus there is a political meeting. The speaker yells into the mike: 'All together cry—*Jai Hind.*' The crowd obeys: '*Jai Hind.*'[79]

This postcolonial city is a picture of chaos, where irrational gestures of the government to change names in order to erase signs of the colonial rule and the abuse or misuse of Gandhian anti-colonial and nationalist slogans by feuding political parties for their petty goals indicate deep entanglements of past and present, history and geography. In this fictional reconstruction of the cartography of the city through human lives spread over centuries, the regularly altering identity of collectivity further underscores the complex morphology of the city. In Musaddi Lal's narrative, "we" is "us Hindus" and "them" are Muslim invaders; in the account of the builder, "we" encompasses Hindus as well as Muslims, while "them"

---

[77] MARLEWICZ 169.
[78] Henri LEFEBVRE, *The Production of Space*, trans. Donald Nicholson-Smith (Oxford: Blackwell, 1991) 44.
[79] SINGH, Delhi: *A Novel* 8.

points towards the British; in the narration of Ram Lakha, a refugee from Pakistan, "we" once again indexes Hindus and Sikhs while "them" implies the "Mussalman"; finally, towards the end of the novel, "we" suggests the supporters of Bhindranwale and the Akal Takht, while "them" refers to Hindus. Throughout the narrative, the identities of victims and victimisers keep changing, but the process of victimization remains constant.[80]

Singh is invited to take Lady Hoity Toity, a VIP anthropologist, around the city. He is writing a TV documentary about the city, and has his own fan club that includes an Army Officer's wife and a few young girls. He moves easily from the diplomatic quarters to the quarters of eunuchs in Lal Kuan, underscoring Delhi's ability to defy the colonial town planners' privileging of reified spaces. The narrative reveals how the urban disenfranchised are alienated from power along the multiple axes of gender, caste and class. Bhagmati and her tribe belong to this category.

The protagonist's assertion, "[i]n Delhi death and drink make life worth living,"[81] sums up the inner paradox of the city. Both death and drink negate life, one permanently and the other temporarily. Likewise, Delhi survives through the coexistence of competing, even contradictory lives, narratives and worldviews. The novel phenomenologically engages with the city and with the way physical spaces act upon the body and shape the emotive and psychological experiences of the people inhabiting these spaces. Recurrent references to spitting, defecating and urinating in public, to farting, sex (both heterosexual and bi-sexual), rape, physical violence and bloodshed, to sloganeering, honking, traffic jams, non-functional traffic lights and power cuts posit the postcolonial city as a conglomerate of contradictions. Pointing to the structure of the novel, Singh writes in the preface: "History provided me with the skeleton. I covered it with flesh and injected blood and a lot of seminal fluid into it."[82]

Dipesh Chakrabarty has argued that public defecation and throwing garbage in the streets are acts of open defiance by the subaltern, embodying their refusal to become citizens of the "bourgeois order."[83] Sudipta Kaviraj also interprets the production of "filth and disorder" by the urban poor as a retaliatory tactic "to symbolically establish their control over that space."[84] According to Joel Lee, such

---

[80]   Cf. Nishat ZAIDI. "Fiction, History and Fictionalised History: A Postcolonial Reading of Khushwant Sigh's *Delhi," The Journal of Indian Writing in English* 34.2 (2006): 37-48.

[81]   SINGH, *Delhi: A Novel* 12.

[82]   SINGH, "Preface," *Delhi: A Novel* n. p.

[83]   Dipesh CHAKRABARTY, "Open Space / Public Space: Garbage, Modernity and India," *South Asia: Journal of South Asian Studies* 14.1 (1994): 15-31.

[84]   Sudipta KAVIRAJ. "Filth and the Public Sphere: Concepts and Practices about Space in Calcutta," *Public Culture* 10.1 (1997): 83-113, here: 107.

readings camouflage the reverse story of the filth produced by the urban elite piling up in the living spaces of the subaltern. Lee also underlines how beyond the optics of garbage, smell transcends and displaces inside/outside and interior/exterior boundaries.[85] The recurrent references to human excreta and public defecation in Singh's novel underline the failure of the modern state to make a difference in the lives of its poor, marginalised citizens.

The visceral aspects of these embodied contacts with space through secreting of waste matter and its sensory impact on an outsider's perception of the place deconstruct the neoliberal privileging of the intellectual and economic order over pre-modern dynamics of caste or religion. In Desai's novel, all descriptions of such contacts are steeped in the language of modernity, where public health and hygiene are privileged, where boundaries between the 'public' and 'private' are treated as sacrosanct and their violations as loathsome. The schematic displacement of such binaries as space/time, sublime and mundane, personal and political, history and geography emerges as Singh's carefully considered strategy to narrate the city. What stands out in his narrative is the foregrounding of corporeality. As Halina Marlewicz argues:

> The history of Delhi in Khushwant Singh's novel is corporeal: much space is given to sexuality, eroticism, physicality, physiology. [...] Much is said about how bodies are made instrumental, exploited, consumed or manipulated in the making of history. At times one has the impression that the interest in what *love, lust, sex, hate, vendetta and violence* do to the body – along with the role all these play in writing the history of the city – approaches obsession.[86]

The deliberate assault on the senses created by Singh's recurrent references to his sexual flings, descriptions of private parts exposed in defecation at public places, and farting reinforce Singh's stance that to appreciate the 'hidden charms' of Delhi, one has to reconcile oneself to its apparent ugliness, disorder and chaos.

---

[85] Cf. Joel LEE. "Odor and Order: How Caste Is Inscribed in Space and Sensoria," *Comparative Studies of South Asia, Africa and the Middle East* 37.3 (2017): 470-490.
[86] MARLEWICZ 170.

3.1.4 'A Lost Memory of Delhi': A Migrant's Re-imaginings of the City in Agha Shahid Ali's Poetry

This section analyses Delhi poems by the Kashmiri-Indian-American poet Agha Shahid Ali, to unpack the various ways in which the city of Delhi shaped the consciousness of a migrant Muslim poet. Ali was born in Delhi. He later returned for his college education[87] before eventually migrating to the USA. Though Delhi appears in his earliest collection, *Bone Sculpture*,[88] which was published while Shahid was still living in the city, its role in shaping his sensibilities is realised fully in his second collection, *In Memory of Begum Akhtar*,[89] which was published after he had migrated to America. References to Delhi keep surfacing in Ali's later collections as well. In poem after poem, Ali returns to the city of his birth and higher education. Through an intergenerational lens, Ali's poems weave the cartography of Delhi within the warp and weft of a larger tapestry of loss, as Ali reminisces about his parents, listens to Qawwali at the mausoleum of the great Sufi saint of the Chishtiya order, Nizamuddin Auliya, meets Muslim butchers, remembers Shahjahan, laments the ravaging of the city due to the colonial aggression of 1857 and recites Bahadur Shah Zafar's poem.

Ali's poem, "A Lost memory of Delhi," reconnects the poet with the topography of Delhi through the memory of his parents, whom the poet imagines as a newly married couple before his birth. Okhla bridge, with the Jamuna flowing underneath, is carefully crafted in the double bind of cyclical time as the young poet, getting off the bus at Okhla, thinks of his father: "At Okhla where I get off / I pass my parents / Strolling by the Jamuna River."[90] The spatial locations are invested with personal memories invoking emotive responses. Repetitions and run-on lines underline the helplessness of the poet in the face of a loss that, given the transience of time, is inevitable.

In the poem "A Butcher," the poet shifts from personal loss to the loss of the Urdu language. He delineates the spatial details of Old Delhi to articulate the decay and degeneration of Urdu, of the majestic Urdu literary culture, and of an entire social order— all indexed on a butcher's shop in a lane near Jama Masjid, from whom the poet purchases a kilo of meat. The poem begins by articulating

---

87   On Agha Shahid Ali's Delhi years, see Akhil KATYAL, "'I swear . . . I have my hopes': Agha Shahid Ali's Delhi Years," *Kafila* (2011), web. For a general introduction to Shahid's life and poetry, see Nishat, ZAIDI, *Makers of Indian Literature, Agha Shahid Ali* (New Delhi: Sahitya Akademi, 2017).

88   Agha Shahid ALI, *Bone Sculpture* (Calcutta: Writers Workshop, 1972).

89   Agha Shahid ALI, *In Memory of Begum Akhtar: Poems by Agha Shahid Ali* (Calcutta: Writers Workshop, 1979).

90   Agha Shahid ALI, *The Veiled Suite* 30.

the location of the Butcher's shop: "In this lane / Near Jama Masjid."[91] The butcher is no longer an individual but a representative of the entire cityscape, which the town planners of a new, sanitised city of Delhi have dismissed as un-hygienic, unwieldy and dirty on the basis of the manner in which the sight of blood, the smell of animals and the sound of butchering knives or the smell of raw meat repel the senses of uninitiated outsiders. The entire edifice of Muslim history and Urdu literature, which in independent India came to be identified as the language of Muslims, is now indexed on the sensorium that the butcher provokes, "Where he wraps kilos of meat / In a sheet of paper / The ink of news / Stains his knuckles."[92] In view of the fact that Muslim butchers were presented as sources of urban violence and unsanitary social practices in colonial archives,[93] an image that has sustained in the post-Partition modern India, Ali's mapping of the Islamicate culture by invoking his interaction with a butcher gains an additional significance.

In the process, the narrow lane in front of the majestic Jama Masjid, the Urdu language and literature, iconic Urdu poets like Mir and Ghalib – all exist in a syntagm forming part of one scene. They all are emblematic of a lost culture, a culture that has been derided and that is being re-membered today only because it is lost:

> the script is wet
> in his palms: Urdu
>
> bloody at his fingertips,
> is still fine on his lips,
>
> the language polished smooth
> by knives
>
> on knives. He hacks
> the festival goats, throws
>
> their skins to dogs
> I smile and quote
>
> a Ghalib line; he completes
> the couplet, smiles.

---

[91]   Agha Shahid ALI, *The Veiled Suite* 47.
[92]   Agha Shahid ALI, *The Veiled Suite* 47.
[93]   Amanda LANZILLO, "Butchers between Archives: Community History in Early Twentieth-Century Delhi," *South Asian History and Culture* (2021), web.

quotes a Mir line. I complete
the couplet.

He wraps my kilo of ribs.
I give him the money. The change

clutters our moment of courtesy,
our phrases snapping in mid-syllable,

Ghalib's ghazals left unrhymed.[94]

Trapped in the money economy of the modern city, both the poet and the butcher, no matter how ill-equipped, become custodians of the grand Urdu literary tradition. Bloody, violated, hacked and discarded, the language survives and though left unrhymed, the poetry is regaled.

In the poem "The Fate of the Astrologer Sitting on the Pavement Outside the Delhi Railway Station" the dust-laden pavement outside the station is invoked once again to articulate a general environment of loss and decay where "The planets gather dust / from passing trucks."[95] The silence of the sky, contrasted with the chaotic movement of trucks and "passers-by" underlines the irreversibility of the change to modern urban ways – a change that has only created apathy towards the bygone. In the poem, "After Seeing Kozintsev's King Lear, in Delhi," the young poet in the modern capital city of Delhi, aspiring to become a global city, watches a Soviet director's staging of an English playwright's play. As he steps out into the Chandni Chowk, Lear's cry "You are men of stones"[96] continues to ring in his ears. In this mood of reverie, he contemplates the grand past of Chandni Chowk that was abuzz with an exotic sensorium of sight, sound and smell: "a street once / strewn with jasmine flowers / for the Empress and the royal women / who bought perfumes from Isfahan, / fabrics from Dacca, essence from Kabul, / glass bangles from Agra."[97] This truly cosmopolitan market is now in a state of utter decay as "Beggars now live here in tombs / of unknown nobles and forgotten saints" while a theatre is showing "a Bombay spectacle."[98] This change in the nature of the sensorium explains the sentiment of repulsion the Old City invokes in the modern populace. The general change in settings is also linked to the travesty of history, as the poet thinks of the last Mughal Emperor Bahadur Shah Zafar, who in a city he once had ruled was "led through this street / by Brit-

[94]   Agha Shahid ALI, *The Veiled Suite* 47-48.
[95]   Agha Shahid ALI, *The Veiled Suite* 49.
[96]   Agha Shahid ALI, *The Veiled Suite* 50.
[97]   Agha Shahid ALI, *The Veiled Suite* 50.
[98]   Agha Shahid ALI, *The Veiled Suite* 50.

ish soldiers, his feet in chains, / to watch his sons hanged."[99] And yet, Old Delhi lives on, as do the Urdu language and literature which are inextricably linked to it, as the poet asks in awe in the poem "Chandni Chowk, Delhi":

> Can you rinse away this city that lasts
> like blood on the bitten tongue?[100]

Old Delhi, thus, continues to be experienced through the sensorium of taste, sound and ideation as the "memory of drought / holds you: you remember / the taste of hungry words / and you chew syllables of salt."[101] These lines resonate Ahmed Ali's *Twilight in Delhi*, where the writer says: "Yet the city stands still intact, as do many forts and tombs and monuments, remnants and reminders of Old Delhis, holding on to life with a tenacity and purpose which is beyond comprehension and belief."[102]

Delhi was not a homeland for Agha Shahid Ali, but it is a constitutive element in his poetic consciousness and central to his community and personal history, his diasporic reality. Delhi's present and the memory of its magnificent past, all unravel multiple ruptures, which the poet can do nothing about but acknowledge. He keeps returning to it in his dreams in his poem "I Dream It Is Afternoon When I Return to Delhi." This dream of return, however, is not of joyful reunion or bliss, but seems surreal, once again beset by betrayal and loss. The poet waits at Purana Qila for a bus to Daryaganj, to be betrayed by the voice of a friend who plays a dirty practical joke, forcing the poet to jump off the bus and run past the Doll's Museum and The Times of India Building to finally reach Golcha cinema, panting, where he again imagines his friend dragging him inside the cinema hall. However, the film is about to end. When the usher comes in, his friend is nowhere, and he discovers his ticket is ten years old. The poet rues his predicament:

> Once again my hands are empty.
> I am waiting, alone, at Purana Qila.
> Bus after empty bus is not stopping.
> Suddenly, beggar women with children
> are everywhere, offering
> me money, weeping for me.[103]

Delhi is not just an urban space, or place for Agha Shahid Ali. It is the vantage point based on the assimilation of history, developmental ecology, colonial and

---

[99] Agha Shahid ALI, *The Veiled Suite* 50.
[100] Agha Shahid ALI, *The Veiled Suite* 51.
[101] Agha Shahid ALI, *The Veiled Suite* 51.
[102] Ahmed ALI 4.
[103] Agha Shahid ALI, *The Veiled Suite* 74.

postcolonial politics of identity, urban planning and demographic distribution. In the poem "I see Kashmir from New Delhi" the poet's location is no longer Old Delhi. He is now in New Delhi, where the corridors of power of India's capital are located, and not surprisingly, this vantage allows Ali a particularly clear perspective on his homeland Kashmir. Kashmir's problems, to Ali, are inextricably linked to the Partition, which had its roots in the colonial history and especially in the events of 1857 with which the minoritization and marginalisation of India's Muslims began. Most of Ali's poems about Delhi are steeped in a description of sensory exuberance leading to nostalgia and exhaustion.

3.1.5 Staged Sound as Mediated Cultural Heritage

Almost all works that we have discussed so far invoke Urdu poetry in their reconstruction of the spatio-temporal setting of Old Delhi. The experience of Urdu poetry is an oral/aural experience realised through the space of the *Mushaira* or poetic symposia,[104] an institution from Persia that formed an important part of the cultural life around princely courts and the urban aristocracy in Mughal India.[105] In their generous citing of Urdu verses of the leading Urdu poets, novels by Ahmed Ali and Khushwant Singh nearly transform the textual space of the novel into a site for *Mushaira*. Conversely, Anita Desai and Agha Said Ali invoke the cultural memory of Urdu poetry in order to juxtapose it with the present state of decay. Anita Desai, who grew up in the elite, Anglophone background of New Delhi, relegates Urdu to the outmoded, pre-modern, aristocratic Muslim society, which now wallows in the dingy, suffocating surroundings of Old Delhi in her novels. But this denigration of Old Delhi and the associated Urdu culture as stagnant, outmoded, and out of tune with the globalising impulse of the New Delhi lifestyle, is not completely true. Questioning the scholars of globalisation who have argued about the adverse impact of the market economy on local cultures,[106] Tylor Cowen has termed the change wrought by globalisation "Creative Destruction." In Cowen's view, globalisation does not necessarily result in the elimination of older cultures or lifestyles, but rather opens avenues for a possible resurgence of local cultures, even in the wake of an increasing transnationalization and

---

[104] Cf. NAIM.
[105] For more information on the musical rendering or recitation of poetry in Mushaira, see Regula QURESHI, "Tarannum: The Chanting of Urdu Poetry," *Ethnomusicology* 13.3 (1969): 425-468.
[106] Jeremy TUNSTALL, *The Media are American: Anglo-American Media in the World* (London: Constable, 1977).

commodification of products, peoples and ideas.[107] In the same vein, the public spaces in New Delhi have brought back the cultural practices associated with Old Delhi such as poetic soirees or *Mushairas, Qawwali Sama* or *Dastangoi* in a renewed form through stage performances that are live-streamed on social media.

Drawing the title from Karin Bijsterveld's work,[108] this section analyses three key cultural events that have come to occupy a prominent place in the cultural calendar of modern Delhi: *Jashn-i-Jamhooriyat* or the Repulic Day *Mushaira* (since 1950 regularly held at the historic Red Fort), the annual *Jashne-i-Rekhta,* and *Jashn-i-Bahar*. My aim is to understand how these sanitised staged performances of *Mushairas* invoke the soundscapes that marked the city in pre-colonial times, their spatial origins rendered invisible in the postcolonial city. Cultural production crafts our understanding of the city and reveals its complex structures of power, its racial and classed cartographies, and demographic shifts. With globalization, there has been an unprecedented incursion of commercialism, bureaucratisation, and large-scale corporate sponsorship. In this context, the transfer of sounds from their original settings to modern spaces turns audiences into consumers rather than active participants in those sonic cultures.

Delhi was one of the centres (Dabistan-i-Dilli), besides Lucknow (Dabistan-i-Lucknow), where Urdu poetry flourished and attained its peak during the last years of the Mughal rule. Many poetic soirees or *Mushairas* were held in the walled city of Delhi in which leading poets of the day recited their latest creations. The Lal Quila *Mushaira*, or the *Mushaira* held at the Red Fort, was one of the most prestigious. Patronised by the last Mughal emperor, a poet of some calibre, it continued until the 1857 rebellion. A detailed description of one such traditional *Mushaira* can be found in Mirza Farhatullah Beg's iconic short narrative *Dilli ki Akhiri Shama,* where apart from the etiquette and material environment of the *Mushaira*, Beg also narrates all the intricate preparations that go in the making of the *Mushaira* venue.[109]

After Independence, the first Prime Minister of India, Jawaharlal Nehru, revived the custom of the *Mushaira* at the Red Fort and the first *Mushaira* of *Jashn-i-Jamhooriyat* in free India was held on February 6, 1950, at *Diwan-e-Aam* (the Hall of Audience) of the Red Fort. Over the years the annual *Jashn-e-Jamhuriat* (Celebration of the Republic) *Mushaira* at the Red Fort has grown in size and popularity. It is attended not only by the connoisseurs of Urdu literature but also

---

[107] Cf. BIJSTERVELD, *Soundscapes of the Urban Past* (Bielefeld: Transcript, 2013).

[108] Tyler COWEN, *Creative Destruction: How Globalisation is Changing the World's Culture* (Princeton: Princeton UP, 2002).

[109] Mirza Farhatullah BAIG, *Dehli ki Aakhri Shama*. [*The Last Mushaira of Delhi.*], trans. Akhta Qamber (New Delhi: Orient Blackswan, 2010).

the general masses.[110] *Mushaira* at *Jashn-i-Rekhta* is another popular event in the cultural calendar of Delhi. The Rekhta foundation, run by businessman Sanjeev Sarraf, successfully launched its website *rekhta.org* in 2013, which has ever since grown to become arguably the largest online repository of Urdu books. Encouraged by the success of the website, the foundation launched its first *Jashn-i-Rekhta* in 2015, which is the annual festival of Urdu. This open-for-all event invites Urdu's finest poets, authors and artists to bring alive the magic of the language. It is usually held in elite spaces like the India International Centre, the Indira Gandhi Centre for the Arts or, as the event continues to grow, the Major Dhyan Chand National Stadium. Even as the *Jashn* has transported Urdu out of its ghettoised location in Old Delhi to modern spaces, it recreates the ambience of Old Delhi by showcasing its signature products like the fragrance of *ittar*, the antiquities of old Delhi, handicrafts, the delicate beauty of *chikankari* as well as an elaborate Book exhibition spanning across Urdu, Hindi and English. The venue usually also features the Food Festival Aiwan-e-Zaiqa, which allows the young and the old to savour cuisines such as Kashmiri, Awadhi, Hyderabadi or Mughlai along with the finest selection of popular street food from Old Dilli. The festival presents Urdu culture in all its versatility through performances, recitations, *Mushairas*, panel discussions, debates, conversation on films, or calligraphy workshops. In this way, the *Jashn* offers the dwellers of the global city an opportunity to enjoy the charms of Old Delhi without having to negotiate its narrow crowded lanes, the smell and noise. *Janshn-i-Bahar Mushaira* is yet another annual event dedicated to Urdu poetry. Organised by the Jashn-i-Bahar Trust, the event aims to promote and nurture India's rich syncretic literary traditions. In the two decades of its existence, the *Mushaira* has invited Urdu poets from across the world "to regale the audience with myriad shades of poetic sensitivities, countless colours of modern day sensibilities and the everlasting elegance of Urdu verse."[111] The thrust once again is on nurturing Urdu sensibilities with a modern day approach, so that Urdu literary culture is not confined to the ghettoised spatial setting of Old Delhi or reductively identified with Islam.

In these events, soundscapes generally associated with one religious identity, location, and culture, are regulated, secularised, and adapted to suit the taste of the modern city dwellers of Delhi. Even as the Old Delhi dwellers, largely Muslims, continue to suffer marginalisation in the colonial and the postcolonial

---

[110]   Parvez SULTAN, "Historic Mushaira at Red Fort to Mark 69th Republic Day," *Hindustan Times* (2018), web.
[111]   Jashn-e-Bahar Trust, web.

city,[112] the overwhelming popularity of the *Mushaira* points towards continuities embedded in outward ruptures. They represent entanglements of two separate structures of power and knowledge underlying the idea of Delhi. If, in its pre-modern form, the agential role in the meaning-making process in the *Mushaira* was invested with patrons and audiences, it now has shifted to poets and performers re-establishing their autonomy. In getting transported spatially, *Mushairas* have also transformed the soundscape of popular culture by deploying emerging technologies. This produces a convergence of the material culture with auditory and visual sensations of memory, affect and poetry/music. YouTube recordings and live Facebook broadcasts of *Mushairas* take the poetry performances beyond the confines of the *Mushaira* venue, wedding the local with the global. Embedded in the poetry recited in the *Mushaira* are layers of locally specific and historically situated references alongside universal emotions, producing "meaning-feeling experiences."[113] *Mushairas* originally served as signifiers of an aristocratic, patriarchal domain of power that did not admit marginalised sections like women and lower-class or lower-caste people.[114] In their present incarnation, however, such hierarchies have been largely removed. The same audience that enjoys movies on OTT platforms and in multiplexes also enjoys the *Mushaira* with equal gusto, thus de-reifying the erstwhile reified realm. In this manner, bearing taints of the Mughal and the colonial past, the capital city of the new, resurgent and globalizing India, has attempted to create modern spaces accommodating tradition and history through the staging of a heritage literary form.

****

The colonial restructuring of the city of Delhi drew stark lines across the spatial, architectural, linguistic and cultural spheres of a social order which had what Sudipta Kaviraj calls "fuzzy identities."[115] It resulted in the production of a collectivity that was constantly engaged with complex cultural negotiations involve-

---

[112] On Muslim marginalisation see Gyanendra PANDEY, "Can a Muslim be an Indian?," *Comparative Studies in Society and History* 41.4 (1999): 608-29. See also Laurent GAYER and Christopher JAFFRELOT, eds., *Muslims in Indian Cities: Trajectories of Marginalization* (London: Hurst, 2011).

[113] John LEAVITT, "Meaning and Feeling in the Anthropology of Emotions," *American Ethnologist* 23.3 (1996): 514-539, here: 530.

[114] In his novel *Umrao Jan Ada,* Mirza RUSWA expresses surprise when Umrao recites her poem in Rekhta and not Rekhti, the language of women. See Mirza Hadi RUSWA, *Umrao Jan Ada,* trans. David Matthews (New Delhi: Rupa, 1996).

[115] Cf. Sudipta KAVIRAJ, *The imaginary institution of India: Politics and Ideas* (New York: Columbia UP, 2010). Kaviraj has argued that in pre-colonial India identities were flexible and "fuzzy." The

ing everyday transactions and textures of memories embedded in language. This chapter has attempted to study textual representations of these negotiations through sensorial signs that embody socio-political dynamics. In the sensorial registering of these 'ruptures of feeling,' often caused by the forces of history, the texts examined in the chapter reconfigure the city as a charged terrain. Foregrounding the intrinsically social character of the sensorium, the chapter has demonstrated how sensorial experiences, often seen as individual and visceral get transformed into archival records indexing individual, communal, national, and even transnational histories.

Sherry Simon has drawn attention to the general neglect the scholars of urban studies have displayed towards language. She has further revealed how language interaction is central to the formation of the public sphere and the shaping of the city's identity.[116] Along this line, this chapter has focused on language as the site where urban imaginaries construe and enact various continuities, traditions, conflicts and negotiations because, as Resina writes, "[a] linguistic continuum is as important to a city's identity as continuity in space."[117] Delhi as a city has witnessed several linguistic, spatial and cultural ruptures rooted in history, which lie embedded in the everyday language of the city. Writings and the performances discussed in the chapter may be viewed as textual sites embodying transactions among the multiple terrains of consciousness that mark the multi-layered city. They present the city as a 'conjunctural space' where the tensions and contradictions between the global, national and local concepts of urban spaces are realised[118] through diverse sensory stimuli. In provoking responses that mark contestations and negotiations between individual autonomy and multiple legacies,

---

colonial census exercise, subsequently adapted by the postcolonial state, categorized and constituted, communities into discrete, "enumerative" categories.

[116]   Sherry SIMON, *Cities in Translation: Intersections of Language and Memory* (London: Routledge, 2012) 7: "Despite the sensory evidence of multilingualism in today's cities, the proliferation of scripts on storefronts, the shouted conversations on cell phones, there has been little more than casual reference to language as a vehicle of urban cultural memory, or of translation as a key in the creation of meaningful spaces of contact and civic participation. There is little sustained discussion of language and language interactions as a feature of a city's identity. This 'oversight' is particularly striking as cities face the challenge of promoting translation practices that will ensure urban cohesion. Translation is the key to citizenship, to the incorporation of languages into the public sphere. This means seeing multilingual, multi-ethnic urban space as a translation space, where the focus is not on multiplicity but on interaction. Understanding urban space as a translation zone restores language to the picture and offers a corrective to the deafness of much current urban theory."

[117]   Joan Ramon RESINA, *Barcelona's Vocation of Modernity: Rise and Decline of an Urban Image* (Stanford: Stanford UP, 2008).

[118]   Rashmi VARMA, *The Postcolonial City and Subjects: London, Nairobi, Bombay* (New York: Routledge, 2012) 14.

asymmetries of power, and the idea of citizenship, Delhi may be viewed as what Rashmi Varma has termed, a "postcolonial city."

3.2 Writing the Globalized City: Socio-Sensorial Dis/Articulations

– Zeno Ackermann

This subchapter turns to major writings on and of Delhi produced since the turn of the millennium. It thus looks at textual responses to the dramatic transformation of the city that was triggered by the decision to implement the prescriptions of the International Monetary Fund and 'liberate' India's economy. The dramatic steps – taken by the new government under Prime Minister P. V. Narasimha Rao and announced by Finance Minister Dr. Manmohan Singh on 24 July 1991 – officially broke with the state-administered capitalism of the postcolonial era. They opened the nearly bankrupt nation to the largely uninhibited international trade and unfettered influx of international capital.

The movement "from state-led development to state-mediated globality"[119] brought about a thorough economic and ideological re-articulation of the relationships – both material and imaginary – between the Indian nation, its big cities, and the wider world. While Mahatma Gandhi had decidedly "looked to the village in defining India,"[120] post-independence programmes for the country's development mostly operated on a grander scale, privileging the paradigms of industrialization and urbanity. In the context of economic liberation, the big cities have now explicitly been moved centre-stage as the operation grounds for re-inventing India. In a speech given in 2005 to launch the Jawaharlal Nehru National Urban Renewal Mission, Manmohan Singh – who had meanwhile become Prime Minister – urged that it was time to "plan big, think big and have a new vision for the future of urban India." As Singh explained, India's welfare has been driven by the country's "urban economy," which represented a "bridge between the domestic and global economy."[121]

---

[119] Rohan KALYAN, Neo *Delhi and the Politics of Postcolonial Urbanism* (London: Routledge, 2017) 25.

[120] Gyan PRAKASH, "The Urban Turn," *Cities of Everyday Life*, ed. Sarai: The New Media Initiative (New Delhi: Sarai, 2002) 2-7, here: 3.

[121] Speech by Prime Minister Manmohan SINGH (2005), qtd. in Gautam BHAN, "The Impoverishment of Poverty: Reflections on Urban Citizenship and Inequality in Contemporary Delhi," *Environment and Urbanization* 26.2 (2014): 547-560, here: 548.

The 'liberalization' of the economy and the attendant reconfiguration of political visions have had a tremendous impact on life within the big cities – not
only in terms of economic processes, administration and planning but also in
terms of social imaginaries and structures of feeling. In this context, Gautam
Bhan provocatively speaks of an "impoverishment of poverty." He comments on
the development of "a 'post-development social formation,' within which even
the 'nominal ethical relationship' between the state, the elite and the poor of a
previous developmentalism stands fractured."[122] Along similar lines, Gyan Prakash suggests that globalization has deepened the material, ideological and sensorial gulf that – ever since the colonialist creation of a 'New' Delhi – has sepa-
rated the "official city" (i.e. the city of grand monuments, ambitious public building projects, imposing commercial enterprises and distinctive middle- or upper-
class homes) from the "unintended city" (i.e. the city of migrant workers camping
in the streets, of slum dwellers or homeless people). "Seen from the lens of mod-
ernisation," Prakash points out, "the huge mass of India's urban poor appears
'obsolete' in the march of progress."[123] And Rohan Kalyan observes how the elites
of cities such as Delhi seem to be well-practiced in placing the poor "out of
sight/out of mind," hoping to shut out "signs of lingering under-development"
from "the hyper-sanitized precincts of the global city."[124]

The phenomena observed by Bhan, Prakash and Kalyan – as, indeed, by many
other scholars and commentators – suggest that contemporary Delhi offers acute
instances of what Richard Sennett described as a "sensate apathy" that is generally typical – and perhaps constitutive – of the atmosphere of big cities.[125] The
following readings are driven by the hypothesis that the topic of socio-sensorial
dis/articulation is at the centre of the contemporary literature of and on Delhi.
However, the last subchapter will return us to Old Delhi as the site for a momen-
tuous (fictional) re-articulation and thus for the vision of a 'worlding' that is alternative to 'globalization.'

---

[122] BHAN 548; the quotations within the quotation are from Vinay GIDWANI and Rajyashree
N REDDY, "The Afterlives of 'Waste': Notes from India for a Minor History of Capitalist Surplus,"
Antipode 43.5 (2011): 1625-1658.

[123] PRAKASH, "The Urban Turn" 5. The frequently quoted concept of the "unintended city" comes
from Ashis NANDY, "Indian Popular Cinema as the Slum's Eye View of Politics," *The Secret Politics of Our Desires: Innocence, Culpability and Indian Popular Cinema*, ed. NANDY (Delhi: Oxford UP, 1998) 1-18.

[124] KALYAN 65.

[125] SENNETT, *Flesh and Stone* 323.

3.2.1 Activating the "Alchemy" of an "Unloved City" –
Delhi: Urban Space and Human Destinies (2000)

Published exactly at the turn of the millennia, the essay collection *Delhi: Urban Space and Human Destinies* stands both as a particularly significant assessment of contemporary Delhi and a particularly interesting attempt of 'writing the city.'[126] Part of the interest of the book, which was brought out by a New Delhi publishing house, is in its articulation of various institutional affiliations, national positionalities, disciplinary methodologies and modes of representation. To begin with, the book project was sustained by a conspicuously complex network of institutions: if the cover advertises the collection as "A Publication of the French Research Institute in India," this is complicated by the book's front matter, where two notes introduce the Institut Français of Pondicherry and the (Delhi-based) Centre de Sciences Humaines (both "part of the same network of research centres of the French Ministry of Foreign Affairs") as responsible bodies; finally, the title page also shows the icon of the IRD (Institut de recherche pour le développement).[127] The book was edited by French researchers who had spent considerable time in India and done systematic research in cooperation with Indian institutions.[128] Moreover, about half of the contributors to the collection were Indian citizens. Yet more significant than this mix of institutional affiliations and national positionalities – a mix clearly presided over by a former colonising power – is the variety of disciplines represented by the authors. These include geography, economic demography, history, sociology, political science, urban planning, development studies and (with several representatives) social anthropology. Additionally, there were two photographers (one French, and one Indian) among the contributors, and both provided intriguing images for the publication.

This multi-facetted cast of contributors came together for a real purpose. According to the editors' introduction, the collection – which might also be referred to as a *collage* – had been born from "the need to break loose from the systems of representations [sic] which successive powers [had] tended to impose on the city and its inhabitants." Véronique Dupont, Emma Tarlo, and Denis Vidal claimed

---

[126] Véronique DUPONT, Emma TARLO, and Denis VIDAL, eds., *Delhi: Urban Space and Human Destinies*. New Delhi: Manohar, 2000.

[127] DUPONT, TARLO, and VIDAL, ed., *Delhi* 2-3.

[128] Cf. "List of Contributors," *Delhi*, ed. DUPONT, TARLO, and VIDAL 253-255. At the time of publication, Véronique Dupont and Denis Vidal were primarily affiliated with the Paris-based IRD, while Emma Tarlo was a Lecturer in Social Anthropology at the University of London's Goldsmiths College.

that the essays, photographs and charts brought together in the volume displayed a shared "concern with challenging conventional images of the city and its populace" and jointly contributed to "the building of alternative images of Delhi."[129] Significantly, the editors felt that it was of particular importance to counter the cliché that Delhi could not "be considered a city in the true sense" but constituted only "an urban patchwork" of irreconcilable sociocultural components.[130] According to the introduction of *Delhi: Urban Space and Human Destinies*, then, the task faced at the turn of the millennium was not only to analyse or re-write Delhi, but to *write it* in the first place – pushing it into the collective (national as well as transnational) imagination as a cohering object that would be susceptible of administrative care and socio-political activity.

In the service of such a writing of Delhi, the first and most interesting part of the book employs social anthropology in order to people the city with communicable human beings. The title of this section, "Life Histories – City History," implies a double proposition: first that the city does in fact have a coherent history, and second that this history emerges from the articulation of the "life histories" of *all* its inhabitants. As the editors put it in their preview of the section: "[A]lthough we begin in Part 1 with the experiences of people who inhabit comparatively marginal spaces – a squatter settlement, a resettlement colony and the rural fringes of South Delhi – we learn how their lives are intimately bound up with wider historical, political and economic developments."[131] While the stories told in the individual chapters are mostly bleak, they still have a function within a constructive project that is to be performatively achieved by the book in its complex totality. The verbal phrase "intimately bound up" hints at the nature of the project: in the final instance, the purpose is to re-position and re-imagine the populace of the city as a cohering citizenship. The explicatory notes with which Saraswati Haider introduces her long contribution on "Migrant Women and Urban Experience in a Squatter Settlement" show that such a feat of socio-political articulation depends on linguistic processes of articulation:

> [I]t must be stressed that if I have been able to elicit expressive, articulate narratives from my protagonists it is, I think, only because of the long time I have spent interacting with them – more than four years – over which time easy rapport eventually became established. Over this long period of association many women have been able to shed at least some of their inhibitions and overcome their initial suspicion of me. Today

---

[129] Denis Vidal, Emma Tarlo and Véronique Dupont, "The Alchemy of an Unloved City," *Delhi*, ed. Dupont, Tarlo, and Vidal 15-25, here: 17.
[130] Vidal, Tarlo, and Dupont, "Alchemy" 16.
[131] Vidal, Tarlo, and Dupont, "Alchemy" 24.

they view me not so much as a stranger, [sic] than as an elderly woman,
who likes chatting with them and means them no harm. [132]

On the surface, this passage serves the function of explaining the methodologies
of a scholarly and analytical project. However, Haider's phrasing just as clearly
signals a different purpose for her article: one that might be described as 'syn-
thetical' rather than analytical. The socially performative dimension of the text –
and of the research activities on which it is based – becomes evident if we focus
on the plethora of phrases that describe feats of contact-making: "elicit expressive
narratives"; "the long time I have spent interacting with them"; "easy rapport
eventually became established"; "long period of association"; "shed their inhibi-
tions and overcome their initial suspicion"; "they view me not so much as a
stranger than as an elderly woman."

As Haider explains, her research is intended to "elicit expressive, articulate
narratives." The goal is to turn the human objects of her research not only into
protagonists of their own stories but also into proponents of a newly articulated
story of Delhi. Accordingly, Haider's text consists mostly of quotations. To be
sure, these quotations have been transcribed, edited and translated. However, rather than processing the life stories, experiences and worldviews of her interview-
ees as scholarly data, the researcher evidently seeks to put them on a stage. It is
interesting to see how her approach serves to transform potential obstacles for
intersectional social contact – especially the problem of defective systems of sanitation and seemingly unenlightened hygienic practices – into a medium of inti-
macy.

The problem of sanitation and hygiene is broached in the contextualising introduction to the respective section in Haider's report: "All squatter settlements
are unhygienic. Rajpur is no different. There are open drains full of muck and
children's faeces with small piles of garbage alongside." As Haider further points
out, the rubbish dumps of the settlement emanate "a horrible smell all around." [133]
Against this backdrop, and after a couple of questions concerning household
management, the interviewer quite directly asks one of her respondents: "Where
do you defecate?" The question triggers an unembarrassed, if cautiously phrased,
answer that ends in the following information: "When the latrines are too dirty I
have no option but to squat on the road." Haider presses further: "And suppose

---

[132]   Saraswati HAIDER, "Migrant Women and Urban Experience in a Squatter Settlement," *Delhi*, ed.
        DUPONT, TARLO, and VIDAL 29-49, here: 30.
[133]   HAIDER 37. "Rajpur," by the way, is not the real name of the settlement where Haider conducted
        her research – cf. 48, note 2: "Because of the sensitive nature of data collected on local politics
        the name of the squatter settlement and all other names in the essay have been changed."

your stomach is upset?" The interviewee's reaction is particularly moving because it is one of the few passages that communicate strong emotion: "My oh my,
then it is a problem. I have to hunt for some private place. It is agony."[134] Zooming in on sensory experience, bodily processes and affective states, the passage
performs a phenomenological transition from the seemingly objective perspective of people such as Haider and her readers (people, that is, who probably take
a flushed toilet for granted) to the lifeworld of the inhabitants of *"jhuggi-jhonpri*
(hutment) clusters."[135] The passage can be read as implementing the sensorial
renegotiation urged by Richard Sennett in *Flesh and Stone*. Firstly, it seems to
underline Sennett's proposition that "urban spaces take form largely from the
ways people experience their own bodies."[136] Secondly, by engineering transi-
tions between different social positions as different experiences of the body,
Haider's report prises open what Sennett describes as dominant "master images
of the body" that tends to "deny us knowledge of the body outside the Garden."[137]

Although Haider's contribution constitutes a performance of articulation in
the double sense of 'expression' and of 'creating a temporary unity,' it still registers the chronic social and socio-political *dis*articulation of the big city. As we
learn from one of the researcher's few explicit interpretative interventions, the
poor are not only divided from the wealthier segments of society but also dis-
united among themselves: "The Rajpur residents may be homogeneous as 'the
poor' but the squatter settlement is definitely not a melting pot but rather a house
divided. [...] The Rajpur cluster is split into ghettos: regional ghettos and within
these, [sic] caste ghettos and within these, [sic] kinship ghettos."[138]

The strong ambivalence of Haider's contribution is characteristic of the entire
collection. Nearly all through *Delhi: Urban Space and Human Destinies* negative
observations – observations that make contemporary Delhi appear as a probably
unsolvable cluster of catastrophic social and administrative problems – are cou-
pled with an overall gesture of hope, a vague yet determined performance of ame-
lioration. The title of the editors' introduction provides a striking example of
such dual voicing: "The Alchemy of an Unloved City." The text does not say what
"alchemy" is supposed to mean here: the heading simply poses the term as the

---

[134] HAIDER 39.
[135] HAIDER 30. Haider's report (but not the entire essay collection) carefully avoids the term 'slum.'
[136] SENNETT, *Flesh and Stone* 370.
[137] SENNETT, *Flesh and Stone* 25. It should be noted, however, the Sennett's focus is exclusively on
        what he terms "Western civilization." See, for example, 15: "Western civilization has had persis-
        tent trouble in honoring the dignity of the body and diversity of human bodies; I have sought to
        understand how these body-troubles have been expressed in architecture, in urban design, and
        in planning practice."
[138] HAIDER 44.

vehicle of an opaque yet seemingly grand claim. To some extent, the word "al-chemy" seems to trigger the potentially Orientalist notion that Asian cities own a particular 'magic,' a capacity for transforming the substantiality of the materi-ally given, tilting reality within the forcefield created by extreme poverty and 'fab-ulous' economic or cultural wealth. However, the final contribution to the vol-ume – a short essay on "Delhi's Place in India's Urban Structure" authored by geographer Phillipe Cadène – indicates a more up-to-date foundation for expect-ing alchemical transformations. Interestingly, the concluding essay features one of only two instances in the entire book where the buzzword 'globalization' comes to be mentioned: "[T]his [i.e. Delhi] is one of the cities which enables India to take part in the massive exchanges induced by the process of globalization." And it is the expected effects of "globalization" that turn the last sentence of the volume into its most hopeful pronouncement: "Due to the recent emergence of Delhi at the regional and national levels, the capital appears capable of assuming the role of a veritable 'international city', at the head of a solid national urban system and of a powerful region."[139]

3.2.2 Moulding the Flows of Globalization and Re-Articulating the Urban Sensorium from Below: *Cities of Everyday Life* (2002)

Two years after the publication of *Delhi: Urban Space and Human Destinies*, Sarai – a highly productive "media initiative" based at the Centre for the Study of De-veloping Societies in Delhi and sustained by various scholars and social activists, writers and artists – brought out a reader on urban life at the beginning of the third millennium.[140] Titled *Cities of Everyday Life*, this Sarai Reader (the second of nine readers produced between 2001 and 2013) may be considered one of the most interesting contributions to this discussion.[141] If *Delhi: Urban Space and Human Destinies* had brought French initiative and finances to the analysis of the Indian capital, *Cities of Everyday Life* almost worked the other way around: here, Indian initiative and curiosity stimulated a process of reflecting on the re-alities and potentialities of (big) cities all over the globe. As a determinate effort of "globalization" in the sense of what Jean-Luc Nancy (in the same historical

---

[139]   Philippe CADÈNE, "Delhi's Place in India's Urban Structure," *Delhi: Urban Space and Human Destinies*, ed. DUPONT, TARLO, and VIDAL 241-249, here: 249.

[140]   See Sarai's website – *sarai: media, information, the contemporary* – for the ongoing vibrant ac-tivity of the initiative. All Sarai Readers can be accessed through this website.

[141]   *Cities of Everyday Life*, The Sarai Reader 02 (New Delhi: Sarai, 2002; web publication).

moment) termed "mondialisation,"[142] the Sarai Reader featured authors from diverse world regions.[143] Accordingly, the list of cities dealt with included Beirut, Berlin, Lagos, London, Mexico City, New York (which, in the immediate aftermath of '9/11,' was prominently discussed) and Sarajevo. The majority of writers, however, came from India. And India's largest cities received the bulk of the attention, Delhi being referred to most frequently.

We have already seen how *Delhi: Urban Space and Human Destinies* was driven by a need to discover the coherence of Delhi as a *city* in the full sense of the term and how Prime Minister Singh urged the development of "a new vision for the future of urban India." Writing at about the same time, the editors of the Sarai Reader pointed out: "*The Cities of Everyday Life* carries within it an argument to take the urban seriously. In the context of India, where a large part of this reader has been edited, this is significant, given the frugality of writing on city life in this part of the world."[144] In this vein, several contributions to the reader – most prominently the opening essay by Gyan Prakash – observed and promoted an "urban turn" in contemporary India. There was a clear sense of ambivalence here: on the one hand, Prakash's essay, as most other contributions to the reader, addressed the problematics inherent in urbanization and globalization, especially the fact of lingering or deepening socioeconomic inequalities; on the other hand, the contributors to the volume joined forces in the attempt of activating a positively evaluated potential of re-inventing the (Indian) city within the context of global processes of communication and transformation. As Prakash put it: "The urban turn, then, offers an opportunity to revise the history of Indian modernity, to bring into view spaces of power and difference suppressed by the historicist discourse of the nation."[145] The project was to re-invent Indian society by using and bending the momentum of globalized urbanity. Disarticulating the contemporary Indian city from the inherited project of post-colonial nationality was part of this movement.

---

[142]   See Jean-Luc NANCY, *The Creation of the World or Globalization*, trans. and introd. François Raffoul and David Pettigrew (Albany: State University of New York P, 2007) passim, see esp. 27-28. The original French version of the book – *La Création du monde ou la mondialisation* (Paris: Galilée, 2002) – was published in the same year as the Sarai Reader.

[143]   Besides India, the biographies and institutional affiliations of the contributors to the Sarai Reader point to the following countries: Australia, Canada, Germany, Italy, Mexico, the Netherlands, Nigeria, the UK, and the USA.

[144]   Ravi S. VASUDEVAN, Ravi SUNDARAM, Jeebesh BAGCHI, Monica NARULA, Shuddhabrata SENGUPTA and Geert LOVINK, "Introduction," *Cities of Everyday Life* vi-ix, here: vi.

[145]   PRAKASH 6.

Similar to the French-edited collection discussed in the previous section, the Sarai Reader appealed to a sort of 'alchemy' that would facilitate the re-articulation of Indian (urban) society. In the later publication, such transformative 'alchemy' was sought in the fabulous potentials of new media systems, especially in computer technology and the internet. This emerges most clearly from a collage of images and texts that the Raqs Media Collective, a subsection of Sarai, contributed to the reader. In this contribution, entitled "The Street is the Carrier and the Sign," the city is envisaged as a media city.[146] Partly, the projected transformation of urban society rests on the new communication and networking options that new media make possible. However, the most important point evidently is in using the generative potential of a newly pervasive concept of mediality for the purpose of elaborating a new social imaginary. Along these lines, the opening paragraph of the Raqs collage figures the city not only in terms of media technology but also as a medium in its own right:

> The things that need saying step out of people, just as people step out of houses and begin to walk the street. Messages find walls, images their imprints, bodies leave traces. People and pictures, objects and subjects, machines and meanings, wires, cables, codes, secrets and the things that need saying out loud crowd the streets, become the streets, and move, overwriting old inscriptions, turning in on themselves, making labyrinths and freeways, making connections, conversations and concentrations out of electricity.[147]

Here the infrastructure of the city ("houses," "walls," "streets") come to be represented as a system of communication (i.e. a system of "messages," "codes," "inscriptions," "connections," and "conversations"). The metaphors used in the quoted passage link to various elements of computer technology: on one level, the urban infrastructure is implicitly compared to the hardware (the "wires" and "cables") inside a PC or a server; on a different level, the passage conjures up the image of a computer screen on which a text is being edited or a graphics programme run. In any case, the kind of machinery evoked forges multiple kinds of 'connections.' It comes to be accentuated as a powerful system of expression,

---

[146]   Cf. Scott MCQUIRE, *The Media City: Media, Architecture and Urban Space* (London: SAGE, 2008).

[147]   RAQS MEDIA COLLECTIVE, "The Street Is The Carrier And The Sign," *Cities of Everyday Life* 93-105, here: 93.

transubstantiation and articulation. "Flow," a keyword in the discourse of globalization,[148] is prominent throughout the Raqs collage.[149] However, as is made painstakingly clear, it is not capital, material resources and goods that are meant to 'flow' through the networks of the transnational urban utopia conjured up throughout the contribution. Rather, the authors are projecting a totally humanized network in which sensorially and affectively charged information is constantly exchanged: "We see, hear, read, glance, surf, so that our 'presence' may get distributed across experiences, moments, information clusters."[150]

The notion – or, indeed, phantasy – of articulation developed by the Raqs Collective is clearly informed by Marshall McLuhan's media theory. Consider, for example, McLuhan's basic proposition in *Understanding Media* (1964): "Rapidly, we approach the final phase of the extensions of man – the technological simulation of consciousness, when the creative process of knowing will be collectively and corporately extended to the whole of human society."[151] According to the same logic, "distributing" one's "presence" across the communication network evidently means merging one's consciousness with a medially integrated collective consciousness. Interestingly, the Raqs contribution indicates that the building of a transnationally articulated and transsectionally integrated urban consciousness rests on a dialectic of personalization and depersonalization, of expressing and shedding established identities: as "the things that need saying" will be said, "old inscriptions" – presumably including the exclusivist affiliation to region, caste and kinship criticized by Haider in *Delhi: Urban Space and Human Destinies* – will simultaneously be "overwritten."[152]

In contrast to the emphatically visionary character of the Raqs contribution, a literary experiment offered by Parvati Sharma in a different section of the Sarai Reader explores actually extant new-media representations and sedimentations of city life. Under the title "decoded+delhi+denuded=Google+Search," Sharma uses seemingly random quotations from the world wide web as jumping boards for critical meditations on the state of both, the net and the Indian capital: "There are two sides to a search: the real and the virtual [...]. Real Delhi online is Delhi

---

[148] See Kimberly DEFAZIO, *The City of the Senses: Urban Culture and Urban Space* (New York: Palgrave Macmillan, 2011) – especially the chapter on the "(Dis)Continuous City" (17-52) – for a critique of this discourse of 'flows' and 'networks' and the attendant imagination of a 'postcapitalist' society.

[149] Indeed, the first four pages of the collage (RAQS MEDIA COLLECTIVE 93-96) are organised around the topic of "flow/s."

[150] RAQS MEDIA COLLECTIVE 97.

[151] Marshall MCLUHAN, *Understanding Media: The Extensions of Man* (1964; London: Routledge, 2001) 3.

[152] See the introductory paragraph of the Raqs collage, as qtd. above.

off-line copied and pasted on an html document. The parameters are complaint, anger, pathos, film reviews, personal reminiscences, alternative perspectives."[153] Interestingly, Sharma's text culminates in an examination of the term 'articulation':

> Etymologically, 'articulation' is the movement of limbs in action, very bodily, organic. A dislocated articulation is, in some ways, a dislocated limb, a broken body – so that most attempts to control articulation begin, logically, by controlling the body. In a place where the body does not exist, however – in NCR Delhi, #delhi, New Delhi, c/o Delhi, Delhi on a tourist map, Delhi Diary – articulation, until it completes a process of transformation, is hesitant, touching, and absurd.[154]

Sharma's concluding passage is deliberately 'open' and thus difficult to decode. It suggests, however, that virtual Delhi suffers from similar problems as real Delhi and that these are problems of articulation, i.e. of establishing a coherent – an "organically" articulated – sense of self and society. Sharma thus casts doubt on the proposition put forward by the Raqs collage and informing most of the Sarai reader. Her montage of media texts implicitly challenges the hope that media networks might be used for building an alternative as well as materially effective urban imaginary.

A different section of the Sarai Reader, however, seems to plausibly demonstrate that computers can in fact help in establishing an articulated sense of self. The respective section is advertised as the "Cybermohalla Diaries."[155] Here, Jeebesh Bagchi's introduction again picks up on the key concerns of the book in its entirety. As the artist and writer explains, in both Hindi and Urdu 'mohalla' means 'neighbourhood': "Sarai's Cybermohalla project takes on the meaning of the word *mohalla*, its sense of alleys and corners, its sense of relatedness and concreteness, as a means for talking about one's 'place' in the city, and in cyberspace." Accordingly, the project is to be seen as "an experiment to engage with media technologies and software 'tactically.'" In the final instance, the project is driven by "a desire for a wide and horizontal network (both real and virtual) of voices, texts, sounds and images in dialogue and debate."[156] This again concretizes the

---

[153] Parvati SHARMA, "decoded+delhi+denuded=Google+Search," *Cities of Everyday Life* 159-163.
[154] SHARMA 163.
[155] "Cybermohalla Diaries," *Cities of Everyday Life* 177-190.
[156] Jeebesh BAGCHI, *Cities of Everyday Life* 177. Of course, Bagchi's use of the idea of 'tactics' gestures to the work and terminology of Michel DE CERTEAU – particularly as delineated in *The Practice of Everyday Life* (1980; trans. Steven Rendall, Berkeley: U of California P, 1984), see esp. 29-42. Although Certeau is only infrequently referred to explicitly, his emphasis on the subversive potential of everyday practices clearly inform the entire Sarai Reader, including the very title of the collection: *Cities of Everyday Life*.

way in which the Sarai Reader proposes to bend the process of globalization: "cyberspace" – which Bagchi oxymoronically couples with the notion of "concreteness" – is meant to be dialectically employed in the service of legitimizing and democratizing local terrains of consciousness.

The section thus introduced by Bagchi collates short writings from the computer diaries of young people (mostly young women) living in Delhi's LNJP basti – a "working-class settlement" which is "constantly threatened by dislocation" and which is situated "in the heart of the city though invisible to Delhi's many millions."[157] A salient property of the texts penned by the young authors in a media lab run by Sarai and the NGO Ankur is their insistence on the significance of concrete sensory impressions – as for example in one of the texts contributed by an author identified as Shahjehan:

> Morning: From every house can be heard the noise of children screaming. And on the tap, the noise of buckets and utensils.
> The sound of utensils being washed *sur sur sur...*
> Of clothes being washed *ghar ghar ghar...*
> Of televisions being switched on and channels being changed *tuk tuk tuk...*
> Of clothes having been washed and being swung in the air to be dried *jhut jhut jhut...*
> From motor cars *suur suur suur...*
> Of stoves being lit *tun tun tun...*
> Of water being drunk *gutuk gutuk gutuk...*
> Of walking *chut chut chut...*
> Of *rotis* being made *thup thup thup...*[158]

The focus of this text, as of several other entries in the "Cybermohalla Diaries," is on the acoustic perception of life activities. Listening in on her environment as a soundscape, Shahjehan evokes the *basti* – a location that many people, both outside and inside India, would simply write off as a 'slum' – as an experientially rich lifeworld, a social space that is both multifaceted and harmoniously integrated. Simultaneously, the diary writer reflects on, re-discovers and empowers her own position in this specific terrain of consciousness as well as in Indian society more generally. In these ways, the short text and its positioning in the Sarai Reader perform the kind of cultural work that Michael Bull and Les Back have

---

[157]   BAGCHI 177.
[158]   Text by SHAHJEHAN, *Cities of Everyday Life* 181. All texts published as part of the "Cybermohalla Diaries" are in English. It is not indicated whether the diary entries were originally penned in English or are translations. The general gesture of the section, however, suggests the former option.

propagated as "deep listening." "What is at stake in deep listening?", Bull and Back ask, thus triggering a series of big claims: "sound," they postulate, "makes us re-think" not only "the meaning, nature and significance of our social experience" but also "our relation to the community," to "power," and to "embodiment itself."[159] In her 2010 study *Listening in to Others*,[160] Tripta Chandola – who was also among the team producing the Sarai Reader – draws on such notions in order to propagate a sonic awareness that challenges the "bourgeois cultural imagination" and significantly positions "slum-dwellers as inquisitors of the city."[161] Chandola's phrasing felicitously captures a programmatic that evidently motivated the Cybermohalla project: to forge a new "cultural imagination" – i.e. a new sociocultural consciousness – by re-articulating the position of "slum-dwellers" within the social structure of the city. As the "Cybermohalla Diaries" suggest, such re-articulation is felt to depend on the detailed articulation – and technologically assisted mediation – of concrete sensory experiences. It needs to be stressed that not only Chandola's study and the "Cybermohalla Diaries" but also Haider's contribution to *Delhi: Urban Space and Human Destinies* imply an underlying common hypothesis: that a city such as Delhi might only become conscious of itself – that it might only gain articulacy – through a process of reconstituting its sensorial awareness from below.

3.2.3 Assessing Infrastructural, Sensorial and Linguistic Disarticulation: *Capital* (2014)

The previous section has discussed the Sarai Reader (2002) as an attempt of bending the discourses of globalized urbanity in order to re-articulate the Indian city. As has been pointed out, the attempt was situated in a specific historical moment. It is this moment to which Rana Dasgupta returns at the beginning of his massive literary reportage *Capital: A Portrait of Twenty-First-Century Delhi* (2014).[162] This revisiting of the recent past has special personal implications for Dasgupta,

---

[159] Michael Bull and Les Back, "Into Sound … Once More with Feeling," [introduction to:] *The Auditory Culture Reader*, 2nd ed. (Abingdon: Routledge, 2020), 1-20, here: 2.

[160] Tripta CHANDOLA, *Listening in to Others: In between Noise and Silence*, PhD thesis, Queensland University of Technology, 2010.

[161] CHANDOLA 18; 24. In the Sarai Reader, Chandola is listed as "production assistance" (ii); she also contributed a short text (353-354) and a couple of graphics.

[162] Rana DASGUPTA, *Capital: A Portrait of Twenty-First-Century Delhi* (2014); rpt. as *Capital: The Eruption of Delhi* (Edinburgh: Canongate, 2015). – It should be noted at least in passing that Dasgupta had also been represented in the Sarai Reader, to which he contributed an essay on "The Face of The Future: Biometric Surveillance and Progress" (290-296).

for it was in the year 2000 that the British author moved to the country where his parents had been raised: "At the time I arrived, Delhi had gone through a decade of the changes resulting from the 'liberalisation' of 1991 – that is to say, the reforms [...] which opened the country to global flows of products, media and capital."[163] Already at this point in the book, Dasgupta constantly emphasizes the negative aspects of these liberated "flows," especially the "enormous transfer of wealth and resources from the city's poorest to its richest citizens."[164] However, he also dwells on the specific sense of possibility that could be felt in the Indian capital around the turn of the millennium. In some respects, Delhi seemed to have the advantage over cities shaped by what Dasgupta refers to as a "Western" model of relatively restrictive "multiculturalism":

> This ability of the Third-World city to embrace utter unintelligibility within its own population, to say not, 'Let me understand you so I may live alongside you,' but 'I will live alongside you without condition, for I will never understand you,' seemed not only more profoundly humane but also more promising as a general ethos of globalisation [...]. Perhaps the Third-World city, long thought of as a place of desolation and despair, might actually contain implicit forms of knowledge that all places could benefit from.[165]

In combination with still obtaining affordable life options, this climate of radical toleration favoured the development of a new scene of artists and intellectuals. The text speaks of "people [...] who staked their lives on a different kind of future" and who "added a whole new range of feelings and possibilities for life to an all-too formulaic city."[166]

Dasgupta is determined to pay attention to the material and economic conditions of life. As a prominently placed quotation from the *Communist Manifesto* underlines,[167] the title of his reportage is purposefully ambiguous: *Capital* is

---

[163]   DASGUPTA 36.

[164]   DASGUPTA 37.

[165]   DASGUPTA 41-42.

[166]   DASGUPTA 84.

[167]   See DASGUPTA 258, where the following famous quotation from Marx' and Engels' 1848 *Communist Manifesto* is used as an epigraph for chapter thirteen of *Capital*: "[The bourgeoisie] has pitilessly torn asunder the motley feudal ties that bound man to his 'natural superiors,' and has left remaining no other nexus between man and man than naked self-interest, than callous 'cash payment'... It has resolved personal worth into exchange value, and in place of the numberless indefeasible chartered freedoms, has set up that single, unconscionable freedom – Free Trade." The Marxist or quasi-Marxist affiliations of Dasgupta's reportage are also brought home in an introductory "Note to the Reader," which clarifies the status of India's 'middle class' as an "elite" and, in fact; as a "bourgeoisie" (xiv).

meant to be read as a rigorous contemporary re-assessment of the workings of capital in India's capital. It needs to be noted, however, that the focus of Dasgupta's attention is on the sensorial and affective aspects of economic processes and historical transformations: his primary interest is in the question of how the potentials and problems of the city come to the fore in terms of "feeling." Here is how the author explains his original motivation: "It felt to me that very wild human energies were at play [...] and that the reality of the city could only be discovered by asking residents how they actually lived and felt."[168] *Capital*, then, is intended as a subjective, yet comprehensive investigation of (dramatically changing) structures of feeling – of what emerges as a kind of 'New Delhi state of mind.' Indeed, Dasgupta's reportage can be read as a phenomenology of globalization – or, more precisely put, as a phenomenology of globalization as experienced on the particular terrain of the city of Delhi.[169]

At the end of his book, Dasgupta briefly returns to what he calls "Delhi's utopian potential."[170] The bulk of the more than 400 pages of *Capital*, however, offer an empathetically observed yet relentless account of Delhi's failure to live up to the promise "felt" around the turn of the millennium. Judging from Dasgupta's report, the stake that was lost in the process was exactly the hope conjured up in the Sarai Reader and remembered at the beginning of Dasgupta's reportage: the hope of activating an alternative form and ethos of globalized urbanity.

In its celebration of Delhi's potential as well as in its critique of the city's failure, Dasgupta's argument is close to Richard Sennett's notions concerning the positive and negative aspects of an urban indifference to difference. Similar to Sennett's, Dasgupta's analysis dwells on the interrelationship between social imaginaries, material infrastructures (i.e. the organization of space and motion, systems of supply and waste management, etc.) and sensorial cultures or regimes. Dasgupta describes the history of Delhi – after Independence just as much or even more so than before – as a history governed by what Sennett calls "sensate

---

[168] DASGUPTA 44.

[169] In the process of such a phenomenology, the very word 'feel' comes to be used in relation to both sensorial and cognitive processes. Cf. 45-46 for an instance of repeating the word 'feel' almost excessively: "I did not FEEL that the scenes I witnessed around me were of concern only to this place. Nor did I FEEL that they were scenes of a 'primitive' part of the system, which was struggling to 'catch up' with the advanced West. They FELT, rather, to be hypermodern scenes which were replicated, with some variations, elsewhere on the rockface of contemporary global capitalism. Indeed, the book I began to write FELT like a report from the global future [...]. It was no longer in the West, I FELT, but in places such as this, that people from all over the world could find their own destiny most clearly writ" (emphases added).

[170] DASGUPTA 422.

apathy," i.e. by the art of ever more rigorously ignoring the poor (i.e. the impoverished manual workforce) and their needs: "Delhi's official urban strategy was to not see those millions of people, to treat them as ghosts who periodically contributed their labour to the feast, but who did not themselves require food or shelter or anything else."[171]

Dasgupta's *Capital* resembles Sennett's *Flesh and Stone* also in its attention to the organisation of urban traffic as both an expression and a medium of social organization. Dasgupta feels that the unfettered individualism of Delhi driving styles bespeaks of a deficit in social perspective. Thus, chapter 10 – which mainly deals with the effects of the Partition on Delhi – takes off from a vignette that describes the irrational behaviour of a driver on a major road. The narrator of the reportage uses this scene as the basis for the following generalization: "There is nothing urban about this place, I think. No metropolitan ethos emerges from all these multitudes who live together."[172] Along similar lines, Dasgupta reads the ways in which not only the homeless but actually all pedestrians have been disregarded in the planning of urban space as both symptom and cause of a defective social imaginary:

> In Delhi, the road is the place from which people derive their image of the entire city. It is a segregated city, a city of hierarchies and clannish allegiances, where very few people from any sector of society enjoy the idea of social distinctions being lost – and it has no truly democratic spaces.[173]

Besides the car and the flyover, Dasgupta's reportage positions the shopping mall as another key figure of Delhi's social dissociation – and, indeed, of the absence of a real democracy. He sees the many malls that 'globalization' brought to the Indian capital as parts of a "carved-up landscape": there is "no continuity" between the world inside the mall and the world immediately outside.[174] Meeting an interviewee in a mall, Dasgupta peers through a screen of trees at the edge of the elegantly furnished terrace on which they are having coffee. He sees a "large slum" where women and children are rushing to get water from an arriving truck. His description and commentary manage to evoke the simultaneity of close proximity and total disconnection. Significantly, the narrator perceives the scene in the slum as if he were watching TV – it seems to resemble "a CNN cliché of ravaged earth." The contrast between the "succulent mall, with all its lawns and fountains" and the "women and children [...] rushing out of their houses with as

---

[171]   DASGUPTA 273.
[172]   DASGUPTA 186.
[173]   DASGUPTA 16.
[174]   DASGUPTA 95.

many plastic containers as they can carry" shows that the distance between the customers in the mall (who are having unnecessary luxuries showered on them while they are comfortably seated or leisurely strolling) and the slum-dwellers (who need to rush in panic so as to hold on to the bare necessities of life) is a distance of access to the supply systems of urban infrastructure.[175] The passage suggests that such glaringly apparent inequality might be seen as determinedly *produced*, as the effect of a wilful act of disarticulation.

In Dasgupta's account of the demise of a North-Indian mixed Hindu-Muslim culture the notion of a wilfully engineered disarticulation becomes concrete. Here, modern Hindi is described as a new language, a "re-invention of traditional Hindustani" that was "fabricated" by "expunging" Persian, Arabic and Turkish words, simultaneously forcing the transition from Arabic script to Devanagari. According to Dasgupta, the Indian Constitution of 1950 had a clear agenda concerning the politics of language: "Indian tongues, henceforth, would not produce Muslim sounds. Nor would Indian hands shape Muslim letters."[176] It is indicative of the harshness with which Dasgupta occasionally approaches his "adopted city"[177] that he sees the destruction of what he describes as an integrated "Hindustani culture"[178] as the reason not only for socio-ideological disarticulation along the lines of religion but also for a general loss of articulateness: "Many members of its [i.e. Delhi's] middle classes ended up speaking no language well – neither English […] nor Hindi," so that "a certain vagueness of speech, a deliberate ignorance of grammar, became the style." Having explained that many Partition refugees forgot much of their Urdu, Dasgupta continues: "but sometimes they heard the speech of the working classes, who had come in from other places where the poetic, ecstatic elements of Hindustani had not become foreign – and they realised how inarticulate they themselves had become."[179]

Dasgupta plays the concept of inarticulateness also in connection to the fraught relations between men and women. Like so many other commentators, he sees Delhi as a hotbed of misogyny – as the site of what he significantly terms

---

[175]   DASGUPTA 118.
[176]   DASGUPTA 175. See, however, Ramachandra GUHA, "How the Filthy Rich Live in Rising Asia," *The New Republic*, 15 October 2014. In this review of *Capital*, Guha mentions Dasgupta's short history of Hindi as one of the signs that the author's "understanding of modern Indian history is, alas, shaky." According to Guha, Dasgupta "assumes that the now-sharp divide between Hindi and Urdu (once cognate languages) began with the Indian Constitution of 1950, whereas in fact the separation had been steadily fueled since the late nineteenth century onward."
[177]   DASGUPTA 44.
[178]   DASGUPTA 77.
[179]   DASGUPTA 176. Similar notions have an important function in Arundhati Roy's *The Ministry of Utmost Happiness* (2017); see the last section of this chapter.

"a low-level, but widespread, war against women."[180] The respective sections of *Capital* dwell on allegedly widespread marital problems among wealthy urbanites. At the same time, Dasgupta discusses the high number of rape cases and the often immense brutality of the sexualized violence inflicted. The main reason offered is that globalization and economic liberalization went along with a dual positioning of women, "whose new mobility made them not only the icons of India's social and economic changes but also the scapegoats."[181] However, Dasgupta also connects the phenomenon to a diminishing power among middle-class men to express their increasingly complex position between the ideals of change and tradition. The narrator of *Capital* (who often uses the past tense even when referring to the present) surmises that the "faultline" between the expectations of these men's traditionalist mothers and their progressivist wives "cut through the most primordial, inarticulate parts of their being," creating a "split" that "could take men beyond words." In consequence, it is suggested, many of these men "turned to blows [...] for they had no words with which to counter their far more clear-headed and articulate wives."[182]

Although the term is used only sparingly and unsystematically, Dasgupta's assessment of contemporary Delhi and its history can be read as a story of multi-layered disarticulation. This means that *Capital* strongly suggests the deep connectedness of various (social, infrastructural, spatial, religious, sensorial, linguistic and even temporal) symptoms of disconnection. Dasgupta's use of the term "inarticulate" ties in with the sensorial and linguistic programmatic we have discovered in Haider's published interviews with slum-dwellers, in Chandola's exercises of "listening in to others", and also in the Sarai Reader's "Cybermohalla Diaries": in unison with these texts and studies, Dasgupta's *Capital* suggests that the predicament of contemporary Delhi comes down to a twin problem of articulation and articulacy – a problem that could only be solved by re-articulating the city from below. In spite of its air of constructedness, the image of wealthy but "inarticulate" Delhiites allegedly encountering a lost cultural heritage in "the speech of the working classes" deftly brings home Dasgupta's message that rampant capitalist exploitation finally impoverishes and silences *all* members of a so-

---

[180] DASGUPTA 139.
[181] DASGUPTA 139.
[182] DASGUPTA 138. It should be noted at this point that while Dasgupta's assessments are always provocative, there is also a tendency towards providing overly clear-cut causes for all kinds of complex phenomena. Moreover, the privileged route for arriving at such causes is psychological or quasi-psychological. For a gentle critique of Dasgupta's strategy of argumentation, see also C. S. Bhagya and G. J. V. Prasad, "'Capital' Consciousness: Reading Rana Dasgupta," *Journal of Postcolonial Writing*, 54.3 (2018): 346-359, esp. 349.

ciety. This message, we are reminded at the end of *Capital*, is significant far beyond the Indian capital. Indeed, Dasgupta argues that contemporary Delhi is of the future rather than the past, that its pronounced problems of articulation should be seen as an indication of where cities are heading all over the globe.[183]

3.2.4 Versions of the Global Fairy Tale: Delhi in *Q & A* (2005) and *The White Tiger* (2008)

So far, our discussion of recent writing on Delhi has concentrated on non-fictional texts wavering between scholarship, activist intervention and literary reportage. We will now turn – briefly – to two novels produced in-between the Sarai Reader (2002) and *Capital* (2014): Vikas Swarup's *Q & A* (2005) and Aravind Adiga's *The White Tiger* (2008). These two fictions have much in common with Dasgupta's (potentially 'epic') literary reportage. One property shared by all three texts is that they primarily aim at an international readership: they constitute examples of writing Delhi for – or at least within the discursive apparatus of – an Anglophone 'wider world' still oriented towards Britain and North America as its cultural centres.[184] Moreover, our texts met with considerable success in the international cultural domain thus addressed: all three books won (sometimes highly prestigious) literary awards,[185] and *Q & A* was also transformed into an Oscar-winning – and hotly debated – feature film by British director Danny Boyle.[186] It might also be noted that the three titles were penned by authors whose biographical experience qualified them for the role of mediating Indian terrains of consciousness to an international audience: Rana Dasgupta's background

---

[183] See esp. DASGUPTA 435.

[184] An Anglophone global orientation – though not necessarily the gesturing towards British and American markets – is also evident with the first two collections discussed in this chapter: the French-edited *Delhi: Urban Space and Human Destinies* (2000) and the largely Indian-edited Sarai Reader.

[185] *Capital* won the Ryszard Kapuściński Award for Literary Reportage and was shortlisted for the Orwell Prize as well as the Ondaatje Prize. *Q & A* won the South African Boeke Prize and the Prix Grand Public at the Paris Book Fair; it was nominated as Best First Book by the Commonwealth Writers' Prize. *White Tiger* won the Man Booker Prize and made the bestseller list of the *New York Times*.

[186] Danny BOYLE (dir.), *Slumdog Millionaire* (UK, 2008). The film won eight Oscars, including "Best Picture" and "Best Director." The film not only boasted a very different title than the novel, but Simon Beaufoy's (Oscar-winning) screenplay had also considerably changed Swarup's story. For a discussion of the debate on the film (and he novel) in India, see Tripta CHANDOLA, "Representing the Slums: The Case of *Slumdog Millionaire*," *Listening in to Others: In between Noise and Silence* 320-332.

combines an Indian family history with an education in Oxford, France and the USA; Vikas Swarup's international work as a diplomat must have equipped him for the task of representing Indian realities to a wider world; Aravind Adiga was born in Madras and raised in Australia, he studied at Columbia and Oxford before working as a Indian correspondent for major American and British periodicals.

As has been seen, Dasgupta's *Capital* focusses on the experiences, views and feelings of Delhi's economic elite. On this basis and from this perspective, the socioeconomic, sensorial and affective disarticulation between the well-to-do or rich, on the one hand, and the poor, on the other, is a constant topic. A particularly striking passage deals with the reaction shown by a powerful entrepreneur on being confronted with the appalling living and working conditions of the labourers who are preparing the city for the 2010 Commonwealth Games:

> It happens that I have come to see Rahul directly from one of the camps set up for the labourers who came to Delhi to work on the infrastructure for the Commonwealth Games, and I am still disturbed by the experience. [...] 'It's not necessary that it be so bad,' I say. 'It's bad by design. It's obstinately bad. It's impossible not to feel it is sadistic.' 'I'm sure if I were to see that I would feel the same,' says Rahul. He pauses, thinking about his feelings, and adds, 'But if I saw those people, I am sure I would also feel contempt.'[187]

The dialogue reported suggests a dual system of insulation that disarticulates the rich from the poor, the masters from their servants, and the entrepreneurs from the workforce. On the one hand, the separation is grounded in a *regime of visuality* that makes it virtually impossible for the powerful to see the powerless: although Rahul seems to be among the people involved in the city's makeover before the Commonwealth Games, he has never so much as glanced at the accommodation of the (or of 'his') workers; were he to take a look, strong feelings might be aroused. However, and this is the second mechanism of insulation or disarticulation, those feelings would finally not be the feelings of compassion felt by the outside observer. Rather, a deeply ingrained *mechanism of affective disposition* would almost automatically transform a stirring sense of compassion into the well-habituated affect of the master class: "contempt."

In spite of Dasgupta's alarm at the exploitation and disparagement of the underprivileged, only one of the 17 chapters in his book is specifically devoted to the life situation of poor people and labourers. However, it is this chapter that

---

[187]   DASGUPTA 223-224.

constructs a counter-image to the story of alienation, disarticulation and inartic-
ulacy that governs *Capital*. As Dasgupta observes about the inhabitants of
Bhalswa, a resettlement colony on the fringes of Delhi whose inhabitants are facing an imminent second displacement: "If these women are so imposing [...] it
has something to do with the fact that no part of their lives is delegated. [...] They
seem to own themselves in a way that most people I know do not."[188] The
women's ownership of their selves is grounded in a dual articulation: not only
with the material environment ("[t]hey know how to make a sewer or a door-
way"), but also with a community: "One senses that they are together in a way
that few middle-class people are. [...] [E]ven in their grammar the 'I' rarely
breaks ranks with the 'we.'"[189] Finally, the women's status of total marginalization
comes to be connected with a partially privileged epistemological position: "It is
the poor who understand how the city is truly managed."[190]

The understanding or knowledge meant by Dasgupta is mostly bitter: it is
knowledge of the enormous endeavours undertaken by the seemingly absent
state to insulate the middle classes from the "ocean of poverty"[191] that surrounds
them. A similar – though more positively inflected – notion forms the basis of
Swarup's *Q & A*. Thus, when lawyer Smita Shah finds it difficult to believe that
her client – the novel's protagonist: an ordinary slum-dweller and waiter – could
have been able to answer (almost) all the questions in a quiz show without trick-
ing, the latter replies:

> 'Well, Madam, we poor can also ask questions and demand answers. And
> I bet you, if the poor conducted a quiz, the rich wouldn't be able to answer
> a single question. I don't know the currency of France, but I can tell you
> how much money Shalini Tai owes our neighbourhood moneylender. I
> don't know who was the first man on the moon, but I can tell you who
> was the first man to produce illegal DVDs in Dharavi. Could you answer
> these questions in my quiz?'[192]

Ram Mohammad Thomas's claim that poor people possess a specific kind of (informal) knowledge triggers the novel's narrative, which consists in the protagonist's account of how his life story equipped him for the quiz show. In the process
it is demonstrated that the knowledge of the poor is grounded in specific terrains
of consciousness, where it has been earned through often painful first-hand experience. In accordance with the assertion quoted above from *Capital*, Swarup's

---

[188]   DASGUPTA 244.
[189]   DASGUPTA 245.
[190]   DASGUPTA 246.
[191]   DASGUPTA 258.
[192]   Vikas SWARUP, *Q & A* (2005; London: Black Swan / Random House, 2006) 29.

novel strongly suggests that such sensorially concrete knowledge is highly significant and potent – that it is necessary for figuring out how the Indian city, and in
fact the country as a whole, is – in Dasgupta's words – "truly managed."[193]

In interview with the *Guardian*, the author of *Q & A* (whose status as a "high-
flying Indian diplomat" is emphasized by reporter Stuart Jeffries) carefully distances his novel from both lyricist ambitions and political intentions: "I'm not
one of those writers," Swarup explains, "who wants to spend four pages describing a sunrise. […] I'm a sucker for thrillers and I wanted to write one. I'm much
more influenced by Alistair MacLean and James Hadley Chase. I'm no Arundhati
Roy."[194] Indeed, *Q & A* is driven by a thrilling dynamic of revelation: How could
the protagonist have known the correct answers? Will he finally get away with
his feat or will the police torture him into submission? It is also clear that the
novel makes a point of unabashedly tuning in on the genres of popular literature
and populist ideologies, including a globalist version of the 'rags to riches' fairy
tale.[195] At the same time, one may well feel hesitant to follow the novel's author
and label *Q & A* as a "thriller." The novel's characteristic combination of populist
expansiveness, melodramatic thrust and picaresque tonality are obviously closer
to the example of Dickens than to that of "Alistair MacLean and James Hadley
Chase."[196] Accordingly, Swarup's ostentatiously innocuous self-characterization
as "a sucker for thrillers" obscures or overplays the political character of *Q & A*.
Thus, in her insightful essay on Boyle's film and Swarup's novel, Alpana Sharma
draws attention to how the former partially "neutralizes" the latter's implications

---

[193]   Cf. Jonathan Shapiro ANJARIA and Ulka ANJARIA, "*Slumdog Millionaire* and Epistemologies of
the City," *Economic and Political Weekly*, 12-18 June 2010, 41-46, who argue that Boyle's film
(but also Swarup's novel) offer a "fairy-world real tale" (46) that plausibly celebrates "the role of
informal knowledge in the navigation of changing urban landscapes" (41).

[194]   SWARUP qtd. in Stuart JEFFRIES, "'I'm the luckiest novelist in the world'" [interview-based feature
on Swarup, *Q & A*, and *Slumdog Millionaire*], *The Guardian*, 16 January 2009.

[195]   Consider, for example, the following passage from the novel's ending: "For the first time, I am
tempted by the prospect of all this money. With a billion I can achieve many things. I can buy
Nita's freedom. I can fulfil Salim's dream of becoming a star. I can light up the lives of thousands
of fellow orphans and street kids like me. I can get my hands on a beautiful red Ferrari. I make
up my mind. It is 'yes' to a billion and 'no' to murder" (353).

[196]   Indeed, Robert L. Patten's assessment of the interplay between picaresque and melodramatic
modes in Dickens' early novels might be directly applied to Swarup's *Q & A*. Cf. Robert L. Patten,
"From *Sketches* to *Nickleby*," *The Cambridge Companion to Charles Dickens*, ed. John O. Jordan
(Cambridge: Cambridge UP, 2001) 16-33, here 25: "The picaresque imagination, which features
provisional solutions to immediate challenges in a universe without absolutes, and the melodramatic imagination, which strongly embeds fundamental, emotionally rendered notions of good
and evil within sharply contrasting characters who act out our deepest fears and desires, combine, despite their apparently contradictory natures, to produce in Dickens's early work a fecund,
turbulent transformative world."

as a "social critique of the nation and its failure to deliver its post-Independence promise of ending poverty and ensuring a better life to all its citizens."[197]

Besides the potent combination of melodramatic and picaresque modes, Swarup shares with Dickens an insistence on providing detailed and reportorially accentuated information on the concrete material conditions and spatial organization of life, especially of life in the city. Here are three examples:

> After the time I spent with the actress Neelima Kumari, living in her flat, I had almost forgotten life in a chawl. A bundle of one-room tenements occupied by the lower-middle classes, chawls are the smelly armpit of Mumbai. Those who live here are only marginally better off than those who live in slums like Dharavi. As Mr Barve told me once, the rich people, those who live in their marble and granite four-bedroom flats, they enjoy. The slum people, who live in squalid, tattered huts, they suffer. And we, who reside in the overcrowded chawls, we simply live.[198]

> All of us live in the servants' quarters attached to the main house. We have one large and two small rooms to ourselves. Bhagwati lives in the large one with his wife and son. Shanti lives alone in the second. And I share the third with Ramu. The room has bunk beds. I sleep in the one on top.[199]

> I live in a corner of Mumbai called Dharavi, in a cramped hundred-square-foot shack which has no natural light or ventilation, with a corrugated metal sheet serving as the roof over my head. It vibrates violently whenever a train passes overhead. There is no running water and no sanitation. This is all I can afford. But I am not alone in Dharavi. There are a million people like me, packed in a two-hundred-hectare triangle of swampy urban wasteland, where we live like animals and die like insects.[200]

Only the second passage refers to Delhi: describing the accommodation of the servants in the household of an Australian embassy official where the protagonist stays as a factotum it describes both a special social world and a special part of

---

[197] Alpana SHARMA, "*Slumdog Millionaire*: The Film, the Reception, the Book, the Global," *Literature/Film Quarterly* 40.3 (2012): 197-215, here: 211-212. However, Sharma also draws attention to what she identifies as the neo-liberal framework of Swarup's critique: "[T]he novel's informing ideology extends beyond nationalism as such to a tacit compliance with India's post-1990s neo-liberal capitalist policies. It demonstrates an obligatory belief in the inherent goodness of downtrodden, disenfranchised, and impoverished people – particularly children and women – but it leaves the status quo unchanged" (210).

[198] SWARUP, *Q & A* 70.

[199] SWARUP, *Q & A* 130.

[200] SWARUP, *Q & A* 156.

the city: 'Lutyen's Delhi.' The other two quotations picture Mumbai localities, both 'imaginary' (the flat of an ageing film actress for whom Ram Mohammad Thomas works) and 'real' (the equally famous and notorious Dharavi settlement, which has often been referred to as 'Asia's biggest slum'[201]). Indeed, the novel's episodically structured plot goes back and forth between three Indian cities: Delhi, Mumbai, and Agra. It is evidently driven by the intention of reconnoitring and inventarising as many sites of Indian life – that is, of Indian life as experienced by the underprivileged – as possible.

The intended audience for this tour of social spaces and life situations seems to be the kind of international audience whose interests and subjectivity the "high-flying Indian diplomat" Swarup is especially competent to address. On closer inspection, however, it appears that the communicative directionality of *Q & A* may be more complicated: while the novel functionalizes spectacular Indian settings (including not only Dharavi but also the Taj Mahal) for the sake of international success, it probably uses the discourse of global Anglophone literature to facilitate a difficult internal debate within India; and if the captivating voice of the first-person narrator gestures to the imagined sensibilities and ethos of a global community of readers, it also seems to enlist these sensibilities and that ethos for breaking through the sensorial regimes and affective mechanisms that insulate many among the Indian elite against considering the life experiences of poor people. The global audience, then, may be both a real marketing target for and an imaginary presence within *Q & A*.

In this context, the discussion of Indian responses to *Slumdog Millionaire* (i.e. to the British film based on Swarup's novel) which Chandola offers as an "Epi-

---

[201] On Dharavi see: Liza WEINSTEIN, *The Durable Slum: Dharavi and the Right to Stay Put in Globalizing Mumbai* (Minneapolis: U of Minnesota P, 2014), Globalization and Community 23; Marie-Caroline SAGLIO-YATZIMIRSKY, *Dharavi: From Mega-Slum to Urban Paradigm* (New Delhi & Abingdon: Routledge, 2013). In relation to our argument and to Dasgupta's portrayal of Delhi, Weinstein's in-depth analysis of the history and present state of Dharavi is interesting because it seeks to counter or complicate what the author represents as a Marxist characterization of the modern city that puts the emphasis on "friction, fragmentation, collage, and eclecticism, all suffused with a sense of ephemerality and chaos" (HARVEY; qtd. in WEINSTEIN 7). While this perspective "captures an important set of dynamics," Weinstein argues, it "fails to account for the actually existing durabilities and the solidity of structures that refuse to melt"(7). Based on two decades of on-site research, Saglio-Yatzimirsky's study also stresses the friction between stereotypical representations of the 'slum's' squalor and the real complexity of a multi-facetted and dynamic urban environment. As it seems to Saglio-Yatzimirsky, this contradiction has widened in the course of globalization, which has created new opportunities for a peculiar culture of enterprise and political empowerment that is presented as a salient characteristic of contemporary Dharavi.

logue" to her study is significant. She suggests that the often condemning assessments of the film voiced by Indian critics and social media users betray a deep-seated problem of articulation: "Lacking vocabularies except the one of absence and alienation, the Indian middle-class discourse finds itself unable to comprehend or articulate the complex language of slums as depicted in *Slumdog Millionaire*."[202] Among the sources quoted by Chandola is a review by film critic by Subhash K. Jha. And indeed, the imagery used in Jha's text seems perplexed as well as perplexing. It opens up a wealth of interpretive options that centre on the twin concepts of (in-)articulateness and (dis-)articulation:

> Cinematographer Anthony Dod Mantle shoots Mumbai with a gun rather than a camera. Every frame conveys the killer instinct. Every shot ricochets across eternity solidifying sounds and feelings that are otherwise intangible.[203]

Jha's assessment of *Slumdog Millionaire* is highly negative: he views the film as an attempt to "exploit the Mumbai slums as a hotbed of tantalising images conveying the splendour of squalidity."[204] However, the passage on the film's cinematography betrays a more fundamental discomfort. Actualizing the dead metaphor of the film 'shot,' Jha triggers a series of strange synesthetic effects: first, the film's intense visuality comes to be described in terms of acoustics; then, it is proposed that such acoustically invasive spectacularity has the power of "solidifying" affective dispositions that would otherwise remain intangible. The idea that the film pushes into the realm of the "intangible" and resonates "across eternity" contradicts the allegation that it is merely exploiting superficial appearances and catering to simplistic stereotypes. Rather than illustrating his criticism of *Slumdog Millionaire* (a criticism, by the way, that may be partly pertinent), Jha's uncontrolled synesthetic conceits capture his experience of the film as a multi-potent sensorial assault on his worldview. They suggest a totally bewildering experience of having ingrained regimes of social compartmentalization and sensorial disarticulation violently transgressed.

---

[202] CHANDOLA, "Epilogue," *Listening in to Others* 320-335, here 332.
[203] Subhash K. JHA, rev. of *Slumdog Millionaire*, qtd. in Chandola 324. For a very different discussion and evaluation of the film's representation of Mumbai, see Vandana BAWEJA, "Architecture and Urbanism in *Slumdog Millionaire*: From Bombay to Mumbai," *Traditional Dwellings and Settlements Review*, 26.2 (2015): 7-24. See also ANJARIA and ANJARIA, who offer a digest of the debate on *Slumdog Millionaire*; comparing the film to the director's earlier *Trainspotting*, the authors suggest that "*Trainspotting*'s Scotland fares much worse than *Slumdog*'s Mumbai in Boyle's filmic vision" (43).
[204] JHA qtd. in Chandola 324.

The problem of socio-sensorial disarticulation – or of what Sennet calls "sensate apathy"[205] – is also an important topic in Swarup's novel. It comes to be explicit in a scene that has the young protagonist complain to the administrator of the Mumbai chawl where he is staying at the time. The object of his complaint is his next-door neighbour, an alcoholic who severely abuses his wife and daughter. Refusing to listen to these problems, the administrator points out that while "wife-beating and abuse and incest and rape" are part of Mumbai's daily life, it is also a universal truth that "no one does anything." He finally condenses his advice in a general rule of how the inhabitants of Indian megacities ought to behave: "We Indians have this sublime ability to see the pain and misery around us, and yet remain unaffected by it. So, like a proper Mumbaikar, close your eyes, close your ears, close your mouth and you will be happy like me."[206]

Towards the end of *Q & A* the protagonist stages a revolt against such apathy. Never shy of unlikely plot constructions, Swarup has the Agra section of his novel feature a subplot centring on a psychically disturbed boy who stays in the same chawl with the protagonist but is really the unacknowledged son of the rich landlady. As no one pays for the expensive medical treatment that might have saved him, the boy dies of rabies. In his grief, the protagonist suddenly decides to take the boy's corpse to his mother who lives in a neighbouring grand villa. He does so while the landlady is giving a sumptuous party:

> The uniformed guards bar my way, but as soon as they see the dead body in my hands they hastily open the gate. I pass along the curved driveway, where the expensive imported cars of the guests are lined up one after the other. I reach the ornate entrance and find it open in welcome. I pass through the marbled foyer into the dining room, where the guests are about to be served dessert. All conversation ceases the moment they see me. I climb on to the table, and place Shankar's body gently in the middle, in between a creamy vanilla cake and a bowl of rasagullas.[207]

The protagonist's revolt against social compartmentalization traverses a visually and semantically rich scenery: there's the guarded gate serving to keep rich and poor apart; there is the corpse of the boy (which works almost in the way of a key); there are the "expensive imported cars" figuring as emblems of globalized capitalism; and there is the "marbled foyer" that needs to be crossed to enter the inner sanctum of the dining room. By finally zooming in on the desserts, however, the climax of the passage performs a synesthetically accentuated transition from sight to taste. Almost, it might be said, the guests at the party and the readers

---

[205]   SENNETT, *Flesh and Stone* 323.
[206]   SWARUP, *Q & A* 83-84.
[207]   SWARUP, *Q & A* 326-327.

of the novel are forced to participate in a ghastly sort of Holy Communion: not only seeing but also tasting the corpse. While this scene of the novel is not in *Slumdog Millionaire*, its interweaving of social, affective and sensorial transgressions is meant to achieve an effect similar to that described in Sha's film review: it is meant to "ricochet[] across eternity solidifying [...] feelings that are otherwise intangible."

The melodramatic tonality and sensorial specificity of the scene in which the protagonist takes Shankar's corpse to the villa is Dickensian.[208] And so is the closure of *Q & A*, which solves nearly all problems by means of a sudden access to fantastic financial means. At the end of the novel, we are invited to imagine Ram Mohammad Thomas – the transsectional and transreligious Indian everyman from the lower ends of the social stratum – inhabiting the world of his dreaming, where he himself owns one of the "expensive imported cars" seen in the driveway of his landlady's villa:

> Smita and I are walking along [Mumbai's] Marine Drive. A pleasant wind is blowing, occasionally sending a misty spray from the ocean where giant waves crash and roll against the rocks. The uniformed driver is following us at a snail's pace in a Mercedes Benz, maintaining a respectful distance. The rear bumper of the Benz carries a sticker. It says 'My other car is a Ferrari.'[209]

What author and narrator are here joining to sell their readers with a pronounced sense of irony is a version of the fairy tale of globalization. Aravind Adiga's Booker-winning novel *The White Tiger* (2008) also draws on this pattern. In comparison to Swarup, however, Adiga offers a decidedly darker version of the pattern. The character of *The White Tiger* as a sardonic improvisation on the discourse of globalization and its invocation of an international readership are both foregrounded through the framing of the narrative. Thus, the novel is presented as a series of (imaginary) letters or e-mail messages in which the protagonist – a man of very simple rural origins who has committed a crime in order to take his life in his own hands and become an entrepreneur – tells the story of his life to Chinese Prime Minister Wen Jiabao. Having heard that Jiabao is about to visit India in order to gain first-hand experience of the country's fabulous economic rise, Balram Halwai tells the PM: "When you have heard the story of how I got to Bangalore and became one of its most successful (though probably least known)

---

[208] On Dickens's use of the entire sensorium, see Michael HOLLINGTON, "Dickens, the City, and the Five Senses," *Journal of the Australasian Universities Language and Literature Association* 113 (2010): 29-38.

[209] SWARUP, *Q & A* 360.

businessmen, you will know everything there is to know about how entrepreneurship is born, nurtured, and developed in this, the glorious twenty-first century of man."[210] It is obvious that the way in which the narrator of *The White Tiger* plays the discourse of economic liberalization, entrepreneurship and globalization is spiked with irony. If Balram has emerged from village life in rural India (a realm that he repeatedly refers to as "the Darkness"[211]) he has since become thoroughly worldly-wise and sees through the mechanisms of exploitation and ideological camouflage: "Never before in human history have so few owed so much to so many, Mr Jiabao."[212] The book provocatively imagines a servant who has not only learnt to understand Indian society better than his increasingly disoriented master, but who has also taken the decision to act on his insights rigorously and brutally.

While the protagonist ends up in Bangalore, most of the story is set in Delhi. Indeed, *The White Tiger* differs from *Q & A* in being specifically a novel about Delhi, focussing on the city's development during the first years of the third millennium. The character of the text as a chronicle of and commentary on the city's rapid development becomes obvious, for example, from descriptions of the building of the Metro Delhi (the first line of which was inaugurated at the end of 2002):

> There is construction work in any direction you look in Delhi. [...] And here too, in the heart of Connaught Place, even in the middle of the night, under the glare of immense spotlights, construction went on. [...] I had heard of this work: they were putting a railway under the ground of Delhi. The pit they had made for this work was as large as any of the coal mines I'd seen in Dhanbad.[213]

The protagonist has been taken to Delhi by his young master, whom he serves as a driver. It is Ram's job to take Mr Ashok to his appointments with politicians whom he bribes with large sums of money to serve the interests of his family. The master and his wife have moved into a flat in Gurgaon, the newly developed settlement of apartment and business towers, which Mr Ashok refers to as "the most American part of the city."[214] In *Capital*, Dasgupta repeatedly dwells on the pri-

---

[210]   Aravind ADIGA, *The White Tiger* (London: Atlantic, 2008) 6.

[211]   Cf. ADIGA 14, where the narrator tells Jiabao as his imaginary addressee: "You see, I am in the Light now, but I was born and raised in Darkness." The term "Darkness" is used nearly all through the book.

[212]   ADIGA 175-176.

[213]   ADIGA 158.

[214]   ADIGA 121.

vate township of Gurgaon as a symptom of the general drift towards the private management of infrastructures for the benefit of the well-to-do:

> An expanse of fields until thirty years ago, Gurgaon's looming apartment blocks and steely towers now look as if they have emerged from a computer game set in some super-saturated future. Gurgaon makes no pretence of being a 'public' space: the great numbers of the poor who clean and guard its houses and offices, for instance, cannot live there.[215]

In Adiga's novel, the servants are in fact accommodated in the same building as their masters and mistresses – albeit in the windowless and only sparsely furnished basement. This location is described as "a warren of interconnected rooms where all the drivers, cooks, sweepers, maids, and chefs of the apartment block can rest, sleep, and wait."[216]

The *new* Delhi emerging around the turn of the millennium may seem to have pushed people like Balram to the margins and into the basements. However, the protagonist of *The White Tiger* actually identifies with the city and with the historical shifts it seems to embody and inspire. Like many people writing about cities – and in particular like many people writing about Delhi[217] – Adiga's protagonist views his urban environment as a person with whom he is in imaginary communion:

> My heart was bitter that night. The city knew this – and under the dim orange glow cast everywhere by the weak streetlamps, she was bitter.
> *Speak to me of civil war*, I told Delhi.
> *I will*, she said.
> An overturned flower urn on a traffic island in the middle of a road; next to it three men sit with open mouths. An older man with a beard and white turban is talking to them with a finger upraised. Cars drive by him with their dazzling headlights, and the noise drowns out his words. He looks like a prophet in the middle of the city, unnoticed except by his three apostles. They will become his three generals. That overturned flower urn is a symbol of some kind.
> [...]
> *And if there is blood on these streets* – I asked the city – *do you promise that he'll be the first to go – that man with the fat folds under his neck?*

---

215   DASGUPTA 3-4. The evolution and character of Gurgaon are an important topic in *Capital*, see esp. 362-365.
216   ADIGA 130.
217   See for example Monica NARULA's "(For) Those Who Live in Cities," *Cities of Everyday Life*, ed. Sarai: The New Media Initiative (New Delhi: Sarai, 2002) 107 – which is the introduction to a section of the Sarai Reader that collects short personal texts on city life. Here, Narula muses about "the cities that speak and are spoken to in this section."

> A beggar sitting by the side of the road, a nearly naked man coated
> with grime, and with wild unkempt hair in long coils like snakes, looked
> into my eyes:
> *Promise*.[218]

The city – invested with the female pronoun "she" – is conjured up as a sensate collective consciousness. It can be spoken to, and it replies – either by means of "symbols" such as disarrayed flowerpots or through the constellations, gestures and looks of its people. The city here imagined by Balram and his author is a social organism on the eve of revolution: it is a place where an "overturned flower urn" must be read as a promise that the entire social order will be overturned, where an imposing Sikh can be seen as a newly emerging general of the people and where an unkempt beggar metamorphoses into a powerful Medusa figure.

When Mr Ashok's family try to falsely frame Balram for a fatal accident caused by the reckless driving of his master's wife, the imaginary reciprocal bond between the servant and his master receives a devastating blow. Balram's eventual revolt consists in murdering and robbing his master, using the cash to start a new life as entrepreneur. The irony of the novel's plot is that this revolt does not resemble the collective endeavour conjured up in the protagonist's quoted dialogue with Delhi. Rather, his crime is a completely self-interested undertaking on which he embarks at a considerable price for others: as Balram well knows, Mr Ashok's relatives will take brutal revenge on his family. Most significantly, the servant's revolt in *The White Tiger* is actually in sync with the dominant system. It simply represents Balram's way of bending the flow of 'liberalization' and 'globalization' for his private empowerment.[219]

---

[218] ADIGA 220-221.

[219] Balram's rhetorical and agential collusion with the dominant neoliberal system and the way this is positioned in the novel have elicited ample commentary. See esp.: Lena KHOR, "Can the Subaltern Right Wrongs? – Human Rights and Development in Aravind Adiga's *The White Tiger*," *South Central Review* 29.1/2 (2012): 41-67; Betty JOSEPH, "Neoliberalism and Allegory," *Cultural Critique* 82 (2012): 68-94; Weihsin GUI, "Creative Destruction and Narrative Renovation: Neoliberalism and the Aesthetic Dimension in the Fiction of Aravind Adiga and Mohsin Hamid," *The Global South* 7.2 (2013): 173-190. KHOR not only observes "that the ruthless form which [Balram] Halwai's thoughts and actions take is but the logical outcome of a world where underdevelopment, modernization, and neoliberal globalization reign" simultaneously but also wonders whether "Adiga himself accepts the structures and systems of neoliberalism as a suspect and regrettable, but ultimately unavoidable reality" (42). GUI's important essay complicates this literalist question: it argues that Adiga's novel – as well as Mohsin Hamid's *How to Get Filthy Rich in Rising Asia* (2013) – explores and interrogates neoliberal discourses by dwelling on their aesthetic dimension, so that "key terms and concepts from neoliberalism and globalization" come to be "appropriated and resignified" in a revealing act of "narrative renovation" (175-176). Along similar lines, JOSEPH returns to the debate on the functions of allegory in 'third-world literature'

This kind of revolt is anchored not in Ram's vision of a Delhi's revolutionary spirit but in his experience of the capital as a prime site of ruthless business activity, unfettered self-interest, and socio-sensorial disarticulation. The representation of this Delhi in *The White Tiger* includes many of the topics and motifs dwelt on in *Capital*. Like Dasgupta, Adiga places a particular emphasis on the traffic system. The protagonist and narrator of his novel clearly is in the position of a picaroon. This results in a highly revealing combination of naivety and shrewdness, of childish enthusiasm and worldly-wise sarcasm – as comes to the fore in Ram's thoughts on the social significance of the automobile:

> With their tinted windows up, the cars of the rich go like dark eggs down the roads of Delhi. Every now and then an egg will crack open – a woman's hand, dazzling with gold bangles, stretches out of an open window, flings an empty mineral water bottle onto the road – and then the window goes up, and the egg is resealed.[220]

The passage apparently strives to disable any innocent view of the automobile as simply a means of transportation. Rather, it is suggested that automobiles constantly emit social messages and enact social hierarchies. The message sent and the system enacted is the total separation of the "rich" from the poor. The process of opening the tinted window and closing it again – the "cracking open" and "resealing" of the "egg" – does not so much disrupt as underline the complete socio-sensorial insulation of one world against the other. Indeed, the act of displaying one's wealth ("dazzling with gold bangles") and disposing of one's trash comes to appear as a poignant gesture of aggrandizement and humiliation. On the streets, the difference between the rich and the poor is felt so acutely, because the two worlds are evidently both so close and so far apart. During a traffic jam, Balram watches the poor people outside the car: "Hundreds of them, there seemed to be, on either side of the traffic, and their life was entirely unaffected by the jam. [...] We were like two separate cities – inside and outside the dark egg."[221]

As it seems from the novel, the two worlds can only meet in terms of a deadly collision. Such a collision first occurs, when Pinky Madam – Mr Ashok's wife – insists on driving the car and kills a little child. It significantly contributes to Ram's growing anger at his subaltern position that he is forced into bearing the consequences of his betters' irresponsibility, first by cleaning the car ("[I]

---

in order to show how "Adiga brilliantly satirizes neoliberalism through ventriloquism": using Balram – the self-styled "White Tiger" as a mouthpiece, Joseph suggests, the novel makes us "hear neoliberal entrepreneurial shibboleths as criminality" (72).

[220] ADIGA 134.
[221] ADIGA 138.

scrubbed out every bit of blood and flesh – there was a bit of both around the wheels"[222]) and then by signing an affidavit that declares him to have been the driver. The second collision between the rich and the poor is Ram's murder of Ashok, which partly results from the latter's wavering between reducing and re-instating the social difference between master and servant. Like the road accident, the murder of Ashok is represented with an almost unbearable amount of sensual detail:

> I rammed the bottle down. The glass ate his bone. I rammed it three times into the crown of his skull, smashing through to his brains. It's a good, strong bottle, Johnnie Walker Black – well worth its resale value.[223]

Adiga's narrator-protagonist describes his act of murder as an act of turning into a "social entrepreneur," which he takes to have been the precondition for his becoming a "business entrepreneur."[224] As the novel shows and as the sardonic comment on the useful properties and market value of the whiskey bottle underlines, Ram's unlikely transition from poverty to wealth and from powerlessness to agency depends on his internalizing the neoliberal and globalist lesson taught him by the big city. This is the lesson of "sensate apathy" or sensorial disarticulation, the lesson of sealing the egg. As the novel strongly suggests, such sealing of the egg entails not only the socio-sensorial insulation of the liberated subject against other human beings but also the imaginary splitting-off of the globalized city from the "Darkness" of its impoverished rural 'hinterland.'[225]

3.2.5 Returning to Old Delhi: *The Ministry of Utmost Happiness* (2017)

In 2017 Arundhati Roy finally published a long-awaited second novel, promisingly titled *The Ministry of Utmost Happiness.* Exactly twenty years earlier, *The God of Small Things,* her Booker Prize-winning debut, had suddenly propelled the author to fame. Written in English and obviously addressing a world-wide readership, *The God of Small Things* had delivered a highly critical assessment of the failures and hypocrisies of the postcolonial nation, specifically of its continuation of casteism as a cultural technology of domination and exploitation. The

---

[222]   ADIGA 164.
[223]   ADIGA 285.
[224]   ADIGA 299; cf. 177.
[225]   See JOSEPH (passim) for a highly productive discussion of the novel's complex discourse on the relationships between the urban and the rural.

innovative character of the novel was primarily in its tone, which systematically combined and contrasted the sardonic exploration of social laws, particularly of the logic of untouchability, with an emphatic politics of sentiment and sentience. Indeed, *The God of Small Things* linguistically instantiated an erotically charged ethics of touchability and thus performed a politically powerful programmatic of 'worlding.'

Roy's skill in managing the collision of a distorted inhuman reality with a striking alternative vision of socio-sensorial articulation was the primary reason for the spectacular world-wide success of *The God of Small Things*.[226] Indeed, while the novel included an urgent critique of the ways in which contemporary India was being packaged for world-wide consumption, Roy's technique of assessing the problems of the postcolonial nation from the point of view of children and according to the fundamental terms of thwarted human needs or desires also resulted in a narrative that almost perfectly leant itself to the mechanics of the globalising literary market. The author's hesitancy in producing a second novel may have been due to an unwillingness of continuing to play into this logic. Rather than sliding along the well-oiled grooves of novelistic stardom, Roy chose to become a political activist, analyst and pamphleteer, using the traction she had earned as the author of *The God of Small Things* as a platform for stubbornly uncompromising interventions into Indian political discourses.

One way of approaching *The Ministry of Utmost Happiness* is in reading it as the author's attempt to not only return to the signature tone of *The God of Small Things* but to also use the tried sensorial and sensational poetics of her first novel in the service of a fictional re-articulation of the entire range of political agendas since put forward in her non-fiction writing. Necessarily, the result is a bulky and heterogeneous kind of novel – a novel which has been described as "overwrought and overwritten," but which has simultaneously, and by the same critic, been praised as impressively integrating the ambitions of a "utopian project" with a consistent "emphasis on the importance of engaging with the reality of present material conditions."[227] In an interview, Roy herself acknowledged the sprawling character of *The Ministry of Utmost Happiness*. At the same time, she used a startling image for defending the novel's diverse combination of digression and design:

---

[226] On the complex relationship between the spectacular global success of *The God of Small Things* and the novel's ambivalent postcoloniality, see esp. Miriam NANDI, "Longing for the Lost (M)Other – Postcolonial Ambivalences in Arundhati Roy's *The God of Small Things*," *Journal of Postcolonial Writing* 46.2 (2010): 175-186.

[227] Samir DAYAL, "Normative Materialist Cosmopolitanism," *New Cosmopolitanisms, Race, and Ethnicity: Cultural Perspectives*, ed. Ewa Barbara LUCZAK, Anna POCHMARA, and Samir DAYAL (Berlin: De Gruyter, 2019) 90-113, here: 91-92.

[My second novel] is like a city – it has form and then that form is am-
bushed, and yet it still has form ... it's not an accretion but it circles
around itself, it has a structure ... It is an Indian city, it has unauthorised
colonies, it has illegal immigrants, it has dogs and cows and creatures and
bats ... it is a porous Indian city with its own plans.[228]

The Ministry of Utmost Happiness may not only be said to resemble the embattled
structure of an Indian megacity but – in contrast to *The God of Small Things* – it
is also a novel *about* urban life and urban space. Moreover, *The Ministry of Utmost Happiness* deals especially with Delhi. On the one hand, the novel explores
the mind-blowing changes undergone by India's capital under the aegis of globalized postmodernity. On the other hand, it elaborates the vision of an alternative
worlding that is based in (as well as productive of) an alternative terrain of consciousness. This latter aspect is most convincingly brought out in Samir Dayal's
reading of *The Ministry of Utmost Happiness* as proposing a "microcosmic cosmopolitanism" by giving voice to "the minoritarian ethicopolitical" and thus to
"the microcosmic that resists being co-opted by the macropolitical."[229] Roy's second novel therefore urgently suggests itself as a reference text for concluding
both our chapter on writing Delhi and our short monograph on "Multilogical
Perspectives on Globalization."

As has been mentioned in the introduction to this book, Jean-Luc Nancy sees
the contemporary megacity – or the world-encompassing network constituted
by such cities – as the primary site, nexus and expression of capitalist globalization and its "unworlding" effects.[230] The present chapter has brought out a consistent tendency of interpreting Delhi – specifically the n/New Delhi jointly created by the British colonizing power, the postcolonial state and the new globalized India – along these lines. Respective interpretations emerge most clearly and
urgently in Adiga's *White Tiger* and Dasgupta's *Capital*, where n/New Delhi is
insistently assessed as the product of globalist articulatory processes and of the
attendant socio-sensorial disarticulation of the local habitat. In these texts, the
automobile, the flyover and the shopping mall emerge as evocative emblems of a
logic of urban development that, in Richard Sennett's words, has "used the technologies of motion, of public health and of private comfort [...] to resist the demands of crowds and privilege the claims of individuals" by creating "sealed

---

[228] Arundhati ROY in conversation with Sirish RAO (*YouTube*); qtd. from Alex TICKELL, "Writing
in the Necropolis: Arundhati Roy's *The Ministry of Utmost Happiness*," *Moving Worlds: A Journal of Transcultural Studies* 18.1 (2018): 100-112, here: 2.

[229] DAYAL 92 and passim.

[230] See NANCY 33-34 and the introduction to our book.

spaces" and air-conditioned bubbles for the individualized few, while resulting in an increasingly uninhabitable environment for the many.[231]

In *The Ministry of Utmost Happiness*, Roy uses her poetic style of prose and her wry powers of irony for delivering devastating articulations of such a view of globalizing New Delhi:

> Around her the city sprawled for miles. Thousand-year-old sorceress, dozing, but not asleep, even at this hour. Grey flyovers snaked out of her Medusa skull, tangling and untangling under the yellow sodium haze. Sleeping bodies of homeless people lined their high, narrow pavements, head to toe, head to toe, head to toe, looping into the distance. Old secrets were folded into the furrows of her loose, parchment skin. [...] But this was to be the dawn of her resurrection. Her new masters wanted to hide her knobby, varicose veins under imported fishnet stockings, cram her withered tits into saucy padded bras and jam her aching feet into pointed high-heeled shoes. [...] It was the summer Grandma became a whore.[232]

Significantly, the subject around whom this evocation of Delhi is made to accrue ("Around her the city sprawled for miles") is a newly arrived outsider: the daughter of a Telugu woman and member of a Maoist guerrilla who has left her baby at Jantar Mantar, hoping she might be adopted by a well-meaning person. It is against the presence of the Adivasi infant that Delhi takes shape as a quasi-mythological character, revealing both its ancient power and its current debasement. In this context, the quoted passage figures the globalist transformation of the city as an act of prostitution and as a ghastly travesty: "Kmart was coming. Walmart and Starbucks were coming, and in the British Airways advertisement on TV, the People of the World (white, brown, black, yellow) all chanted the Gayatri Mantra."[233] As Roy's narrative suggests, the new globalist splendour of the "tormented city"[234] is a distorting imposition, while Delhi's 'real' character emerges only in the presence and in the consciousness of its normal, poor inhabitants[235] – and thus of the very people whom the joint regime of capitalist globalism and vapid nationalism is making homeless and invisible:

---

[231]   SENNETT, *Flesh and Stone* 369, 347-349.

[232]   Arundhati ROY, *The Ministry of Utmost Happiness* (London: Hamish Hamilton / Penguin, 2017) 96.

[233]   ROY, *Ministry* 97.

[234]   Thus the epigraph to this part of the novel, which quotes Pablo Neruda (ROY 93).

[235]   Cf. ROY, *Ministry* 301, where the narrative boasts a particularly moving and shrewd image for the relation between the city and its dispossessed. It does so by having Tilo look out of her window very early one morning and watch "migrant workers from roadworks nearby," standing "around a tiny boy as he squatted like a comma on the edge of an open manhole": "The spirit moved him. He made a pool. A yellow leaf. His mother put down her axe and washed his bottom

All day long the roads were choked with traffic. The newly dispossessed, who lived in the cracks and fissures of the city, emerged and swarmed around the sleek, climate-controlled cars, selling cloth dusters, mobile phone chargers, model jumbo jets, business magazines, pirated management books […], gourmet guides, interior design magazines with colour photographs of country houses in Provence, and quick-fix spiritual manuals […]. On Independence Day they sold toy machine guns and tiny national flags mounted on stands that said *Mera Bharat Mahan*, My India Is Great. The passengers looked out of their car windows and saw only the new apartment they planned to buy, the Jacuzzi they had just installed and the ink that was still wet on the sweetheart deal they had just closed.[236]

The keynote of this passage (and of many similar passages in the novel) is social apathy or socio-sensorial disarticulation. The frenzy of globalist change, Roy suggests, is creating a discourse and a sociocultural climate in which the poor majority (who has been written off as a "surplus"[237]) is rendered invisible, voiceless and untouchable. Indeed, Roy's narrative insists that globalist modernization is far from abolishing casteism. Rather, it results in grafting new forms of untouchability on top of the traditional ones. Roy strikingly expresses this correlation in her portrayal of how Biplab's tenant treats her young maid. Initially, the narrative presents the tenant – from Biplab's perspective – as the typical representative of an upwardly ambitious and globally conscious new middle class:

"I'm Ankita," she said over her shoulder as she led me in. Her long, chemically straightened hair streaked with blonde highlights was damp and I could smell her tangy shampoo. She wore solitaires in her ears and a fuzzy white wool sweater. The back pockets of her tight blue jeans – 'jeggings',

---

with muddy water from an old Bisleri bottle. With the leftover water she washed her hands, and washed the yellow leaf into the manhole. Nothing in the city belonged to the women. Not a tiny plot of land, not a hovel in a slum, not a tin sheet over their heads. Not even the sewage system. But now they had made a direct, unorthodox deposit, an express delivery straight into the system. Maybe it marked the beginning of a foothold in the city." Contrasting their total exclusion from actual citizenship to their centrality to the city's upkeep and meaning, the passage strikingly captures both the powerlessness and the power of the dispossessed workers.

[236] ROY, *Ministry* 100.

[237] Cf. ROY, *Ministry* 100-101: "On the city's industrial outskirts, in the miles of bright swamp tightly compacted with refuse and colourful plastic bags, where the evicted had been 're-settled', the air was chemical and the water poisonous. […] Surplus mothers perched like sparrows on the debris of what used to be their homes and sang their surplus children to sleep. […] The surplus children slept, dreaming of yellow 'dozers."

my daughters say they're called – stretched over her generous behind
were embroidered with colourful forked-tongued Chinese dragons.[238]

However, the signally 'liberal' costume and bearing of the hostess are starkly at
odds with the outrageous theatre of submission and domination that she stages
in presenting her maid: "At one point we had to clasp our knees and lift our feet
off the floor while her maid passed below us, shuffling on her haunches like a
small duck, swabbing the floor with something that smelled sharp, like citron-
ella."[239] Significantly, Biplab is able to clearly locate the servant's status in the
caste system: "The maid was obviously a Gond or a Santhal from Jharkhand or
Chhattisgarh, or perhaps one of the aboriginal tribes in Orissa."[240]

As has been indicated, however, the major point of *The Ministry of Utmost
Happiness* – the point that saves the novel's title from being (merely) ironic – is
in evolving a counterpoint to the bleak portrayal of n/New Delhi as a dismal instance of unworlding. In order to craft the vision of an alternative present and a
better future, Roy returns to Old Delhi, which the discourse of the novel frequently refers to as "the old city" or as "Shahjahanabad." Thus, we learn that
Anjum – the main protagonist of *The Ministry of Utmost Happiness* – was born
"in Shahjahanabad, the walled city of Delhi."[241] While the newer parts of the capital are made to appear as an unreal and unworldly network of flyovers, the novel
carefully evokes the concrete presence of Old Delhi as an experientially graspable
and felt though complex site – an urban landscape which has deep roots in stories
or histories and which connects to a rich spiritual topography. Consider the following passage, which paints a picture of how Anjum (who is here still referred
to by her original boy's name: Aftab) spent her/his childhood days:

> Aftab spent hours on the tiny balcony of his home looking down at Chitli
> Qabar – the tiny shrine of the spotted goat who was said to have had su-
> pernatural powers – and the busy street that ran past it and joined the
> Matia Mahal Chowk. He quickly learned the cadence and rhythm of the
> neighbourhood, which was essentially a stream of Urdu invective – I'll
> fuck your mother, go fuck your sister, I swear by your mother's cock –
> that was interrupted five times a day by the call to prayer from the Jama
> Masjid as well as the several other smaller mosques in the old city. As
> Aftab kept strict vigil, day after day, over nothing in particular, Guddu

---

[238] ROY, *Ministry* 148.
[239] ROY, *Ministry* 148.
[240] ROY, *Ministry* 148-149. Cf. 260, where Biplab's first-person narration refers to the servant as
       "Ankita['s] […] little Adivasi child-slave."
[241] ROY, *Ministry* 7. This is the first of many times that the name Shahjahanabad is used. Cf. the
       following instructively worded entry in Roy's list of acknowledgements: "The Jhinjhanvis […]
       for a home in Shahjahanabad" (441).

Bhai, the acrimonious early-morning fishmonger who parked his cart of
gleaming fresh fish in the centre of the chowk, would, as surely as the sun
rose in the east and set in the west, elongate into Wasim, the tall, affable
afternoon naan khatai-seller who would then shrink into Yunus, the
small, lean, evening fruit-seller, who, late at night, would broaden and
balloon into Hassan Mian, the stout vendor of the best mutton biryani in
Matia Mahal, which he dished out of a huge copper pot.[242]

Joining Anjum/Aftab on the "tiny balcony," the reader is made to experience or
imagine Old Delhi as a world of details, an engaging tapestry of visual and acoustic impressions that link to specific forms of localized or culture-specific
knowledge. The scene is rendered insistently authentic by listing the names of
concrete localities such as Chitli Qabar, Matia Mahal Chowk and Jama Masjid –
and although these names (with the exception of Jama Masjid) are probably unknown to most of the novel's international readers, they are used as if they were
naturally familiar. The specific local knowledge thus displayed in the passage
constitutes a world – a world that comprises not only places but also people, linking both in an articulatory circuit of mutual animation and identification. In this
spirit, the narrative goes out of its way to report the names and trades of a roaster
of characters who have no further importance to the plot: Guddu Bhai, Wasim,
Yunus, Hassan Mian. The locationally grounded and intimately peopled world
thus evoked is characterized by what the sociologist Hartmut Rosa terms "resonance": it draws the subject into its network of connectivities by meaningfully
responding to her or his inquisitive attention.[243] In this resonant world, people,
practices and objects are integrated by means of the specific "cadence and rhythm
of the neighbourhood."

Moreover, the quoted passage relates that "cadence and rhythm" to linguistic
practices – specifically to Urdu and to the "call for prayer" issued in that language
"five times a day." It would not be going too far to say that *The Ministry of Utmost
Happiness* sets up Urdu as both the constitutive articulatory characteristic of a
specific terrain of consciousness and as the medium of a worlding – i.e. a cultural
articulation or re-articulation of the social in its relation to the natural – that may
offer resonant alternatives to the destructive aspects of globalization. In line with
similar tendencies in Dasgupta's *Capital*, however, this gestural positioning of
Urdu as a privileged articulatory device should not be read as an argument for a

---

[242] ROY, *Ministry* 17-18.
[243] See Hartmut ROSA, *Resonanz: Eine Soziologie der Weltbeziehung* (Berlin: Suhrkamp, 2016). The
       title of Rosa's book, which works an alternative introduction to and as a fundamental recalibra-
       tion of sociology, might be translated as: "Resonance: A Sociology of Relating to the World."

Muslim India but rather as plea for returning to culturally, ethnically and linguistically more pluralist and integrative Indian legacies – legacies that might be described as both more (or differently) 'traditional' and more 'cosmopolitan.' The drift of the implied argument becomes clearer, if we consider one of the many similar passages in Dasgupta's analysis of Delhi. Commenting on his experiences on visiting a retired colonel who writes poetry, the literary reporter muses:

> Severe and regimented in his general dealings, something tender and mellifluous emerges from Colonel Oberoi in our conversation about poetry. It comes, in part, from the memory of stupendous nature in the mind of this man who has lived so long in what has become one of the world's largest conurbations. But his Urdu poetry asserts also his allegiance to a lost culture, one that Hindus like him once shared with Muslims, a cosmopolitan, multilingual culture in which poetry and the life of the spirit found more ample expression.[244]

As we have seen in my discussion of *Capital*, Dasgupta hears Urdu as conserving traces of a lost cultural and linguistic elegance that he identifies as once having been the shared characteristic of an integrated "Hindustani culture" that has been sacrificed in the traumatic process of Separation. Moreover, he points out that these traces survive most clearly in the spoken language of the underprivileged – or, as he puts it, in "the speech of the working classes, who had come in from other places where the poetic, ecstatic elements of Hindustani had not become foreign."[245]

Interestingly, Roy makes exactly the same point in *The Ministry of Utmost Happiness*. Thus, when Anjum interferes in the commotion caused by the unattended baby at Jantar Mantar the narrator comments: "Those who could understand what she was saying were a little intimidated by the refinement of her Urdu. It was at odds with the class they assumed she came from."[246] Anjum's language – and her facility with or relationship to language – is a vehicle of her primary function in the novel: to serve as an agent of the alternative worlding imagined and proposed by Roy. In his role as the first-person narrator of one of the novel's sections, Biplab reports his first encounter with the protagonist: "The woman-man speaks to me in a voice that sounds like two voices. She speaks the most beautiful Urdu. She says her name is Anjum."[247] On the figurative level, the impression that Anjum's voice "sounds like two voices" connects to her ability to build communities by integrating diverse ways of speaking and diverging subject

---

[244] DASGUPTA 184.
[245] DASGUPTA 174-177; quotation: 176.
[246] ROY, *Ministry* 119.
[247] ROY, *Ministry* 207.

positions. At the same time, the twofold quality of Anjum's voice expresses her special identity as a "hijra" – i.e. as what Biplab thinks of as a "woman-man," a person who integrates male and female identities. Indeed, *The Ministry of Utmost Happiness* resembles Khushwant Singh's *Delhi: A Novel* (1990) in suggesting a hijra as the representation of India's capital – of its specific articulatory powers of integration and transformation as well as of the specific tensions underlying its heterogeneity.

Yet more insistently than Singh, however, Roy proffers her 'hermaphrodite' character not only as an allegory of the capital but also as an allegory of the nation – more precisely speaking: as a traditionally legitimated alternative allegory of the nation, a provocatively different version of 'Mother India.' In this role, Anjum's difficult and painful task consists in embodying and rearticulating the postcolonial programmatic of 'unity in diversity.' In a way that is characteristic for Roy's writing – and especially for *The Ministry of Utmost Happiness* – the novel insistently foregrounds the functionality of its dramaturgy and poetics. Thus, the motto displayed on the novel's back cover – "How to tell a shattered story? By slowly becoming everybody. No. By slowly becoming everything" – proves a variant of Anjum's most important self-characterization: "I'm a gathering," the protagonist is made to declare close to the beginning of the novel, "[o]f everybody and nobody, of everything and nothing. Everyone's invited."[248]

As Anjum's dramatic life story shows, being or becoming a "gathering" is a struggle. This struggle – which is clearly to be read as alluding to the struggle of Delhi and of India in total – figures on the biographical level in Anjum's painful but determined exertions to come to terms with her ambiguous gender and her difficult sexuality. The first major step she takes is to move into a community of hijras: the Khwabgha or "House of Dreams,"[249] which is situated in the heart of Old Delhi. In this line of the story, the accent is on the proposition that coming to terms with one's identity is not possible on the level of individuality but can only be achieved by means of building a community. Significantly, the Khwabgha community represented in the novel not only includes hijras who possess various kinds of bodies and desires, but it also stands as a largely successful experiment of interreligious cohabitation: it features Hindus as well as Muslims, and there is even one Christian household member.

However, a traumatic experience Anjum makes with interreligious violence results in a depression to which the hijra household cannot adequately respond. Eventually, Anjum decides to leave the Khwabgha and singlehandedly restart her life. She does so by literally *moving* to a Muslim graveyard in Old Delhi. This

---

[248] ROY, *Ministry* 4.
[249] ROY, *Ministry* 19.

graveyard, which figures as the main site of Anjum's – and the novel's – worldmaking or worlding, is first introduced in the novel's opening vignette:

> At magic hour, when the sun has gone but the light has not, armies of flying foxes unhinge themselves from the Banyan trees in the old grave- yard and drift across the city like smoke. When the bats leave, the crows come home. Not all the din of their homecoming fills the silence left by the sparrows that have gone missing, and the old white-backed vultures, custodians of the dead for more than a hundred million years, that have been wiped out. The vultures died of diclofenac poisoning. Diclofenac, cow-aspirin, given to cattle as a muscle relaxant, to ease pain and increase the production of milk, works – worked – like nerve gas on white-backed vultures. Each chemically relaxed, milk-producing cow or buffalo that died became poisoned vulture-bait. As cattle turned into better dairy ma- chines, as the city ate more ice cream, butterscotch-crunch, nutty-buddy and chocolate-chip, as it drank more mango milkshake, vultures' necks began to droop as though they were tired and simply couldn't stay awake. Silver beards of saliva dripped from their beaks, and one by one they tum- bled off their branches, dead. Not many noticed the passing of the friendly old birds. There was so much else to look forward to.[250]

This highly atmospheric and simultaneously wry opening makes the reader come to the novel – and to Delhi – from an ecological perspective. Even before we en- counter Anjum as an agent of community building, she is introduced as a lone chronicler of the environmental damage done by "the city" – i.e. by n/New Delhi as a hub of capitalist consumerism and globalist progressivism. For all its deso- lateness, Anjum's new life practice in the graveyard has a purpose: to become aware of the damage done by "the city" and to remember the victims of its hunger or thirst. Indeed, Anjum restarts her life by restarting her relationship to the city as a natural habitat: "She lived in the graveyard like a tree."[251] The work done by the protagonist here is the work of breaking with what Sennett characterizes as the "sensate apathy" that results from the mode of life characteristic of the mod- ern city, where "[i]ndividualism and the facts of speed together deaden the mod- ern body" so that it becomes unable to "connect."[252]

Having re-connected to nature by building a resonant community with ani- mals and with the ghosts of animals, Anjum's next step is to re-connect to her human environment and to re-construct a social community with other people. Here is how the novel not only describes but downright forces this process:

---

[250] ROY, *Ministry* 1.
[251] ROY, *Ministry* 3.
[252] SENNETT, *Flesh and Stone* 323-324.

Gradually the Fort of Desolation scaled down into a dwelling of manage-
able proportions. It became home; a place of predictable, reassuring sorrow – awful, but reliable. [...] As the Fort of Desolation scaled down,
Anjum's tin shack scaled up. It grew first into a hut that could accommodate a bed, and then into a small house with a little kitchen.[253]

These passages develop a theme that had already been prepared for in the previous descriptions of the Khwabgha household: domesticity. Anjum and the novel
respond to the increasing uninhabitability of "the city" by creating habitable in-
teriors, i.e. by a strategy of home-making:

So as not to attract undue attention, she left the exterior walls rough and
unfinished. The inside she plastered and painted an unusual shade of
fuchsia. She put in a sandstone roof supported on iron girders, which
gave her a terrace on which, in the winter, she would put out a plastic
chair and dry her hair and sun her chapped, scaly shins while she sur-
veyed the dominion of the dead.[254]

The narrative literally revels in the thrilling and potentially cosy contrast of inside
and outside. At the same time, it marks out Anjum's expanding graveyard dwelling as a quasi-utopian space – a space that can (at present) exist only in the imagination or only as long as it remains undetected by the agents of order. The
quoted passage also reinforces the notion, introduced in the opening vignette,
that Anjum's power of worldmaking depends on her ability and willingness to
remember: "Over time Anjum began to enclose the graves of her relatives and
build rooms around them. Each room had a grave (or two) and a bed. Or two."[255]
The habitable space created by and around Anjum includes both the dead and
the living. Habitability, hospitality and commemoration go hand in hand. What
began with Anjum sleeping in the open on the graves of her relatives ends up by
her running a combined guest house and funeral service that she chooses to name
"Jannat" – an Urdu term that the narrative translates as "Paradise."[256]

   Among the various people drawn and accepted into the orbit of the Jannat
Guest House are the drug addicts who regularly hang out on the fringes of the
graveyard. The most important associate in Anjum's enterprise of worlding or
worldmaking, however, is a young Hindu Dalit who has responded to the trauma
of anti-minoritarian violence by posing as a Muslim, provocatively taking on the
name Saddam Hussain. The novel reaches its closure when these two heterogeneous characters finally welcome Tilo into the community they have assembled

---

[253] ROY, *Ministry* 66-67.
[254] ROY, *Ministry* 67.
[255] ROY, *Ministry* 68.
[256] ROY, *Ministry* 68.

around themselves. She is to inhabit the room built around the grave of Ahlam Baji, a former midwife and Old Delhi institution:

> Saddam and Anjum showed Tilo to the room they had readied for her on the ground floor. She would share it with Comrade Laali and family, Miss Jebeen and Ahlam Baji's grave. Payal-the-mare was tethered outside the window. […] Anjum introduced Tilo to Ahlam Baji as though Ahlam Baji were still alive. She recounted her accomplishments and achievements and listed the names of some of Shahjahanabad's luminaries that she had helped bring into the world – Akbar Mian the baker, maker of the best sheermal in the walled city, Jabbar Bhai the tailor, Sabiha Alvi, whose daughter had just started a Benarasi Sari Emporium in the first-floor room of their house. Anjum spoke as though it was a world that Tilo was familiar with, a world that everybody ought to be familiar with; in fact, the only world worth being familiar with.[257]

These sentences share many of the characteristics highlighted above in reference to the passage on Anjum's childhood. This indicates that the "Ministry of Utmost Happiness" created at the end of the novel (and postulated in the title of the respective chapter) successfully returns to the specific terrain of consciousness as which the novel makes us see Old Delhi. However, the passage represents a return with a difference: it marries traditionalism to an ameliorative version of progress. Indeed, the highly inclusive patchwork family created by the hijra protagonist and her Dalit aide can be read – and is intended to be read – as a *modern* institution of its own kind. In the integrative, open and expandable micro-society here dreamt up by Roy, Tilo significantly feels "[f]or the first time in her life" that "her body [has] enough room to accommodate all its organs."[258] "World" is the keyword and keynote of the passage: "Anjum spoke as though it was a world that Tilo was familiar with, a world that everybody ought to be familiar with; in fact, the only world worth being familiar with." Roy thus presents the vision of a terrain of consciousness which comprises a *world* – and which is still firmly opposed to the precepts of *globalization*.

---

[257]   ROY, *Ministry* 304-305.
[258]   ROY, *Ministry* 305.

Works Cited

ADIGA, Aravind. *The White Tiger.* London: Atlantic, 2008.

AHMAD, Na'im, ed. *Shahr-Ashob.* Translated by Frances W. Pritchett. Delhi: Maktabah Jami'ah Ltd., 1968.

AHMED, Sara. "The Orient and Other Others." *Queer Phenomenology: Orientations, Objects, Others.* Durham: Duke University Press, 2006. 109-156.

ALI, Agha Shahid. *Bone Sculpture.* Calcutta: Writers Workshop, 1972.

-----. *In Memory of Begum Akhtar: Poems by Agha Shahid Ali.* Calcutta: Writers Workshop, 1979.

-----. *The Veiled Suite: The Collected Poems.* New York: WW Norton, 2010.

ALI, Ahmed. *Twilight in Delhi.* 1940. New Delhi: Rupa, 2007.

ALI, Semeen. Dilli: *An Anthology of Women Poets of Delhi.* Eastern Cape: The Poets Printery, 2014.

ANDERSON, Benedict. *Imagined Communities: Reflections on the Origin and Spread of Nationalism.* London: Verso, 1983.

ANDERSON, Emma. "German Teen Launches Global Feminist Trend." *The Local* (German Edition), 20 March 2015. Web (accessed on 7 July 2021).

ANJARIA, Jonathan Shapiro, and Ulka ANJARIA. "*Slumdog Millionaire* and Epistemologies of the City." *Economic and Political Weekly* 45.24 (2010): 41-46.

APPADURAI, Arjun. *Fear of Small Numbers: An Essay on the Geography of Anger.* Durham: Duke University Press, 2006.

-----. *Modernity at Large: Cultural Dimensions of* Globalization. Minneapolis: Minnesota University Press, 1996.

ARMSTRONG, Philipp. *What Animals Mean in the Fiction of Modernity.* New York: Routledge, 2008.

AYYUB, Rana. "Bilkis: The Hundred Most Influential People of 2020." *Time*, 22 September 2020. Web (accessed on 7 July 2021).

AZAD, Nikita. "Pinjra Tod: Stop Caging Women behind College Hostel Bars." *Feminism in India: Intersectional Feminism – Desi Style!*, 30 September 2015. Web (accessed on 7 July 2021).

BAIG, Mirza Farhatullah. *Dehli ki Aakhri Shama*. [The Last Mushaira of Delhi.] Trans. by Akhta Qamber. New Delhi: Orient Blackswan, 2010.

BANERJI, Rita. "The Pink Panties Campaign: The Indian Women's Sexual Revolution." *Intersections: Gender and Sexuality in Asia and the Pacific*, 23 January 2010. Web (accessed on 7 July 2021).

-----. "Besharmi Morcha, 'Shameless Protest.'" *Remember Our Sisters Everywhere*, 24 July 2011. Web (accessed on 7 July 2021).

-----. "SlutWalk to Femicide: Making the Connection." *The Women's International Perspective*, 2 September 2011. Web (accessed on 7 July 2021).

BASNET, Minu. "Disrobed and Dissenting Bodies of the Meira Paibi: Postcolonial Counterpublic Activism." *Communication and the Public* 4.3 (2019): 239-252.

BAVISKAR, Amita. "Between Violence and Desire: Space, Power, and Identity in the Making of Metropolitan Delhi." 2003. Rpt. in *International Social Science Journal* 68 (2018): 199-208.

BAWEJA, Vandana. "Architecture and Urbanism in *Slumdog Millionaire*: From Bombay to Mumbai." *Traditional Dwellings and Settlements Review*, 26.2 (2015): 7-24.

"BBC 100 Women 2020: Who is on the list this year?" *BBC News*, 23 November 2020. Web (accessed on 7 July 2021).

BELGIOJOSO, Ricciarda. *Constructing Urban Space with Sounds and Music*. Farnham: Ashgate, 2014.

BHAGYA, C. S., and G. J. V. PRASAD. "'Capital' Consciousness: Reading Rana Dasgupta." *Journal of Postcolonial Writing* 54.3 (2018): 346-359.

BHAN, Gautam. "The Impoverishment of Poverty: Reflections on Urban Citizenship and Inequality in Contemporary Delhi." *Environment and Urbanization* 26.2 (2014): 547-560.

BHATTACHARYA, Rakhee. "Identity Consolidation of Meitei Women: Reflections on Women's War." *Nationhood and Identity Movements in Asia: Colonial and Post-Colonial Times.* Ed. Swarupa GUPTA. New Delhi: Manohar, 2012.

BIJSTERVELD, Karin, ed. *Soundscapes of the Urban Past: Staged Sound as Mediated Cultural Heritage.* Bielefeld: transcript, 2013.

Blank Noise. *Blank Noise.* Web (accessed on 7 July 2021). <http://www.blanknoise.org/>

BLEWETT, David. "The Iconic Crusoe." *The Cambridge Companion to 'Robinson Crusoe.'* Ed. John RICHETTI. Cambridge: Cambridge University Press, 2018. 159-190.

BUCK-MORSS, Susan. *Hegel, Haiti, and Universal History.* Pittsburgh: University of Pittsburgh Press, 2009.

BUELL, Lawrence. "Space, Place, and Imagination from Local to Global." *The Future of Environmental Criticism: Environmental Crisis and Literary Imagination.* Malden, MA: Blackwell, 2005. 62-96.

BULL, Michael. *Sound Moves: iPod Culture and Urban Experience.* London: Routledge, 2007.

BULL, Michael, and Les BACK. "Introduction Into Sound ... Once More with Feeling." *The Auditory Culture Reader.* 2nd ed. Abingdon: Routledge, 2020. 1-20.

CADÈNE, Philippe. "Delhi's Place in India's Urban Structure." *Delhi: Urban Space and Human Destinies.* Ed. Véronique DUPONT, Emma TARLO, and Denis VIDAL. New Delhi: Manohar, 2000. 241-249.

CHAKRABARTY, DIPESH. *The Crises of Civilization: Exploring Global and Planetary Histories.* Oxford: Oxford University Press, 2016.

-----. "The Global and the Planetary: Some Thoughts on Our Times," SPARC (online) conference "New Terrains of Consciousness." February 2021, Keynote Lecture.

-----. "Open Space / Public Space: Garbage, Modernity and India." *South Asia* 14.1 (1994): 15-31.

CHAKRABORTY, Madhurima. "Introduction: Whose City?" *Postcolonial Urban Outcasts: City Margins in South Asian Literature.* Eds. Madhurima Chakraborty and Umme Al-Wazedi. New York: Routledge, 2017. 1-18.

CHANDOLA, Tripta. *Listening in to Others: In between Noise and Silence.* PhD thesis, Queensland University of Technology, 2010. Web.

CHATTERJEE, Debangana. "Masooma Ranalvi – Fighting the Odds of Female Genital Cutting in India." (Excerpts from interview with Masooma RANALVI, 22 August 2018) *Be! Life Beyond Numbers,* 28 April 2020. Web (accessed on 7 July 2021).

CHATTERJEE, Partha. *The Politics of the Governed: Reflections on Popular Politics in Most of the World.* New York: Columbia University Press, 2004.

CHAUDHURI, Maitrayee, eds. *Feminism in India.* New Delhi: Kali for Women/ Women Unlimited, 2004.

CHEA, Pheng. "Worlding: The Phenomenological Concept of Worldliness and the Loss of World in Modernity." *What is a World? On Postcolonial Literature as World Literature.* Durham: Duke University Press, 2016. 95-130.

ÇINAR, Alev, and Thomas BENDER, eds. *Urban Imaginaries: Locating the Modern City.* Minneapolis: University of Minnesota Press, 2007.

COELHO, Karen, Lalitha KAMATH, and M. VIJAYBASKAR, eds. *Participolis: Consent and Contention in Neoliberal Urban India.* New Delhi: Routledge, 2013.

Consortium of Pub-Going, Loose and Forward Women, "The Pink Chaddi Campaign." Blog, 8 Feb. – 11 Apr. 2009. Web (accessed on 7 July 2021).

COWAN, Alexander, and Jill STEWARD, eds., *The City and the Senses: Urban Culture Since 1500.* Aldershot: Ashgate, 2007.

Cowen, Tyler. *Creative Destruction: How Globalisation is Changing the World's Culture.* Princeton: Princeton University Press, 2002.

CRUTZEN, Paul J. "Geology of Mankind." *Nature,* 3 Jan. 2002: 23.

DASGUPTA, Rana. *Capital: A Portrait of Twenty-First Century Delhi.* 2014. Rpt. as *Capital: The Eruption of Delhi.* Edinburgh: Canongate, 2015.

DAYAL, Samir. "Normative Materialist Cosmopolitanism." *New Cosmopolitanisms, Race, and Ethnicity: Cultural Perspectives.* Ed. Ewa Barbara LUCZAK, Anna POCHMARA, and Samir DAYAL. Berlin: De Gruyter, 2019. 90-113.

DE CERTEAU, Michel. *The Practice of Everyday Life.* Trans. Steven Rendall. Berkeley: University of California Press, 1984.

DEB, Siddhartha. *The Beautiful and the Damned: Life in New India.* New Delhi: Penguin, 2010.

DEFAZIO, Kimberly. *The City of the Senses: Urban Culture and Urban Space.* New York: Palgrave Macmillan, 2011.

DEFOE, Daniel. *A New Voyage Round the World by a Course Never Sailed Before.* Ed. George A. AITKIN. London: Dent, 1902.

-----. *The Novels of Daniel Defoe.* Ed. W. R. OWENS, W. R. FURBANK, John MULLAN. 10 vols. London: Pickering & Chatto, 2008-2009.

DESAI, Anita. *In Custody.* 1984. London: Vintage, 1999.

DEVI, Ksh. Bimola. "Women in Social Movements in Manipur." *Social Movements in North-East India.* Ed. M.N. KARNA. New Delhi: Indus, 1998.

DIACONU, Mădălina, Eva HEUBERGER, Ruth MATEUS-BERR, and Lukas Marcel VOSICKY, eds. *Senses and the City: An Interdisciplinary Approach to Urban Sensescapes.* Wien: LIT, 2011.

DONALD, James. "Metropolis: The City as Text." *Social and Cultural Forms of Modernity.* Ed. Robert BOCOCK and Kenneth THOMPSON. Cambridge: Polity Press / Open University, 1992. 417-461.

DUPONT, Véronique, Emma TARLO, and Denis VIDAL, eds. *Delhi: Urban Space and Human Destinies.* New Delhi: Manohar, 2000.

DVORAK, Marta. *The Faces of Carnival in Anita Desai's* In Custody. Paris: Presses Universitaires de France, 2008.

FALLON, Ann Marie. *Global Crusoe: Comparative Literature, Postcolonial Theory and Transnational Aesthetics.* Farnham: Ashgate, 2011.

FARIDI, A. H. "Hamare Mushaire." *Tarikh o tanqid.* Ed. H. H. QADIRI. Agra: Lakshmi Narayan Agarwal. 2nd ed., 1947.

FARUQI, Shamsur Rahman. "A long history of Urdu literary culture, Part 1: Naming and placing a literary culture." *Literary Cultures in History: Reconstructions From South Asia*. Ed. Sheldon POLLOCK. Berkeley/Los Angeles: University of California Press, 2003. 805-863.

FREE, Melissa. "Un-erasing *Crusoe: Farther Adventures* in the Nineteenth-Century." *Book History* 9 (2006): 89-130.

GANDY, Matthew, and B. J. NILSEN, eds. *The Acoustic City*. Berlin: Jovis, 2014.

Gayer, Laurent, and Christopher Jaffrelot, eds. Muslims in Indian Cities: Trajectories of Marginalization. London: Hurst, 2011.

GHOSHAL, Devjyot. "A Brief History of #HokKolorob, the Hashtag that Shook Kolkata." *Quartz India*, 9 October 2014. Web (accessed on 7 July 2021).

GIDDENS, Anthony. *The Consequences of Modernity*. Cambridge: Polity Press, 1990.

GIDWANI, Vinay, and Rajyashree N. REDDY. "The Afterlives of 'Waste': Notes from India for a Minor History of Capitalist Surplus." *Antipode* 43.5 (2011): 1625–1658.

GUHA, Ramachandra. "Chipko: Social History of an 'Environmental' Movement." *The Unquiet Woods: Ecological Change and Peasant Resistance in the Himalaya*. Delhi: Oxford University Press, 1991. 152-184.

-----. "How the Filthy Rich Live in Rising Asia." Rev. of *Capital*. *The New Republic*, 15 October 2014.

GUI, Weihsin. "Creative Destruction and Narrative Renovation: Neoliberalism and the Aesthetic Dimension in the Fiction of Aravind Adiga and Mohsin Hamid." *The Global South* 7.2 (2013): 173-190.

HABERMAS, Jürgen. *Strukturwandel der Öffentlichkeit*. 1962. Frankfurt: Suhrkamp, 1990.

HAIDER, Saraswati. "Migrant Women and Urban Experience in a Squatter Settlement." *Delhi: Urban Space and Human Destinies*. Eds. Véronique DUPONT, Emma TARLO, and Denis VIDAL. 29-49.

HARAWAY, Donna. "Situated Knowledges: The Science Question in Feminism and the Privilege of Partial Perspective." *Feminist Studies* 14.3 (1988): 575-599.

-----. *Staying With the Trouble: Making Kin in the Chthulucene.* Durham: Duke University Press, 2016.

-----. *When Species Meet.* Minneapolis: University of Minnesota Press, 2005.

HARDGRAVE, Robert L. Jr. "The Breast-Cloth Controversy: Caste Consciousness and Social Change in Southern Travancore." *The Indian Economic & Social History Review* 5.2 (1968): 171-187.

HARVEY, David. *Spaces of Global Capitalism: A Theory of Uneven Geographical Development.* London: Verso, 2006.

HEISE, Ursula. *Sense of Place and Sense of Planet: The Environmental Imagination of the Global.* Oxford: Oxford University Press, 2008.

HIGHMORE, Ben. "Formations of Feelings, Constellations of Things." *Cultural Studies Review* 22.1 (2016): 144-167.

HOLLINGTON, Michael. "Dickens, the City, and the Five Senses." *Journal of the Australasian Universities Language and Literature Association* 113 (2010): 29-38.

HOLSTON, James, and Arjun APPADURAI. "Cities and Citizenship." *Public Culture* 8 (1996): 187-204.

-----, eds. *Cities and Citizenship.* Durham, NC: Duke University Press, 1999.

INGOLD, Tim. "Building, Dwelling, Living." *The Perception of the Environment: Essays on Livelihood, Dwelling and Skill.* New York: Routledge, 2011. 172-188.

JACOB, Cristian. *The Sovereign Map: Theoretical Approaches in Cartography through History.* Trans. Tom Conley. Chicago: Chicago University Press, 2006.

Jashn-e-Bahar Trust. *Jashn-e-Bahar.* Web (accessed 10 August 2021). <http://jashnebahar.org/>

JEFFRIES, Stuart. "'I'm the luckiest novelist in the world.'" Interview-based feature on Swarup, *Q & A*, and *Slumdog Millionaire. The Guardian*, 16 January 2009.

JOHARI, Aarefa. "'Red Alert: You've Got a Napkin' campaign – Kerala activists fight menstrual taboos #Vaw." *Kractivism: Bridge the Gap Bring the Change*, 1 January 2015. Web (accessed on 7 July 2021).

JOHN, Mary E., ed. *Women's Studies in India: A Reader*. New Delhi: Penguin Books India, 2008.

JOSEPH, Betty. "Capitalism and Its Others: Intersecting and Competing Forms in Eighteenth-Century Fiction." *Studies in Eighteenth-Century Culture* 45 (2016): 157-173.

-----. "Neoliberalism and Allegory." *Cultural Critique* 82 (2012): 68-94.

-----. "Worlding and Unworlding in the Long Eighteenth Century." *Eighteenth-Century Studies* 52.1 (2018): 27-31.

KALYAN, Rohan. *Neo Delhi and the Politics of Postcolonial Urbanism*. London: Routledge, 2017.

KATYAL, Akhil. "'I swear ... I have my hopes': Agha Shahid Ali's Delhi Years." *Kafila: 10 Years of a Common Journey. Kafila Online*, 2011. Web.

KAVIRAJ, Sudipta. "Filth and the Public Sphere: Concepts and Practices About Space in Calcutta." *Public Culture* 10.1 (1997): 83-113.

KHAN, Pasha Mohamad. *The Lament for Delhi*. 1863.

KHILNANI, Sunil. *The Idea of India*. Delhi: Penguin, 2003.

KHOR, Lena. "Can the Subaltern Right Wrongs? – Human Rights and Development in Aravind Adiga's *The White Tiger*." *South Central Review* 29.1/2 (2012): 41-67.

KING, Anthony D. "Re-Presenting World Cities: Cultural Theory/Social Practice." *World Cities in a World-System*. Ed. Paul Leslie KNOX and Peter J. TAYLOR. Cambridge: Cambridge UP, 1995. 215-231.

"Kiss of Love." Facebook page (accessed on 7 July 2021). <https://www.facebook.com/kissoflovekochi/>

LABELLE, Brandon. *Acoustic Territories: Sound Culture and Everyday Life*. New York: Continuum, 2010.

LAL, Vinay. *The Oxford Anthology of the Modern Indian City*. 2 vols. New Delhi: Oxford University Press, 2013.

LANZILLO, Amanda. "Butchers between Archives: Community History in Early Twentieth-Century Delhi." *South Asian History and Culture* (2021). Web.

LASHUA, Brett, Stephen WAGG, Karl SPRACKLEN, and M. Selim YAVUZ, eds. *Sounds and the City*. 2 vols. Houndmills: Palgrave Macmillan, 2014-2019.

LATOUR, Bruno. *Facing Gaia: Eight Lectures on the New Climatic Regime*. Transl. Catherine Porter. Cambridge: Polity, 2017.

LCWRI (Lawyers Collective Women's Rights Initiative), and Speak Out On FGM. Female Genital Mutilation: Guide to Eliminating the FGM Practice in India, Lawyer's Collective, 21 May 2017. Web (accessed on 7 July 2021).

LEAVITT, John. "Meaning and Feeling in the Anthropology of Emotions." *American Ethnologist* 23.3 (1996): 514-539.

LEE, Joel. "Odor and Order: How Caste Is Inscribed in Space and Sensoria." *Comparative Studies of South Asia, Africa and the Middle East* 37.3 (2017): 470-490.

LEFEBVRE, Henri. *The Production of Space*. Translated by Donald Nicholson-Smith. Oxford: Blackwell, 1991.

LEGUIN, Ursula. "The Carrier Bag Theory of Fiction." *Dancing at the Edge of the World: Thoughts on Words, Women, Places*. New York: Grove, 1989. 165-70.

LOKUR, Madan B. "Five Questions on the Shameful Proceedings against Natasha Narwal, Devangana Kalita, Asif Iqbal." *The Wire*, 22 June 2021. Web (accessed on 7 July 2021).

LOW, Kelvin E. Y., and Devorah KALEKIN-FISHMAN, eds. *Senses in Cities: Experiences of Urban Settings*. London: Routledge, 2017.

MACINTOSH, Alex. "Crusoe's Abattoir: Cannibalism and Animal Slaughter in *Robinson Crusoe*." *Critical Quarterly* 53.2 (2011): 24-43.

MAHMOOD, Saif. *Beloved Delhi: A Mughal City and Her Greatest Poets*. New Delhi: Speaking Tigers, 2018.

MAHMUDABAD, Ali Khan. *Poetry of Belonging*. New Delhi: Oxford University Press, 2020.

MANDAL, Dilip. "Why Indian history has forgotten Fatima Sheikh but remembers Savitribai Phule." *The Print*, 9 January 2019. Web (accessed on 7 July 2021).

MARKLEY, Robert. *The Far East and the English Imagination: 1600–1730*. Cambridge: Cambridge University Press, 2006.

-----. "'I have now done with my island, and all manner of discourse about it': Crusoe's *Farther Adventures* and the Unwritten History of the Novel." *A Companion to the Eighteenth-Century English Novel*. Ed. Paula R. BACKSCHEIDER and Catherine INGRASSIA. Oxford: Blackwell, 2008. 25-47.

MARLEWICZ, Halina. "Heterotopian City: Khushwant Singh and His *Delhi: A Novel*." *Politeja* 40 (2016): 159-176.

MCLUHAN, Marshall. *Understanding Media: The Extensions of Man*. 1964. London: Routledge, 2001.

MCQUIRE, Scott. *The Media City: Media, Architecture and Urban Space*. London: SAGE, 2008.

MIN, Eun Kyung. *China and the Writing of English Literary Modernity, 1690–1770*. Cambridge: Cambridge University Press, 2018.

MISHRA, Anupam, and Satyendra Tripathi. *The Chipko Movement*. New Delhi: People's Action/Gandhi Peace Foundation, 1978.

MUKHERJEE, Sajni. "The movement that shook Kolkata." *India Today*, 27 February 2015. Web (accessed on 7 July 2021).

NAIM, Choudhary M. *Readings in Urdu: Prose and Poetry*. Honolulu: East-West Center Press, 1965.

NAIR, Janaki. *The Promise of the Metropolis*. New Delhi: Oxford University Press, 2005.

NANCY, Jean-Luc. *The Creation of the World, or Globalization*. Transl. François Raffoul and David Pettigrew. New York: SUNY, 2007.

NANDI, Miriam. "Longing for the Lost (M)Other – Postcolonial Ambivalences in Arundhati Roy's *The God of Small Things.*" *Journal of Postcolonial Writing* 46.2 (2010): 175-186.

NANDY, Ashis. "Indian Popular Cinema as the Slum's Eye View of Politics." *The Secret Politics of Our Desires: Innocence, Culpability and Indian Popular Cinema.* Ed. NANDY. Delhi: Oxford University Press, 1998. 1-18.

NAQVI, Zehra. "The Nanis and Dadis of Shaheen Bagh … not just Dadis." *The Indian Express*, 3 February 2020. Web (accessed on 7 July 2021).

NARULA, Monica. "(For) Those Who Live in Cities." *Cities of Everyday Life.* Ed. Sarai: The New Media Initiative. New Delhi: Sarai, 2002. 107.

NEPRAM, Binalakshmi. "A Narrative on the Origin of the Meira Paibis." Webcast lecture, 9 January 2005. Pub. in *E-Pao: Now the World Knows.* Web (accessed on 7 July 2021).

NEUMAN, Daniel M. *The Life of Music in North India: The Organisation of an Artistic Tradition.* Chicago: University of Chicago Press, 1990.

NINGTHOUJA, Malem. "Nupi Lan: Women's War in Manipur." *Reflections* 1.2 (2007): 27.

NOWKA, Scott. "Building the Wall: Crusoe and the Other." *Digital Defoe* 2.1 (2010): 41-57.

OINAM, Sunil. "TOI Social Impact Awards: Lifetime Contribution – Meira Paibi." *Times of India*, 10 January 2013.

PALLASMAA, Juhani. *The Eye of the Skin: Architecture and the Senses.* Chichester: John Wiley & Sons, 2005.

PANDEY, Gyanendra. "Can a Muslim be an Indian?" *Comparative Studies in Society and History* 41.4 (1999): 608-629.

PANDUIT, Rahul. *Hello Bastar: The Untold Story of India's Maoist Movement.* Chennai: Westland/Tranquebar Press, 2011.

PATTEN, Robert L. "From *Sketches* to *Nickleby.*" *The Cambridge Companion to Charles Dickens.* Ed. John O. JORDAN. Cambridge: Cambridge University Press, 2001. 16-33.

PETTIGREW, David. Albany: SUNY Press, 2007.

PLOURDE, Lorraine. *Tokyo Listening: Sound and Sense in a Contemporary City.* Middletown: Wesleyan University Press, 2019.

PRAKASH, Gyan. "Imagining the Modern City, Darkly: Introduction." *Noir Urbanisms: Dystopic Images of the Modern City.* Ed. Gyan PRAKASH. Princeton: Princeton University Press, 2010. 1-14.

-----. "The Urban Turn." *Cities of Everyday Life.* Ed. Sarai: The New Media Initiative. New Delhi: Sarai, 2002. 2-7.

PRATT, Mary Louise. *Imperial Eyes: Travel Writing and Transculturation.* London: Routledge, 1992.

PULAPAKA, Venkat. "The History of Breast Tax and the Revolt of Lower Caste Women in 19th Century Travancore." *STSTW Media,* 17 May 2019. Web (accessed on 7 July 2021).

QUAYUM, Mohammad A., and Md. Mahmudul HASAN, eds. *A Feminist Foremother: Critical Essays on Rokeya Sakhawat Hossain.* Hyderabad: Orient BlackSwan, 2017.

QURESHI, Regula. "Tarannum: The Chanting of Urdu Poetry" *Ethnomusicology* 13.3 (Sep. 1969): 425-468.

RAHBAR, Daud. *Urdu Letters of Ghalib.* New York: State University of New York, 1987.

RAQS MEDIA COLLECTIVE. "The Street Is The Carrier And The Sign." *Cities of Everyday Life.* Ed. Sarai: The New Media Initiative. New Delhi: Sarai, 2002. 93-105.

RAZZACK, Bushra Alvi. *Dilliwali: Celebrating the Woman of Delhi through Poetry.* New Delhi: Authors Press, 2018.

Rekhta Foundation. *Jashn-e-Rekhta.* Web (accessed on 10 August 2021). <https://jashnerekhta.org/>

RESINA, Joan Ramon. *Barcelona's Vocation of Modernity: Rise and Decline of an Urban Image.* Stanford: Stanford University Press, 2008.

RICHETTI, John. "Eurocentric Crusoe: *The Farther Adventures of Robinson Crusoe.*" *Études Anglaises* 72.2 (2019): 213-224.

Rosa, Hartmut. *Resonanz: Eine Soziologie der Weltbeziehung.* Berlin: Suhrkamp, 2016.

Roy, Ananya. "Postcolonial Urbanism: Speed, Hysteria, Mass Dreams." *Worlding Cities: Asian Experiments and the Art of Being Global.* Eds. Ananya Roy and Aihwa Ong. Hoboken: Wiley-Blackwell, 2011. 279-306.

Roy, Arundhati. *Broken Republic.* New Delhi: Penguin, 2013.

-----. *The God of Small Things.* London: Flamingo, 1997.

-----. *The Ministry of Utmost Happiness.* London: Hamish Hamilton / Penguin, 2017.

-----. *Walking with the Comrades.* New Delhi: Penguin, 2011.

Ruswa, Mirza Hadi. *Umrao Jan Ada.* Translated by David Matthews. New Delhi: Rupa, 1996.

Sabisch, Petra. *Choreographing Relations: Practical Philosophy and Contemporary Choreography.* München: epodium, 2011.

Saglio-Yatzimirsky, Marie-Caroline. *Dharavi: From Mega-Slum to Urban Paradigm.* New Delhi: Routledge, 2013.

Sahiyo – United against Female Genital Cutting. Web (accessed on 7 July 2021).

Santhosh, Keerthana. "Dress as a Tool of Empowerment: The Channar Revolt." *Our Heritage* 22.1 (2020): 532-536.

Sarai: The New Media Initiative, ed. *Cities of Everyday Life.* The Sarai Reader 02. New Delhi: Sarai, 2002. Web Publication.

Sarfaraz, Kainat. "In Jamia – How #PadsAgainstSexism Turned into People against Sanitary Pads." *Youth Ki Awaz*, 26 March 2015. Web (accessed on 7 July 2021).

Sarwar, Firoj High. "Christian Missionaries and Female Education in Bengal during East India Company's Rule: a Discourse between Christianised Colonial Domination versus Women Emancipation." *IOSR Journal of Humanities and Social Science* 4.1 (2012): 37-47.

Schafer, R. Murray. *The Vancouver Soundscape.* Burnaby: World Soundscape Project / Simon Fraser University, 1973.

SCHLEIFER, S. Abdallah, ed. *The Muslim 500: The World's 500 Most Influential Muslims 2021.* Amman: The Royal Islamic Strategic Studies Centre, 2020. Web (accessed on 7 July 2021).

SCHMIDGEN, Wolfram. *Eighteenth-Century Fiction and the Law of* Property. Cambridge: Cambridge University Press, 2002.

SEAGER, Nicholas. "Crusoe's Crusade: Defoe, Genocide, and Imperialism." *Études Anglaises* 72.2 (2019): 196-212.

SENNETT, Richard. *Building and Dwelling: Ethics for the City.* New York: Allen Lane, 2018.

-----. *Flesh and Stone: The Body and the City in Western Civilization.* New York: W. W. Norton, 1996.

SHARMA, Alpana. "*Slumdog Millionaire*: The Film, the Reception, the Book, the Global." *Literature/Film Quarterly* 40.3 (2012): 197-215.

SHARMA, Parvati. "decoded+delhi+denuded=Google+Search." *Cities of Everyday Life.* Ed. Sarai: The New Media Initiative. New Delhi: Sarai, 2002. 159-163.

SHARMA, Sunil. "The City of Beauties in Indo-Persian Poetic Landscape." *Comparative Studies of South Asia, Africa and the Middle East* 24.2 (2004): 73-81.

SHIVA, Vandana. "Women in the Forest." *Staying Alive: Women, Ecology and Development.* New Delhi: Zed Books, 1989. 55-95.

SIMMEL, Georg. "The Metropolis and Mental Life." *On Individuality and Social Forms.* Ed. Donald N. LEVINE. Chicago: University of Chicago Press, 1903.

SIMON, Sherry. *Cities in Translation: Intersections of Language and Memory.* London/New York: Routledge, 2012.

SINGH, Khushwant. *City Improbable: Writings on Delhi.* London: Penguin, 2004.

-----. *Delhi: A Novel.* New Delhi: Penguin, 1990.

SINGH, N. Joykumar. *Colonialism to Democracy: A History of Manipur, 1819-1972.* Guwahati & Delhi: Spectrum Publications, 2002.

SLACK, Jennifer Daryl. "The Theory and Method of Articulation in Cultural Studies," *Stuart Hall: Critical Dialogues in Cultural Studies*. Ed. David MORLEY
and Kuan-Hsing CHEN. London: Routledge, 1996. 113-129.

Slumdog Millionaire. Dir. Danny BOYLE. Fox Searchlight Pictures, 2009. Film.

SOJA, Edward. *Postmetropolis: Critical Studies of Cities and Region*. Oxford:
Blackwell, 2000.

SPIVAK, Gayatri Chakravorty. "Planetarity." *The Death of a Discipline*. New York:
Columbia University Press, 2003. 71-102.

SRIVASTAVA, Sonakshi. "The Pink Chaddi Campaign: Women's Fight for Right
to Public Spaces." *Feminism in India: Intersectional Feminism – Desi
Style!,* 20 June 2019. Web (accessed on 7 July 2021).

SULTAN, Parvez. "Historic Mushaira at Red Fort to Mark 69th Republic Day."
Hindustan Times, 11 January 2018. Web.

SUNDAR, Nandini. *The Burning Forest: India's War in Bastar*. Delhi: Juggernaut,
2016.

SUSAN, Nisha. "Valentine's Warriors: The Pink Chaddi Campaign – Why It Began and How." *Tehelka Magazine* 6.8, 28 Feb. 2009.

SWARUP, Vikas. *Q & A*. 2005. London: Black Swan/Random House, 2006.

TAMBE, Anagha. "(Hyper)Visible 'Women'/Invisible (Dalit) Women: Challenging the Elusive Sexism in Indian Universities." *Strategies for Resisting Sexism in the Academy: Higher Education, Gender and Intersectionality*. Ed.
Gail CRIMMINS. Cham, Switzerland: Palgrave Macmillan, 2019. 129-152.

"The Woman Who Cut off Her Breasts to Protest a Tax." *BBC News*, 28 July 2016.
Web (accessed on 7 July 2021).

TICKELL, Alex. "Writing in the Necropolis: Arundhati Roy's *The Ministry of Utmost Happiness*." *Moving Worlds: A Journal of Transcultural Studies* 18.1
(2018): 100-112.

TODD, Dennis. "*Robinson Crusoe* and Colonialism." *The Cambridge Companion
to* Robinson Crusoe. Ed. John RICHETTI. Cambridge: Cambridge University Press, 2018. 142-156.

TUNSTALL, Jeremy. *The Media are American: Anglo-American Media in the World*. London: Constable, 1977.

Velivada Team. "Life Sketch of Savitribai Phule – Timeline." *Velivada: Educate, Agitate, Organize*, 2017. Web (accessed on 7 July 2021).

VERGHESE, Leah, et.al. (script), and Sumon CHITRAKAR (illustrations), *Savitribai: Journey of a* Trailblazer. Bangalore: Azim Premji University, 2014.

VIDAL, Denis, Emma TARLO and Véronique DUPONT. "The Alchemy of an Unloved City." *Delhi: Urban Space and Human Destinies*. Ed. Véronique DUPONT, Emma TARLO, and Denis VIDAL. 15-25.

We Speak Out. 2021. Web (accessed on 7 July 2021). <https://wespeakout.org/>

WEBER, Thomas. *Hugging the Trees: The Story of the Chipko Movement*. New Delhi: Viking Penguin, 1988.

WEINSTEIN, Liza. *The Durable Slum: Dharavi and the Right to Stay Put in Globalizing Mumbai*. Minneapolis: University of Minnesota Press, 2014. Globalization and Community 23.

WHEELER, Roxann. *The Complexion of Race: Categories of Difference in Eighteenth-Century British Culture*. Philadelphia: University of Pennsylvania Press, 2000.

WILLIAMS, R. John. "Naked Creatures: *Robinson Crusoe*, The Beast, and The Sovereign." *Comparative Critical Studies* 2.3 (2005): 337-48.

YAMBEM, Sanamani. "Nupi Lan: Manipur Women's Agitation, 1939." *Economic and Political Weekly*, 21 February 1976: 325-331

YAQIN, Ameena. "The communalization and disintegration of Urdu in Anita Desai's In Custody." *Alternative Indias: Writing, Nation and Communalism*. Eds. Peter MOREY, and Alex TICKELL. Amsterdam/New York: Rodopi, 2005. 89-114.

ZAIDI, Nishat. "Fiction, History and Fictionalised History: A Postcolonial Reading of Khushwant Singh's *Delhi*." *The Journal of Indian Writing in English* 34.2 (2006). 37-48.

-----. *Makers of Indian Literature, Agha Shahid Ali*. New Delhi: Sahitya Akademi, 2017.

The Authors

ZENO ACKERMANN is Professor of British Cultural Studies at the University of Würzburg, Germany. His research focuses on correlations between poetics and ideology, on the reverberations of war, on the position of the novel vis-à-vis audiovisual mass media, on the concept of articulation and the problem of the voice, and on the afterlives of Shakespeare's works inside as well as outside the theatre. With Sabine Schülting he has recently published a monograph entitled *Precarious Figurations: Shylock on the German Stage, 1920–2010* (De Gruyter, 2019), a cultural history of the functionalization of Shylock on German stages and in German discourses since the beginning of the twentieth century.

ISABEL KARREMANN is Professor of English Literature at the University of Zurich, Switzerland, where she teaches early modern and eighteenth-century literature, focussing on questions of memory, affect, space and gender. While still at Würzburg University (2013-2019) she established there the Indo-German research and teaching collaboration "Literature in a Globalized World," funded by the DAAD and UGC, and became the co-PI of the SPARC project "New Terrains of Consciousness." Her main interest lies in the critical discourse and the literary history of globalization, for which Defoe's *Robinson Crusoe* proves a key text. Having published several articles on this novel, she is now planning a monograph entitled *Other Robinsons* that draws on the rich reception history of Defoe's novel in different cultural contexts.

SIMI MALHOTRA is Professor and Head of Department at the Department of English, Jamia Millia Islamia, Delhi. Her research interests include contemporary literary and cultural theory, culture studies, and heterodox Indian philosophies, theology, and aesthetic practices, particularly Sikhism. Her latest publications are the edited books *Food Culture Studies in India: Consumption, Representation and Mediation*, and *Inhabiting Cyberspace in India: Theory, Perspectives and Challenges* (both Springer, 2021). She is the recipient of several grants and awards, the latest being the 2020 DUO-India Professor Fellowship Award.

NISHAT ZAIDI is Professor and Former Head of Department at the Department of English, Jamia Millia Islamia, Delhi. She has taught at Aligarh Muslim University and Vasanta College for Women, Varanasi, before joining Jamia Millia Islamia. Her publications include *Day and Dastan* (With Alok Bhalla), *Between Worlds: The Travels of Yusuf Khan Kambalposh* (With Mushirul Hasan), and

Makers of Indian Literature: Agha Shahid Ali. Her forthcoming book is her translation of Premchand's historical play *Karbala.*